Helping Library Users
with Legal Questions

Helping Library Users with Legal Questions

Practical Advice for Research, Programming, and Outreach

Deborah A. Hamilton

LIBRARIES UNLIMITED®

An Imprint of ABC-CLIO, LLC

Santa Barbara, California • Denver, Colorado

Library of Congress Cataloging-in-Publication Data

Names: Hamilton, Deborah A., author.
Title: Helping library users with legal questions : practical advice for research, programming, and outreach / Deborah A. Hamilton.
Description: Santa Barbara, California : Libraries Unlimited, [2021] | Includes bibliographical references and index.
Identifiers: LCCN 2020053010 (print) | LCCN 2020053011 (ebook) | ISBN 9781440872006 (paperback ; acid-free paper) | ISBN 9781440872013 (ebook)
Subjects: LCSH: Law libraries—United States. | Law libraries—Reference services—United States. | Legal research—United States.
Classification: LCC Z675.L2 H36 2021 (print) | LCC Z675.L2 (ebook) | DDC 025.5/27634—dc23
LC record available at https://lccn.loc.gov/2020053010
LC ebook record available at https://lccn.loc.gov/2020053011

ISBN: 978-1-4408-7200-6 (print)
      978-1-4408-7201-3 (ebook)

25 24 23 22 21   1 2 3 4 5

This book is also available as an eBook.

Libraries Unlimited
An Imprint of ABC-CLIO, LLC

ABC-CLIO, LLC
147 Castilian Drive
Santa Barbara, California 93117
www.abc-clio.com

This book is printed on acid-free paper ∞

Manufactured in the United States of America

I would like to dedicate this book to my mother, Rita Hamilton. Through example she taught me the powerful impact that education can have upon one's life, the importance of fighting for justice, and the value of including everyone at the table. Although she is no longer with us, I hope that part of her spirit can live on through my work.

Contents

Acknowledgments

There are a few people and organizations I would like to thank and without whom the publication of this work would have not been possible. To the great team of people who make up the Pikes Peak Library District—first and foremost, Jim Stolz, Janice McPherson, and Kaitlin Roeder—thank you for taking a chance on hiring a librarian with no legal background to fill the law librarian position. I thank my current supervisor, Amy Rodda, and my colleagues, Heidi Buljung, Sandy Hancock, Jenny Pierce, and Tammy Sayles for all their support and encouragement. I would also like to thank the many wonderful librarians of the Colorado Association of Law Librarians and the Southwest Association of Law Librarians. Both of these organizations have provided me with tremendous support and guidance.

In addition, I want to thank members of the access to justice and legal communities of Colorado Springs. These groups have helped me to better serve my community and to fully understand the complex challenges that self-represented litigants face. First and foremost, I extend my thanks to the Justice Center, their board of directors, former executive director Charles Simon, and current executive director Britt Kwan. Also, Kristi Dorr at the El Paso County Bar Association and Sarah Lipka at Colorado Legal Services have both helped me to forge meaningful connections with local attorneys. I am grateful to the Access to Justice Committee of the Fourth Judicial District in Colorado for their innovative approaches to assisting self-represented litigants, and last but definitely not least, to the Self Represented Litigant Coordinators and Family Court Facilitators of the Fourth Judicial District in Colorado, especially Lisa Younger Anderson for her great attitude and tireless work to help pro se litigants.

Outside of my professional world, I also extend thanks to my partner of many years, Richard Buxton. Your work ethic and dedication are an inspiration to me.

ONE

The Justice Gap

Who Are We Serving and Why Do They Need Us?

Our country is facing a justice crisis. Many low- and moderate-income people cannot afford the legal help they need to resolve civil legal disputes. According to Legal Services Corporation's last major report from 2017, entitled *The Justice Gap: Measuring the Unmet Civil Legal Needs of Low-income Americans*, "86% of the civil legal problems reported by low-income Americans in the past year received inadequate or no legal help" (Legal Services Corporation 2017, 6). This justice gap creates a two-tiered justice system where those who can afford an attorney have better chances of receiving justice than those who cannot. This gap fundamentally alters our perception of how the justice system works and who it is designed for. I will begin this chapter by examining what the justice gap is and who it affects. Next, I will explore some of the causes for this gap and what is being done by the justice system and legal-service providers to address this issue. Last, I will propose some ideas for how public libraries can help patrons in the position of having to represent themselves in court, ideas I will explore in more depth in subsequent chapters.

THE JUSTICE GAP

The Colorado Access to Justice Commission has defined the justice gap as "the difference between the civil legal needs of low-income people and our system's capacity to meet those needs" (Colorado Access to Justice Commission 2014, 5). This gap can be found in all fifty states and results in many people having to represent themselves in court or in other legal matters. These parties are referred to as "pro se" or "self-represented litigants." Many of us are familiar with the right established by the U.S. Supreme Court case *Gideon v. Wainwright*, which states that if a defendant in a criminal matter cannot afford an attorney one will be provided to him by the state. This right to an attorney if you cannot afford one applies only to criminal matters, so those who are involved in civil cases are left to try to seek help from legal aid organizations that are overwhelmed by the volume of requests or to go it alone.

It is difficult to capture statistics that show the full breadth of the issue. Joy Moses writes: "There's no nationwide snapshot of the problem. We don't know how many people represent themselves in civil legal matters in the United States, and we can't make year-over-year comparisons. Still, 60 percent of judges in a 2009 study reported increases in self-represented litigants" (Moses 2011, 15). Here are a few figures to consider. In their last major report released in 2017, Legal Services Corporation, the largest provider of legal aid services in the country, estimated that 1.7 million people would seek their services in 2017 but they would have the resources to assist only half of them (Legal Services Corporation 2017, 6). Legal Services Corporation offices can offer a range of help from legal advice to full representation. However, due to the large volume of people seeking assistance, not all cases can receive full representation, which explains the statistic that 86 percent of civil legal problems of low-income Americans received inadequate or no legal help I quoted at the beginning of this chapter.

Legal Services Corporation is only allowed to take cases of people who meet strict income qualifications, which is currently those who live at 125 percent of the poverty level. In 2020, this amount for a single person is an annual income of $15,950 and, for a family of four, $32,750 (U.S. Department of Health and Human Services 2020). In 2017, 60 million Americans were living at 125 percent of the poverty level. This included 6.4 million seniors, 11.1 million people living with disabilities, 1.7 million veterans, and 10 million rural residents (Legal Services Corporation 2017, 6). Further, there are still many people who earn more than these amounts each year who cannot realistically afford an attorney, thus making the problem greater than these numbers indicate.

In her work *Access to Justice*, Deborah L. Rhode finds that, "According to most estimates, about four-fifths of the civil legal needs of the poor, and two- to three-fifths of middle-income individuals, remain unmet" (Rhode 2004, 3). In the state where I live, Colorado, a report of our Access to Justice Commission found that legal services providers had to "turn down at least one of every two eligible applicants for services because of inadequate staffing and resources" (Colorado Access to Justice Commission 2014, 1). This resulted in the Commission also finding that "More than 50 percent of all civil litigants and nearly 76 percent of parties in domestic cases are self-represented" (Colorado Access to Justice Commission 2014, 1). Robert Frank wrote in the *New York Times* that "more than 70 percent of low-income American households had been involved in eviction cases, labor law cases, and other civil legal disputes during the preceding year, and in more than 80 percent of those cases they lacked effective legal representation" (Frank 2018). The New York State Courts Access to Justice Program found that, in 2015, an estimated 1.8 million people appeared in New York State courts without an attorney. And in 2013, in eviction cases in New York State courts, 98 percent of tenants were unrepresented, and in child-support cases 95 percent of parents had no attorney (Legal Services Corporation 2017, 9).

While these numbers seem high, they probably do not capture the full picture. In general, low-income Americans will seek professional legal help for "only 20% of the civil legal problems that they may face" (Legal Services Corporation 2017, 7). This is due to a number of reasons. Some want to handle the problem on their own. Others are not sure where to turn for help. And also, people might not even realize that their problem has a legal remedy: they are more likely to seek legal help for problems that are more overtly legal, like custody issues, or wills and estates, and less likely to seek it for problems with creditors or difficulty claiming benefits to which they are entitled.

Legal Services Corporation found that 71 percent of low-income households faced at least one legal problem per year. That percentage can be higher for specific groups within that population—97 percent of domestic violence survivors, 80 percent of parents or guardians with children under eighteen, and 80 percent of disabled persons face at least one problem per year. Of the issues that people are facing, the Corporation found that 41 percent had a legal problem related to health; 37 percent had legal problems related to consumer and finance issues; 29 percent had a legal problem related to rental housing; 27 percent had a legal issue with children and custody; 23 percent faced a legal problem relating to a disability; and 22 percent had a legal problem related to income maintenance (Legal Services Corporation 2017, 7). So it is evident that the problem of accessing legal services is widespread and that it disproportionately effects vulnerable populations.

CAUSES OF THE JUSTICE GAP

A number of factors contribute to the justice gap. At the root of the problem is rising income inequality rates. Robert Frank outlines a number of ways in which rising inequality contributes to the justice gap. He asserts that "Rising inequality has reduced the supply of legal aid by kindling resistance to taxation" (Frank

2018). We will examine below how the various funding streams to legal aid providers have dwindled over time despite the rising demand for those services. In addition, many Americans are unaware of this civil justice gap and the impacts that it has on both their community and the justice system, so they might not see the need for more robust access to justice funding.

Author Jason Tashea describes how inequality is growing in the United States: "between 1971 and 2014, the share of aggregate income held by middle income households—a family of four in 2014 making at least $48,347—shrunk from 62 percent of the total population to 43 percent." Also, "Between 2000 and 2012, median income for all families dropped eight percent while common expenses increased, like childcare (24 percent), higher education (62 percent), rent (seven percent) and medical expenses (21 percent), according to the Brookings Institute" (Tashea 2018). As the cost of other expenses rise, housing, food, and so on, less is left over to pay for something like attorney's fees. And the cost of those fees has also been on the rise while wages remain stagnant.

As already mentioned, while income inequality is on the rise, legal aid providers have had to struggle to maintain services due to dramatic decreases in their funding. The most numerous providers of legal aid in the country are organizations that are a part of the Legal Services Corporation, which receives funding primarily from the federal government. During the last two decades, this federal funding has been cut by one-third, while more restrictions have been placed on the types of cases on which this government funding can be spent (Rhode 2004, 3). The United States spends around $2.25 per capita on supporting legal assistance. Rhode concludes that this is "a ludicrously inadequate amount for a nation in which roughly a seventh of the population is in or near poverty and eligible for aid" (Rhode 2004, 106). Our spending pales in comparison to that of other countries, such as England, which spends $32 per capita, or New Zealand, which spends $12 per capita (Rhode 2004, 112).

In Colorado, our Access to Justice Commission found that funding for Colorado Legal Services had declined by 10 percent since 2009 (Colorado Access to Justice Commission 2014, 6). This decline in funding has occurred while the number of people who would qualify for legal services has been on the rise. The Commission found that "In 1980, 396,775 people in Colorado were at or below 125 percent of the federal poverty level. By 2005, that number had increased to 692,505 and today it is at 880,224. These numbers translate to significantly limited access to legal representation for Colorado's poor" (Colorado Access to Justice Commission 2014, 10). Colorado Legal Services receives not only federal funding but funding from some state resources as well. These state funding sources have either fluctuated greatly over the years or have been declining while the need for these services has been growing.

In addition to the lack of funds, Rhode outlines many of the restrictions that are placed on how the Legal Service Corporation and other legal aid organizations that receive federal funding can use those funds: "Legal services offices that receive federal funds generally may not use those funds, and in some instances may not use any other revenue, for a broad range of matters including school desegregation, labor boycotts, abortion, political redistricting, military service, welfare reform, undocumented aliens, prisoners, and public housing tenants facing eviction because of alleged drug activities" (Rhode 2004, 105). In addition, given the large demand of cases that do not fall into any of those restricted areas, most legal-service providers also have to establish priority lists of the remaining clients, so a divorce case involving domestic violence is more likely to receive help than an uncontested divorce where no domestic violence has occurred. Tough choices must be made by these legal-service providers due to a lack of staff and resources.

This overall lack of funding means there are fewer attorneys serving those who need legal assistance. In Colorado, there was one legal aid attorney for every 4,839 eligible people in 1980. By 2008 there was one legal aid attorney for every 16,890 eligible people. And in 2014 there was one legal aid attorney for every 18,728 eligible people. This varies greatly from the ratio of attorneys to those who can afford them, which is one attorney for every 203 people (Colorado Access to Justice Commission 2014, 10–11). The situation in Colorado is worse than the national average. In the United States, for every 6,415 low-income people there is one free legal services attorney (Moses 2011, 18).

Some attorneys who are not employed by legal aid organizations also take on pro bono work, but again we see that these efforts fall well below the demand. The American Bar Association and state codes of conduct for attorneys usually set aspirational standards for attorneys to provide some service to those who cannot afford legal representation. However, there are no enforcement mechanisms that actually require attorneys to take on those cases. In practice, "fewer than 10 percent of lawyers accept referrals from legal aid or bar-sponsored poverty-related programs" (Rhode 2004, 17).

This lack of legal representation forces many lower-income people to represent themselves in court. Here they face even more hurdles, as they are navigating a system that is not designed for laypeople. They need to research and understand the law. They need to decipher courtroom etiquette. They need to be able to effectively write and argue on their own behalf. Forms and court procedures are difficult to understand, but many clerks and court employees are not allowed to give legal advice, and judges are also limited in the amount of guidance they can give to parties because they are obliged to remain impartial. This has put a huge burden on the legal system as it tries to figure out how to deal with self-represented litigants while still maintaining impartiality and keeping the courts running efficiently.

INNOVATIONS IN ACCESS TO JUSTICE

In order to respond to this crisis a group of court employees, judges, attorneys, community service providers, and technologists have created what is known as the Access to Justice movement. Access to Justice encompasses a wide range of efforts to make the legal system more navigable to those who are not represented by attorneys. I will now examine some of the many creative approaches that are being taken. Many of these efforts are cost-effective and not only save the courts time but also save taxpayer money, as they enable the courts to run more efficiently.

There are a wide range of developments that have helped make self-help resources more available to self-represented litigants. One example is the creation of many websites geared toward this audience. There are too many examples to list here, but these websites contain information ranging from explanations of laws, access to legal research sources, where to find court forms, how to connect with legal-service providers and legal clinics, and explanations of court procedures. There are two good places to locate these sites as they aggregate a number of different legal resources: first is LawHelp.org; and the other is the Public Librarian Toolkit available from the Legal Information Services to the Public Special Interest Section of the American Association of Law Libraries.

Some jurisdictions are working on simplifying court forms to make them easier for the lay user to understand. This usually means converting the form into what is known as "plain language" and stripping it of complex legal terminology. Having court forms translated into multiple languages and making interpreters available through the courts are some other ways in which jurisdictions are easing the burdens on self-represented litigants. Another measure is the creation of what are known as "interactive forms." These digitally based forms ask litigants to answer a set of plain-language questions, after which the computer can populate the court form with the information provided by the litigant.

We are also seeing more and more jurisdictions creating self-help centers within the courts where court employees have the ability to assist litigants in ways they previously were not allowed to do. This generally requires the jurisdiction to expand some of their rules on what types of information court employees are permitted to give. In the state of Colorado, our Self-Represented Litigant Coordinators, also known as the Sherlocks, can help litigants select the correct form and answer questions regarding court procedures. Their offices may also offer legal clinics, depending on the resources available in their community.

Another project that we are currently developing in Colorado is allowing self-represented litigants access to the court's electronic filing system. Previously, only registered attorneys could use this system. However, in the past couple of years the state has let a few counties run a pilot where simple domestic cases could let pro se patrons file in this system. The e-filing system makes it easier for litigants to follow their cases and to keep track of documents. The state judicial branch hopes to expand this service to more counties and additional areas of the law.

Some of these creative responses may require jurisdictions to establish judicial directives or to ease court rules that are currently in place. In the case of the Sherlocks, a judicial directive had to be established in order to allow them to help self-represented litigants select forms and to give procedural recommendations. Previously those two actions would have been considered legal advice and thus illegal given the state's prohibition on the unauthorized practice of law.

Many states are also considering changing some of the professional conduct rules for attorneys. One of the advantages of this is that attorneys could "unbundle" their services. Unbundling would allow them to offer their services à la carte, which would make it easier for a person to afford some legal assistance even if it was not full representation.

Many of these changes will require funding from somewhere. The Colorado Access to Justice Commission made recommendations on where that money could come from in their 2014 report. They were going to seek additional funding from the state legislature and try to restore state funding that had been cut back during the recession. Another suggestion was to use a portion of attorneys' registration fees to go to access to justice initiatives and amend court rules so they could increase the fees for out-of-state attorneys and then apply those funds to these initiatives. The Commission was also examining the possibility that another court rule could be amended to require that at least 50 percent of residual funds from class-action lawsuits go into the Colorado Lawyer Trust Account Foundation (COLTAF), which already supports civil legal aid programs. The Commission was working with the Colorado Supreme Court to see if a filing fee surcharge could also be created to accrue additional funds (Colorado Access to Justice Commission 2014, 2–3).

The good news is that many of these steps taken to help self-represented litigants and provide legal aid are cost-effective. The Colorado Access to Justice Commission found that, for "every dollar invested in CLS (Colorado Legal Services), Colorado receives $6.35 in financial benefit" (Colorado

Access to Justice Commission 2014, 6). John Greacen found similar savings in his 2009 report that looked at courts in the San Joaquin Valley in California. Workshops were found to reduce not only the amount of time that staff at public counters needed to take with self-represented litigants but also the overall number of hearings in those cases. This amounted to a cost of $0.13 for every dollar saved. When courts were able to provide one-on-one assistance, this eliminated at least one hearing per case, reduced the overall amount of time in those hearings by five to fifteen minutes, and saved court staff one to one-and-a-half hours of time processing paperwork and working with those self-represented litigants. These efforts cost $0.33 to $0.26 for every dollar saved. If courts were able to provide assistance that limited the cases to only one court appearance, this amounted in services that cost $0.14 for every dollar saved (Greacen 2009, 1).

Many other benefits to these access to justice initiatives are a bit more difficult to measure. Laura Abel lays out some of these in her report on the "Economic Benefits of Civil Legal Aid." She contends that domestic violence is reduced when legal aid is provided, which in turn saves the public money through reduced medical and mental health costs, but also through allowing victims to maintain their jobs and keep hold of their property. Another benefit she writes about is that civil legal aid allows children to leave foster care more quickly. Evictions can also be reduced when civil legal aid is provided. Civil legal aid may also foster better health by connecting people with benefits, maintaining insurance, and removing environmental hazards from rental homes (Abel 2012, 1–2). So, in many ways, not only is providing access to justice the right thing to do, it is also the most cost-effective step that leads to a more just society for all.

WHAT LIBRARIES CAN DO

Libraries are in a unique position to assist self-represented litigants. As trusted sources of information with easy access to technology, there are many ways in which our libraries can extend the services we already provide into the area of law. Richard Zorza writes: "To be effective in this important work, a public library's staff needs to know: 1. Where the information is; 2. How to access and share it; 3. That it is appropriate for them to assist in providing that information; and 4. How they can do so without inappropriately acting as lawyers who give legal advice" (Zorza 2010, 127). We will work through these areas in the subsequent chapters of this book.

Chapter 2 will discuss how to develop library materials and resources. This will include looking at what to consider when putting together a legal reference policy. The chapter will also discuss what to consider when training staff in this area. For instance, look for partners when developing training: you may find that your state has a law library that does outreach to public libraries; a local law school might also offer training; or professional organizations may also provide these services. Chapter 2 will also examine ideas about how to build a collection of materials in the area of law and what types of resources your library can create to assist self-represented litigants.

Chapter 3 will focus on legal outreach and programming. Assisting patrons with legal questions is much easier to do if you are familiar with the legal service providers in your area. I would encourage you to familiarize yourself with your local courts. Try to find out what services they offer to self-represented litigants. Do the courts have a self-help center? Are forms available online? Is there day care at the court? What about interpreters or translation services? Also, locate who may provide free and low-cost legal services in your area. Then you can refer patrons to clinics and pro bono service providers so they can get more in-depth information than what the library can provide. All of these organizations may also be looking for partners to host classes and workshops. The library can provide the space and technology, and your partners can provide the legal content.

Chapter 4 will address how to conduct a legal reference interview. We will see how working with legal questions is different and what sort of issues are in play. I will also cover how to avoid the unauthorized practice of law, so you are not providing the patron with legal advice but rather with legal information.

Chapters 5–9 discuss how to approach legal reference work and the types of sources you will use. In Chapter 5 I look at some of the concepts at play in legal research such as jurisdiction and authority and why they are important to be aware of. Chapter 6 covers what legal secondary source materials are and how they can assist you in finding laws. Chapter 7 discusses laws that are created in the legislative branch and how to locate them. Chapter 8 looks at laws generated in the judicial branch, and Chapter 9 covers laws from the executive branch. This section of the book, hopefully, will help you to better understand the basics of legal research, the variety of laws that are created, and how to assist patrons in locating them.

Chapter 10 will offer some last pieces of advice and encouragement as well as some lessons I have learned during my time as a law librarian. The goal of this book is to make you more comfortable fielding questions in the area of law, but also to give you a better understanding of the issues that self-represented litigants are facing. I believe that when librarians build partnerships with the legal community, their libraries will have a lot to offer those who are seeking access to the law and legal information.

REFERENCES

Abel, Laura. 2012. "Economic Benefits of Civil Legal Aid." Accessed March 22, 2020. https://ncforaj.files.wordpress.com/2012/09/final-economic-benefits-of-legal-aid-9-5-2012.pdf.

Colorado Access to Justice Commission. 2014. "Justice Crisis in Colorado 2014: Report on Civil Legal Needs in Colorado." Colorado Bar Association. Accessed October 14, 2019. http://www.cba.cobar.org/repository/Justice%20Crisis%202014%20text.pdf.

Frank, Robert H. "How Rising Inequality Has Widened the Justice Gap." *New York Times,* August 31, 2018.

Gideon v. Wainwright, 372 U.S. 335 (1963).

Greacen, John. 2009. "The Benefits and Costs of Programs to Assist Self-Represented Litigants: Results from Limited Data Gathering Conducted by Six Trial Courts in California's San Joaquin Valley." Accessed March 22, 2020. https://www.courts.ca.gov/partners/documents/Greacen_benefit_cost_final_report.pdf.

LawHelp.org. Accessed April 16, 2020. https://www.lawhelp.org/.

Legal Services Corporation. 2017. "The Justice Gap: Measuring the Unmet Civil Legal Needs of Low-Income Americans." Accessed March 5, 2020. https://www.lsc.gov/sites/default/files/images/TheJusticeGap-FullReport.pdf.

Moses, Joy. "Grounds for Objection." In *Closing the Justice Gap: How Innovation and Evidence Can Bring Legal Services to More Americans.* Washington, D.C.: Center for American Progress, 2011.

Public Library Toolkit, American Association of Law Libraries. Accessed October 14, 2019. https://www.aallnet.org/lispsis/resources-publications/public-library-toolkit/.

Rhode, Deborah L. *Access to Justice.* New York: Oxford University Press, 2004.

Tashea, Jason. 2018. "Access-to-Justice Gap? It's the Economy." *ABA Journal.* Accessed March 22, 2020. https://www.abajournal.com/lawscribbler/article/access_to_justice_gap_its_the_economy_stupid.

United States Department of Health and Human Services. "Poverty Guidelines." Accessed March 22, 2020. https://aspe.hhs.gov/poverty-guidelines.

Zorza, Richard. 2010. "Public Libraries and Access to Justice." In *Future Trends in State Courts 2010.* Accessed March 22, 2020. https://www.srln.org/node/217/report-public-libraries-and-access-justice-richard-zorza-future-trends-state-courts-2010.

TWO

Developing Library Legal Materials and Resources

In this chapter I cover a wide range of resources you can develop that will help you and your fellow staff members better serve patrons with legal questions. I begin by discussing the need for a legal reference service policy; a policy can help staff to have a clearer understanding of their role when working with patrons who have legal questions. Next, I discuss what other types of staff training you may want to consider when preparing those working on the desk who may have to field legal questions. I then switch gears to discuss items to consider when building your collection, and close with a look at other types of resources you may be able to provide your patrons in order to help them to access legal information and services.

LEGAL REFERENCE SERVICE POLICY

I would encourage you and your institution to consider either developing a legal reference service policy or adding language to your current policy that addresses legal information. The most important reason to do this is to protect your institution, your employees, and your patrons from what is known as the unauthorized practice of law. All fifty states have some sort of law that prohibits people who are not licensed attorneys from giving legal advice or representation to others. While no librarian has been charged with this crime, these are still actions that we want to avoid when assisting patrons who are looking for legal information. And while most patrons realize that we are information professionals and not attorneys, we still want to provide information in good faith and not do anything that might unintentionally harm our patrons. In chapter 4, we will look more closely at the unauthorized practice of law and how to avoid it. While we want to be cautious not to provide legal advice, there are still plenty of other ways that we can help patrons find legal information, and a policy can help to outline what those actions and services are. Another reason to develop a policy around legal reference services is to help define the distinction between legal information that can be provided and what is considered legal advice. This helps both patrons and staff know where the limits are.

At my institution, the Pikes Peak Library District, we have a separate policy for legal reference services. Since we have a specialized legal research collection, we felt this warranted a separate policy. A number of other institutions just insert language within their general reference policy to address legal information and legal advice. Let me first outline what is in our policy; then I will discuss different approaches so you can get a sense of what you might want to draft for your institution.

The Pikes Peak Library District policy begins with a short section outlining what is in the collection and explaining that it is a noncirculating reference collection. Next the policy contains a section labeled "District Procedures," which explains that library staff can assist patrons in locating items and can provide assistance in how to use those items. It goes on to explain that the unauthorized practice of law is illegal in Colorado and explains that library staff cannot provide legal advice or interpretations.

The last section of the document is labeled "Guidelines." It first lists services that library staff may offer and then lists services that staff may not offer. Activities that are allowed include demonstrating how to search for and use legal materials; finding legal definitions of terms; pulling up laws if a patron has an exact citation; helping to brainstorm search terms; and referring patrons to legal resources, but it is up to the patron to choose which sources to use. Activities that are not permitted include selecting legal forms for a patron; helping patrons to fill out forms or write legal documents; giving legal advice; interpreting legal sources; recommending specific laws or cases; and recommending specific attorneys. I find the guidelines section particularly helpful in that it clearly spells out, for staff and patrons, which activities staff are allowed to engage in and which are not permitted. Often people will shy away from offering any type of legal information because they are afraid they might stray into advice or interpretation, so offering clear guidelines empowers people to assist patrons with legal questions to some extent even if there are limits.

Other institutions choose to include legal questions in their general reference service policy. Most of these examples express in brief language that library staff cannot offer legal interpretations or advice. Others will also include that library staff is not allowed to conduct legal research on behalf of a patron. Some even limit legal reference services only to specialized librarians. What these examples fail to do is to outline what services can be offered in terms of legal information. So while they do a good job of preventing the unauthorized practice of law, they fail to illustrate how staff can assist patrons with legal questions. I see over and over again people refraining from offering any kind of help because they are afraid even to approach legal questions in any capacity. It is as if when they hear legal terminology they assume they do not need to offer any type of assistance. With our policies we want to assist staff to understand the difference between legal information and legal advice so we can then best assist patrons while still operating within the bounds of the law.

STAFF TRAINING

Another way to assist staff in understanding the difference between legal information and legal advice is to implement some type of staff training to address these topics. Currently I train staff in a few different ways. I teach a class that is part of our library system-wide Finding Info at Our Library series. I also teach shorter classes to staff who work more closely with legal patrons that focus on a particular area of law or legal research. And lastly, I will do one-on-one trainings with newly hired staff who work on the reference desk next to the law collection to familiarize them with the collection and the services we offer. Below I will outline each of these types of training in more detail.

Within our library system we offer a series of classes for staff development called Finding Info. The classes cover a wide range of topics from conducting a reference interview to an overview of our databases to subject-specific classes such as legal resources, business resources, and so on. The Finding Info classes were initially offered as two-hour in-person classes. In them I would attempt to cover everything one might need to know in order to help patrons with legal questions. A class consisted of what is included in our legal reference policy; how to conduct a legal reference interview; how to work with patrons who have legal questions; what types of law there are; what resources are available for doing legal research; and where people can go in the community for legal assistance. Advantages to this format are is its comprehensive coverage of the subject so staff understand the full range of topics and resources. Disadvantages are that staff retain less of the information overall because so much is covered. Also, as the classes would take longer, it was more difficult to find a time when a good number of staff could attend.

Prior to the pandemic, we offered the legal resource class only once a year, not as frequently as I would like. The library is now developing an asynchronous online Finding Info curriculum, which I feel will make it easier for staff to access this information. These classes are initially offered as live webinars that are recorded for staff to also access at a later date. As I reconstruct this class, I am planning to break up the two-hour presentation into several shorter sessions in order to help maintain focus and retention.

I have also developed a few shorter classes to teach staff who work in the building where the law collection resides. These classes run from forty-five minutes to an hour and will just focus on one area of the law or on a particular resource. In the longer Finding Info course I focus on resources that can be accessed throughout the whole library system, but in these shorter classes I will highlight specific resources that are housed in the law collection. Topics for these classes have included the Colorado Revised Statutes, legal secondary sources, how to use WestlawNext (one of our legal research databases), finding legal forms, and more. I think the shorter time frame and the ability to focus on just one particular resource helps staff to retain the information better. These classes can also be offered more frequently, which can help new staff to understand the legal collection more quickly.

The last type of training I offer consists of one-on-one meetings with all newly hired staff who will work the reference desk near where the law materials are housed. These meetings cover the "need to know" items for staff in case it might be a while until any other formal legal reference training is offered. They are an hour long, and in them we cover the most frequently asked-for items. I begin with explaining the legal reference service policy. Then we look at where to refer people for different types of legal assistance. Because we get a lot of requests for legal forms, I show people where to find court forms on the state judicial branch's website as well as our Legal Forms database from Gale. Last I will review how to use the Colorado Revised Statutes. The one-on-one appointments are great, as I can also focus on any specific questions that a staff member may have. Additionally, it is a good opportunity to connect with new hires and hopefully to dispel any anxiety they may have about working with legal questions.

I have learned a few things from developing staff training over the years. First, in order to effectively explain what legal resources are available, you need to make sure that staff have a basic understanding of how our government is structured and how laws are created. Second, sometimes you need to take a triage approach to training staff. Because the law is such a broad area, it is best to focus on training staff in the areas where you receive the most questions. Third, make sure staff are aware of what community resources are available in this area. A lot of the work I do is referring people to other places where they can receive the assistance they are looking for. Last, make sure that staff understand the difference between legal information and legal advice. We do not want staff unwittingly falling into the trap of the unauthorized practice of law, but we also want them to feel confident in assisting patrons with accessing legal information. From my own experience, I have found that the three most important areas in which to offer training are where to refer people for legal assistance, where to find court and other legal forms, and how to locate and use your state statutes. Your patrons may have different needs, but these may be good areas in which to start.

Also, keep in mind that you may not need to develop your own set of training resources; there may already be other trainings out there that you can access in order to build a curriculum. Check the websites and YouTube channels for law schools and state law libraries. The Federal Depository Library Program has a webinar series that covers a wide range of government information. Webjunction also offers training on providing civil legal reference services.

COLLECTION DEVELOPMENT

The unfortunate reality is that many of the published legal resources are quite expensive, and therefore it is not feasible to purchase and maintain them with a public library's budget. One of the challenges with certain types of legal sources is that they need to be updated through subscriptions to supplements, meaning you will have an initial cost up front to purchase the set and then a yearly cost to maintain it so it is up-to-date with the most current laws. In this section, I would like to highlight some of the more inexpensive resources available and then discuss some other items to consider if you are able to invest more in legal resources.

The publisher Nolo offers inexpensive books on a wide range of legal matters. The Nolo books are also written in easy to understand language geared toward a lay audience, so they are perfect for people who are representing themselves. The books will offer a general overview of a particular legal topic. The only drawback is that, if the book is covering an area that falls under state jurisdiction, the content will not be specific to your state's laws. However, these books are great for getting a foundational understanding of the various legal concepts at play in a particular area. They will also help patrons to better understand the legal terminology for that topic. This will help them be more successful when they go to search for their specific state's laws.

Nolo books can also be found electronically through the EBSCO database Legal Information Reference Center. This database can sometimes be included as part of bundled EBSCO packages, so if you have already purchased a bundle of EBSCO databases you should check to see if you already have access to this particular database title. In addition to the Nolo titles, Legal Information Reference Center also includes some legal forms. I would proceed with caution in using these forms, as they tend to be very general and not state-specific. (I will discuss a couple of other legal-form databases below if that is the type of content you are interested in.) Nolo also has some free content available; if you visit the Nolo website, you will also find a section labeled "Legal Articles" that will give you a brief overview of a particular legal area. While it does not give the same level of coverage as the books, it still can offer some help.

The Nutshell Series from West Academic is another affordable series of books that covers a wide range of legal topics. The Nutshell books will generally be more technical and dense than the Nolo books, but again, they do a good job of giving a legal novice an overview of legal concepts and terminology. Just like the Nolo titles, these books will not be state-specific. You can also find the Nutshell Series on Overdrive if you were interested in building an electronic collection.

When I visit public libraries in other cities, the majority of what I see in their legal section are Nolos and Nutshells. If you have funds for some more expensive purchases, I would first recommend seeing what it would cost to purchase and maintain a copy of your state's statutes. Again, this would be a situation where you would pay the initial price for the set and then would need to also pay to maintain it. Our state statues are by far our most used print legal resource. Granted, you can find your state's statutes online for free, but there are some advantages to having a print set. Many patrons still prefer using print resources as opposed to websites. Additionally, a print set will include an index, which most websites do not. Since it can sometimes be difficult to determine the preferred legal terms for some things, an index can lead to you to the preferred term more quickly than full text searching and browsing through the table of contents can.

Another item to consider for purchase would be a copy of your city's code or ordinances if they are available. Many cities have their codes available online for free, but some do not. Also, you will have the benefit of the index once again if you have this resource in print. A number of libraries also invest in *Black's Law Dictionary* for their reference collections. We do get patrons who will ask for this resource by name. I would also check is to see if your state bar association publishes any affordable titles. Sometimes these will be referred to as continuing legal education (CLE) materials. What is nice about these materials is that they will be specific to your state's laws and will help self-represented litigants identify the key laws and cases in a particular area.

CLE materials can also help patrons to better understand legal procedures and which forms to use.

Lastly, you may wish to investigate the cost of a legal forms database. We subscribe to Gale Legal Forms, but I have seen a number of public libraries who use the database NuWav to access legal forms. You will find a number of other vendors who sell legal forms online, sometimes for pretty steep fees. What can be useful about a forms database is that you can help provide access to many of those legal documents and forms that will not be available through your state courts' website. Also, with our subscription to Gale, we are able to purchase a collection of forms that will be specific to Colorado laws. This will help our patrons to access forms that are relevant to the state laws at hand. We want to remember that we cannot recommend specific forms to patrons, but these databases can help patrons to find more trustworthy content rather than just searching on the open Web.

Every library is going to have a different amount of money that they can direct to legal resources. Given the cost of many of these books and databases, you may not be able to invest as much as you would like. So if you can purchase only a few sources, that is okay, but take the time to figure out what types of legal matters you are getting the most questions about so you can then purchase the sources that best match those needs. Our main areas for questions tend to fall into the areas of family law, landlord–tenant, and estate and probate. Your library patrons may have different needs. Generally, you may find that your patrons are more interested in legal matters that tend to fall under state jurisdiction, so this may be what you need to focus your resources on.

OTHER RESOURCES

In this last section I am going to cover a wide range of resources that you can potentially develop in order to better serve patrons with legal questions. You may have to create some of these resources on your own. On the other hand, you may find that others have already been created by a different agency or organization. So even if your library cannot afford to build a robust print legal collection, there may be other types of resources that can be just as helpful to your patrons.

Two of our most useful legal resources were created by the self-help center at our district court. The first is a listing of all of the legal assistance providers in our area. This handout lists and gives a brief description of all of the organizations that provide either free or low-cost legal help in our region. This list makes it easier for staff to make referrals, and it can be a great starting place if we are not sure what to do to help a patron. The second item created by the self-help center in the courthouse is a monthly calendar that lists all of the free legal clinics in our area. Again, this calendar helps tremendously with referring patrons to free legal services. While we are lucky in that another organization has created these resources, if you cannot find something similar in your community these could be the resources that you could compile and share with other organizations. I would first check, though, to see if your courthouse or area legal services offices has similar documents before creating your own. Also, depending on the size of your community, you may have fewer resources or events to compile, so a different format might work better, depending on what resources are available.

I also maintain a display of various pamphlets and handouts that contain various types of legal information. Some of these are informational pamphlets that have been created by the Colorado Bar Association and cover such subjects as "Wills in Colorado," "What To Do When Someone Dies," "So you Have Been Named a Conservator," "Financial Powers of Attorney," and so on. If you are located in Colorado, I have included the link to the brochures available from the Colorado Bar Association in the reference list. In the pamphlet collection, I also have a series of flowcharts created by the courts that outline the steps and forms needed for different types of family law actions. These flowcharts are extremely helpful, as we cannot recommend specific forms but patrons can use them to determine for themselves which forms they will need. Other information in this display includes pamphlets for area service providers, such as help for victims of domestic violence, veteran services, child-support enforcement, and so on. If you are looking for these types of informational flyers, I would first check at your local courthouse to see if they have any self-help offices or check at the clerk's office. You may also find some available resources at your state bar association.

If you house research guides on your website, then you may wish to consider creating one that focuses on legal resources. On my legal research page, I have several sub-guides in order to break up the topic by interest: Laws and Legal Forms (where patrons can find primary laws and access court forms); Understanding the Law (this page covers secondary sources that help explain the law); Representing Yourself in Court; Getting Legal Help; Special Legal Topics; and Government. While you may not want to develop something this robust, you still may want to consider something that can provide easy access to the primary laws for your jurisdiction, any court forms that may be available, and legal service providers in your area. In addition to the websites listed on the research guide, I have also created a few tutorials for how to navigate commonly used websites and databases. These tutorials come in two formats: print and video. The videos are housed on YouTube and then embedded into the research guide. In the tutorials you will find step-by-step directions for how to access and use these resources. I have found that many patrons requesting legal information are generally not comfortable finding and using online resources; hopefully these tutorials can assist those patrons. Currently, I have tutorials for the following: How to Find Colorado Court Forms; Searching the Colorado Revised Statutes; Using Gale Legal Forms; Using Legal Information Reference Center; and Using WestlawNext. In terms of views, the guides for how to find court forms and searching the statutes have been viewed three to four times more often than the ones on using our databases.

REFERENCE SCENARIO

Patron: I need to find an attorney to help me with my case.

Librarian: Sure, I would be happy to show you what resources we have that can help you locate an attorney.

Patron: Don't you have one you can recommend?

Librarian: I am unable to recommend a specific attorney for you, but I can show you how the directories work, or I can give you information for the free and low-cost legal services organizations in town. Are you looking to hire an attorney, trying to find one who will work pro bono, or do you just want to chat with an attorney at a free law clinic?

Patron: Ideally, I would like to get a pro bono attorney if I can.

Librarian: Great, we have two organizations in town you can contact. Just a heads up, they do require income verification to make sure that you qualify for their services, and they also have some limits on the types of cases that they can take. I would recommend calling first to see what the income requirements are and if they can take your type of case. The first is Colorado Legal Services, and here is their number. The second is a nonprofit called the Justice Center, and this is their number. One thing to note is that, in addition to pro bono services, the Justice Center has a Modest Means program. So if you find out that you make too much money to qualify for pro bono, you still might be able to get a lower-cost attorney through the Justice Center. I am also going to give you a handout that has all of the free clinics in town just in case. And if you find that you don't qualify for a free attorney, here is my card; please reach back out if you find you need to hire an attorney and I can show you how to go about that.

In these types of interactions there are a few things to note. First, library staff should never recommend a specific attorney to represent someone. Just as we would never recommend a specific doctor or health professional, the same is true for attorneys and legal professionals. Next, in terms of pro bono services I find it easiest just to have the patron call the organization to see if they qualify.

I personally do not feel comfortable assessing someone's income to see if they meet the requirements. Also, while a number of legal services organizations may list their areas of service on their websites, sometimes they have special grant funds you might not be aware of that cover a new area or population. If patrons talk to the organization directly, they will get the most complete information about what it does. Additionally, even if the organization cannot provide full pro bono representation for the patron, they still might offer a clinic or partial service. You should also check to see if other nonprofits that serve specific populations provide legal assistance. Many times you may find legal assistance at domestic violence shelters, veterans service organizations, senior centers, and so on.

Finally, if a patron does wish to hire an attorney then you can demonstrate how to use one of the many attorney directories available. I would first see if there is one available through your state or local bar association. If not, there are a number of online services like Martindale Hubbell or Avvo that provide attorney listings and reviews. When using these directories, you will want to ask the patron what the general legal area is that they need the attorney for, and you will also need to find out if he or she is planning to pursue this action locally or in another state. Attorneys have a state license to practice law, so if a person is suing for divorce in California, finding an attorney from Colorado is not particularly helpful unless that attorney is actually licensed in both states. Last, I almost always give someone a copy of the legal clinic calendar, as they might decide not to hire an attorney but still want to speak with one. I also always give them my card and invite them to follow up with me if they need further assistance.

CONCLUSION

There are many ways in which you can assist patrons with legal questions through clear policies, staff training, collection development, and other resources. A good policy will clarify expectations and can help staff to focus on what they can do rather than what they cannot do. We always want to avoid the unauthorized practice of law, but still want to help people to access the information they need. When training staff, find a model that works best for your organization. You may need to experiment with length and coverage. Initially, you may need to take a triage approach so you can quickly address the greatest needs first. In my organization, the need-to-know items have been where to refer people for legal assistance, where to find court forms, and where to find the state laws. Your community may have different needs.

Developing a legal research collection can be expensive, but there are some less expensive resources out there. Be sure to see if you can afford a copy of your state's statutes, as this can be an invaluable resource, and pay attention to what legal topics you are fielding questions in so you can then build your collection based on the needs of your community. Last, there are a number of other resources you can either track down within your community or develop on your own. Check to see what resources the organizations in your community have developed, but two of our most useful resources include the legal aid list and the free legal clinic calendars.

REFERENCES

Colorado Bar Association. "Legal Informational Brochures." Accessed February 10, 2020. https://www.cobar.org/For-the-Public/Legal-Brochures.

Nolo. Accessed February 10, 2020. https://www.nolo.com/.

Pikes Peak Library District. "Law and Legal Resources." Accessed February 10, 2020. https://research.ppld.org/lawandlegalresources.

Pikes Peak Library District. "Legal Reference Service Policy." Accessed February 10, 2020. https://research.ppld.org/c.php?g=563686&p=3906116.

Webjuction. "Webjunction Course Catalog." Accessed February 12, 2020. https://learn.web junction.org/?_ga=2.122768712.2143837485.1581546098-2061862348.1581454600

THREE

Legal Outreach and Programming

In this chapter we will be looking at developing outreach partnerships and creating legal programs. Finding community connections can be a great way to support current legal programs and to develop your own. First, I will begin by discussing library outreach and why it is important. Next, I will outline where to look for potential partners in the community and how to develop relationships with those individuals and organizations. Then we will switch gears to walk through some programming best practices. Finally, we will conclude by looking at a number of different sample program types.

OUTREACH

Library outreach can perform a number of important functions. First, it is a great way for you to stay on top of what services and resources are available in your community. When working with legal patrons it is extremely useful to know where to refer people to for legal assistance and information outside of the library. Building relationships with those outside organizations also gives you a way to provide support from the library for those groups.

Second, outreach is also an excellent way to bring nonusers and underserved populations into the library. When you are out in the community it gives you a chance to connect with those who may not use the library. Outreach provides you an opportunity to extend library services beyond the physical space of the library. This way you can meet people where they are in the community rather than waiting for them to come to you.

Unfortunately, there is no set rubric for how to provide outreach services successfully. Every community is going to be different, and so you may need to try different approaches in order to find what works for your community and the population you are trying to reach. It will require you to be adaptable in order to meet those community needs.

FINDING POTENTIAL OUTREACH PARTNERS

Finding potential outreach partners will help you to locate organizations who may be providing services to self-represented litigants. Below is a detailed listing of possible organizations to look into. Please note that some areas may not have all of these organizations and your area might have additional service providers not on this list.

Bar Associations—Every state will have a bar association, and there may also be local bar associations that represent your county or city. Bar associations may sometimes offer legal clinics or free and low-cost legal representation to people who qualify. Many bar associations have special-interest groups that you can use to find attorneys who may be able to present in a specific area of the law.

Legal Services Corporation—Legal Services Corporation provides funding to 133 different legal aid nonprofits around the country. Most of these legal aid organizations will provide pro bono representation to people who meet both income and case-type requirements. Some of these legal aid services may also provide clinics or other types of help to people who are representing themselves. They are another place where you may find potential presenters for library programming.

Access to Justice Commissions—A number of states have created access to justice commissions to make sure that their state's judicial system is taking proactive steps to assist self-represented litigants. These commissions will often form local committees to help with this work. I serve on the committee for the Fourth Judicial District for the Access to Justice Commission for the State of Colorado. Our committee hosts legal resource days for self-represented litigants. We also offer CLE classes for attorneys in high-need areas and offer the credits for free if attorneys agree to take on pro bono cases. In addition, we also worked on a grant-funded project to create a web resource for issues pertaining to senior law. So the work of these groups can take many forms. The committees tend to be made up of a variety of individuals who represent different stakeholder groups in the Access to Justice Movement. On our committee we have judges, legal aid attorneys, court employees, and me, the lone law librarian. The American Bar Association provides a map of all of the active access to justice commissions in the county. The link can be found in the references section below.

Other Service Providers—Check with groups that provide other services to see if they include an element of legal help in what they offer. Domestic violence assistance groups, senior focused groups, and veterans' groups are just a few places to look. Catholic Charities in your area may provide assistance with family immigration issues as well. Some of these service providers may have attorneys on staff to help members of a designated population.

City and Local Government—City and local governments may also be interested in providing legal information to the community, and they have a great reach for promoting events.

Self-Help Groups in Courts—Some states offer self-help offices in their courts. These offices can help people with selecting court forms and understanding court procedures. They may also offer legal clinics or other services. It is good to know if your state's judicial system offers this type of service. These self-help groups can be a great place to which to refer patrons. Be aware that each state will differ in how much legal help a person can get from someone who is not a licensed attorney. For example in Colorado, Chief Justice Directive 13-01 gives some court employees the authority to recommend specific court forms to people. Not all states have this directive, so court employees in other states may be more restricted in the types of information that they can provide.

Law School Faculty and Students—Some law schools may offer legal clinics or other types of legal information to the public. Law school faculty may be another potential source for speakers for library programming.

Department of Corrections: Parole Officers and Re-entry Specialists— Parole officers and re-entry specialists may have clients who have legal issues they need to address as they re-enter the community. Often people coming out of prison may have to address domestic or consumer-credit legal issues. Also, this population can benefit from all types of library programming and resources.

Law Libraries—It is helpful to know where your closest public law library is so you will know where to refer patrons with more in-depth questions. These institutions may also make great partners for creating and offering legal programming to your patrons.

DEVELOPING PARTNERSHIPS

After you have located potential groups to work with, you will want to spend some time thinking about what type of relationship with each organization will be most helpful to your library patrons. Perhaps an organization is already providing some sort of service that the library can support and refer people to. If this is the case, try to get information from the organization on how to best refer people. The library can support the work of other organizations in many ways—through publicity, providing space, distribution of information, and so on. Perhaps an organization can provide speakers for a library-planned event. Or, perhaps you and an organization can work together on a joint venture. In either case, you may wish to outline a partnership agreement, which I will discuss below.

When looking for potential partners, it helps to know about the groups and individuals that you may be working with. Try to find out an organization's mission or strategic plan. This can help you to know if the partnership is a good match. For individuals, see if they have affiliations with any professional organizations. Do they have any degrees or credentials in their area of expertise? Vetting presenters and partners can help you to avoid any unsettling surprises.

Once you have identified potential partners and have committed to working together on an event, it can be helpful to formulate some sort of agreement to clarify expectations. If you are paying for services, you will want to draft a formal contract. If you are not paying for services, it is still helpful to have some sort of partnership agreement or memorandum of understanding in writing that people can refer back to. In whatever type of document you choose to use, you will want to outline who is responsible for what. Details to consider are: what services and types of content will the presenter provide; when you would like the presenter to show up; will the presenter have a role in advertising and promotion? Then outline what services the library will provide: what types of audiovisual equipment will the library have available; will the library advertise and promote the event; will the library make copies of any handouts or presentation materials; is the library responsible for registration? These are all items you will want to address in the agreement.

Remember that it takes time to build relationships. Finding partners in the community can be a lengthy process, and it usually involves going out to meet people where they are in the community. Also keep in mind that some organizations may already have multiple partners that they are already juggling. So if they seem disinterested, it may have nothing to do with you, your organization, or your project; it may just be that they are already stretched too thin. Try not to be discouraged, as perseverance and patience will be your friends in building relationships.

PROGRAMMING

Designing library programs can be challenging, but hopefully this section will alert you to some of the pitfalls and outline some of the best practices. Before you begin you will want to consider what type of program you are hoping to offer. This presents the challenge of anticipating what an audience will want to hear about. Sometimes what you think an audience needs differs from what they actually want. For example, when I began, I thought my audience needed to know how to access legal information on their own; so I designed a few classes where people could learn basic legal research skills and become familiar with which community organizations could help them. Attendance at these classes has been consistently low. I have kept tinkering to see if there is a different way I can frame or advertise the classes, but ultimately they do not seem to be what the masses want to attend. Programs where there is an attorney who can address questions or speak more in depth about a legal topic seem to draw larger crowds, so they seem to be the type of programs my patrons want. Every community is going to have different needs and wants, so do not be afraid to try different approaches to discover what speaks to your audience.

It can be helpful to try to think about who your audience is and what may motivate them. You will also want to assess what type of program you want to offer. Do you want something with a broad appeal that gets lots of people in the door? Or you do you want to offer something smaller in scope, where patrons may get more one-on-one attention? Both approaches have value, and your decision may be based upon what kind of resources you can dedicate to the program. I still keep offering the legal research classes mentioned above because the few people who attend each time really do get something out of them. For me with those classes it is still a better use of time to teach three people at once for an hour and a half, rather than to make three separate hour-long appointments with each person. Every library will need to find a way to assess whether a program is worth the time and effort spent on development and execution.

After you have a sense of what it is that you are hoping to offer, then you will want to find potential partners if they are needed. Please see the section above regarding where to look and what to consider when drafting a partnership agreement. If you are working with an outside presenter or organization, communication will be key to a successful event. Communicate how you intend to communicate. That way people will know when to expect to hear from you. People need to be reminded of things, so I always feel it is best to err on the side of overcommunicating so everything is clear.

Advertising is essential to drawing an audience. Use the traditional methods of advertising such as your website, library calendar, newsletters, and social media channels. The adult programming team at the library I work at has set up their own Meetup group to communicate programs to their followers. They also use the neighborhood networking group Nextdoor to advertise events. Do not underestimate the effectiveness of older forms of advertising as well. Community calendars, local newspapers, radio, and television stations will have a great reach. We also still use posters and flyers, and if you can post them outside of the library, even better. Try to use as many different communication channels as possible.

While not totally necessary, having a way to register attendees can provide some distinct benefits. First, it can provide you with an estimated headcount. Keep in mind that not everyone who registers for a free event will show up, and you may also get folks who did not register showing up at the door. A registration list also allows you to communicate with attendees. Generally, your attendance will be higher if you can send out a reminder a few days in advance. Or if you need to unexpectedly cancel the event, the list allows you to communicate that change. Our library system has meeting-room software that we can use for program registration, but there are some free alternatives out there. Eventbrite is free to use if your event is free. Google Forms is another possibility, and there are probably other free services available too.

When you are a week away from your event, you will want to touch base with your presenter and whoever is hosting the event if you are not holding it in-house. Be sure to provide the presenter with directions to the venue, any relevant parking information, and the best way to reach you on the day of the event. If you are expecting inclement weather, outline any contingency plan. Cover questions about any last-minute needs that the speaker may have and confirm her audiovisual needs. If you are working with a host location, also touch base with the people there to confirm that the space will be configured the way you need it to be and the staff will be informed of your event so they can direct people on the day.

On that day you will want to plan to arrive thirty to sixty minutes early. This way you can check the room setup and make any necessary modifications. The extra time will also prove useful if you need to do any audiovisual troubleshooting. It is nice to always provide water for speakers. You may also consider having refreshments if your budget allows; snacks tend to make for a happier, more attentive audience. Then, as people arrive, greet them so they feel welcome and know they are in the right place. Last but not least, remember it is supposed to be fun! It can be easy to get swept up in the stress of event planning, but try to stay focused on the value of the information that you will be providing to the community.

Even the best-planned events can hit some snags. If you are working with a host location, be sure to have clear and frequent communication with the people in charge there. There is nothing worse than showing up to a building you are unfamiliar with to find that no chairs have been set out or you don't have the equipment you need. Discouraging as it is, you can still do everything right and still have no one show up. Some factors will just be out of your control. If this happens, try a different time of day or day of the week, or possibly a different venue. Your audience may still be out there, just not where you expected. It also helps to be aware of any community conflicts. This will vary by community, but it might include things like school holiday schedules or large sporting events.

For some general resources concerning formulating library programming for adults there are a few places to look in addition to the wide range of print literature out there. WebJunction is one place for information. The ALA website Programming Librarian also has a number of programs outlined on their website. You may also find that your state library has available resources.

PROGRAM EXAMPLES

In this section, I would like to offer examples of legal programs, including some in which I have directly participated. Some are programs that I created; others are ones that my library partnered on. I also list some examples of programs I have collected from other law libraries around the country. This is not an exhaustive list, and you should be creative when designing programs and activities in order to meet the particular needs of your community.

Virtual Pro Se Clinic of Colorado

The first program I would like to discuss is a legal clinic program that our library participates in. This program was created and is administered by attorney Ric Morgan. The goal of the clinic is to connect self-represented litigants in more rural, underserved areas with attorneys from around the state. Each clinic site is hosted by a public library. The library provides a private space, generally a study or meeting room that has a computer or laptop with a Wi-Fi connection, microphone, and camera. These computers are outfitted with the free version of the Zoom videoconferencing software. Libraries log in at their designated time, and then patrons generally have between ten to twenty minutes to meet with trained attorneys to discuss any civil legal matter. The overall budget for this program is relatively low. Monthly clinics for forty-two sites can be offered for a few thousand dollars per year. The costs go to website hosting, attorney training, and the Zoom subscription for the attorney volunteers so they can share their screen with participants when necessary.

We have had great success with this clinic model. The clinic is offered at one of our library district's rural libraries where no other legal services were available in the community. We generally serve between five to seven people each month. Participants come in with all kinds of questions, ranging from domestic violence, landlord tenant, probate, consumer credit, and more. Patrons generally leave with a better sense of what steps they need to take, and we do get repeat visitors as folks work through their legal journeys. A number of other libraries around the country offer different kinds of legal clinics; some are in person, some are over the phone, so there are a number of ways that you can tweak this model depending on the resources available.

Estate and Probate Classes

We have offered two separate sets of estate planning classes. The first class, "Top Ten Estate Planning Mistakes" is taught by an attorney who was recommended to me by the Estate and Elder Law Section of our local bar association. This class focuses on common mistakes that people make when planning their estates. The second class is a two-part class that covers "Basic Estate Planning" and "Basic Probate Issues." It is taught by two volunteer attorneys from Colorado Legal Services. In these classes, since the legal expertise comes from the attorneys, I am only responsible for reserving the space, managing registration, advertising, making sure that the room is set up correctly, and that the audiovisual equipment works.

Legal Research Basics Classes

I have designed and offered a few different iterations of these classes. One class, entitled "Legal Ease," covers many of the tools and resources that pro se litigants will need to familiarize themselves with, such as how to find court forms, how to locate laws, and what free and low-cost legal services are available in the community. I have also offered classes on how to use WestlawNext, our main legal research databases, and one that focuses specifically on the Colorado Revised Statutes, as that is our most commonly used legal resource.

Renter's Rights Workshops

This program is a collaboration between the City of Colorado Springs, Colorado Legal Services, the Justice Center, and the Pikes Peak Library District. The Community Development Office of the City of Colorado Springs wanted a way to provide information to the community in order, hopefully, to mitigate the high eviction rates in our community. The city organized the events and brought in an attorney from Colorado Legal Services to provide the content, while the library provides the space and assists with the advertising. In 2020, we started to offer this program online using Microsoft Teams. We have participants register ahead of time and then e-mail them a link to a watch a live webinar.

Legal Resource Days

Our Access to Justice Committee has three legal resource days throughout the year. There is Family Law Day, Senior Law Day, and a Legal Resource Day that covers a wide range of civil legal topics. Each of these days offers free one-on-one appointments with attorneys, classes on various legal topics, and access to other community services providers related to that particular legal area. In 2020, this program also shifted to a virtual format. We built a website to host pre-recorded videos on a wide range of legal topics, offered a call-in clinic, and created an online directory of local service providers.

Continuing Legal Education Classes

Attorneys need to take Continuing Legal Education (CLE) classes in order to keep their licenses. Our Access to Justice Committee offered a CLE class on landlord–tenant law for free if attorneys agreed to take on two full representation pro bono eviction cases or to provide limited advice for six cases. Attorneys could still pay for the class without taking on cases, but most chose the free option, which helped many people facing eviction by providing them legal representation.

Record Sealing/ Expungement Clinics

The Criminal Defense Bar of Colorado obtained grants to for two years to offer record sealing/expungement clinics around the state. These clinics required volunteer attorneys and paralegals to search for records, check the statutes, and assist with the paperwork. Laws will vary from state to state about who is eligible to have criminal records sealed or removed. There is a detailed example of this type of program found at the website Programming Librarian.

Topic-Specific Classes

A number of law libraries offer classes that focus on a particular area of law. These classes may be taught by attorneys or librarians. L.A. County's

Law Library offers an extensive set of classes. Topics include Debt Collection Defense; Civil Lawsuit Basics; Family Law; Unemployment Appeals; Becoming a Conservator; Paternity; Business Contracts; Evictions; Accessing Court records; and more.

Name-Change Clinics

Many law libraries around the county also offer name-change clinics where attorneys can assist with the forms and paperwork for this process.

Copyright and Patent Classes

Another type of topic-specific class that a number of libraries offer covers the basics of intellectual property law. Local authors and inventors could benefit from this type of information.

Legal Reference Hours

Law librarians from the Minnesota State Law Library regularly hold legal research hours at several of the public library locations around St. Paul.

REFERENCE SCENARIO

Patron: I need information on garnishment.

Librarian: Okay, what type of information are you looking for? General information? Laws? Forms?

Patron: I got behind on my state taxes and now they are garnishing my wages. I am having trouble paying other bills. Can they even do this?

Librarian: Well, let's see what we can find. Was it here in this state that you fell behind in the taxes?

Patron: Yes.

Librarian: Okay, let's first see what we can find about garnishment in general and then we can see if there is any relief you can get if you're having trouble with other expenses. So let's just start with a simple search, like wage garnishment Colorado. I would always put the state in there in case the laws vary from state to state.

Patron: It's just so messed up. If I didn't have money to pay the taxes, why do they think I have money now?

Librarian: Yeah, that sounds very frustrating and difficult. Okay, here is an article from Nolo that talks about wage garnishment in Colorado. It does look like wages can be garnished for missed tax payments, but it also sets limits on how much they can take. Let's print this out, so then you can see if they are taking too much. Okay, and the article is pointing us to the Colorado Department of Labor and Employment for more information, so let's look there.

Okay, I don't see garnishment listed in any of the main titles on their homepage, so let's use their search box to see if we can find the right page for you. It looks like the information on this wage deductions page is pretty much the same information as what we found on the other site. So while it doesn't give us anything new, it does help confirm what we found. It also looks like it cites the specific Colorado laws about garnishment, so let's print those out for you to read.

Since it is the Department of Revenue that is taking your wages, let's see if there is anything on their website that might help. So let's search something like Colorado Department of Revenue garnishment. Okay, now we are starting to get somewhere. Here it looks like they have an explanation of the garnishment process and then at the bottom is the application for financial hardship. Do you want me to print out all of this stuff?

Patron: Yes, please. Is there someone here at the library that can fill out these forms for me?

Librarian: Unfortunately, no. We are not allowed to complete paperwork like this for people. It does look like it is going to require a bit of financial information, so you are going to want to carefully read through it all and take a look at your finances to make sure you qualify. If you have questions about that part of the process, there are some free legal clinics where you can speak with an attorney. Let me get you that calendar.

When helping a patron find information, I try to model how best to go about searching for facts. Explain why you include the jurisdiction in your search. Demonstrate what to do if you don't immediately find what you are looking for. In this scenario, one might be tempted to jump into the statutes to see what the law says, but first consulting a secondary source like Nolo may help give you a clearer picture and point you to resources that will list the actual statutes so they are easier to find. This scenario is also a good reminder of the wealth of information that is on government agency websites. Many times those sites will help you to quickly find the relevant laws and forms.

CONCLUSION

In this chapter I began with a discussion of how outreach to legal organizations can benefit your library. It is a great way to identify community services and to build partnerships with community organizations. Going out into the community can be an excellent way to find and connect with people who are not are using the library. I identified several places to look for potential partners, though your community may have different resources available. You will want to be intentional about how your partnerships will work, so be sure to look carefully into potential partners and draft some kind of agreement.

Legal programming can assume many forms. It is important to take some time to consider what type of scope and impact you want to have. Try to figure out what will appeal to your audience, though sometimes that will become evident only through trial and error. Thorough advertising and frequent communication will contribute to a successful event. Using some way to track registration will also help. Don't be discouraged if things don't work out the first time; sometimes programs need to be revised in order to make the desired impact. There are many different types of programs you can try, but also be creative in your efforts to best respond to the needs of your community.

REFERENCES

"Access to Justice Commissions." American Bar Association. Accessed April 24, 2019. https://www.americanbar.org/groups/legal_aid_indigent_defendants/resource _center_for_access_to_justice/atj-commissions/.

"Chief Justice Directive 13-01." Colorado Judicial Branch. Accessed April 24, 2019. https:// www.courts.state.co.us/Courts/Supreme_Court/Directives/13-01.pdf.

Eventbrite. Accessed April 26, 2019. https://www.eventbrite.com/.

"Expunge Your Criminal Record." Programming Librarian. June 12, 2015. Accessed April 24, 2019. http://programminglibrarian.org/programs/expunge-your-criminal -record.

"Find Legal Aid." LSC. Accessed April 24, 2019. https://www.lsc.gov/what-legal-aid/find -legal-aid.

Google Forms. Accessed April 26, 2019. https://www.google.com/forms/about/.

Meetup. Accessed April 26, 2019. https://www.meetup.com/.

Nextdoor. Accessed April 26, 2019. https://nextdoor.com/.

Programming Librarian. Accessed April 24, 2019. http://www.programminglibrarian.org/.

WebJunction. Accessed April 24, 2019. https://www.webjunction.org/home.html.

FOUR

Legal Reference Interview

When working with a library user who has questions about a legal matter, it is essential to conduct a legal reference interview. This process will be relatively similar to carrying out a regular reference interview where you ask a patron open-ended questions in order to determine what information she is looking for and how she plans to use that information. However, the legal interview has a few distinct elements that I will now examine. First, I will explain the purpose of the legal reference interview so you understand what you are hoping to accomplish and what you want to avoid doing. Next, I will outline the process for the interview and explain the reasons for the various steps. Then I will address the concerns of the unauthorized practice of law and liability, which will be followed by a discussion of the difference between legal information and legal advice. Finally, I would like to wrap up with some other considerations to keep in mind when working with legal patrons.

PURPOSE OF THE LEGAL REFERENCE INTERVIEW

During the legal reference interview you are trying to accomplish a couple of things. First, you want to help the patron locate and navigate resources as well as instruct him in the research process so that he will be able to locate binding primary authority for the legal issue at hand. What is binding primary authority? We will discuss that in more detail in chapter 5, but briefly it is the law or laws of the jurisdiction the patron is from that apply to his situation. The other thing we want to accomplish, or rather avoid, is to not offer any legal advice or interpret legal resources for the patron. Providing legal advice or interpretations can be considered the unauthorized practice of law, something you must avoid.

The legal reference interview is slightly different from your usual reference interview in that it tends to focus more on the process of research rather than on determining an exact answer. As we will see, the law is complex, and providing a patron with an exact answer might require you to interpret laws or to give legal advice. When conducting a legal reference interview, I like to approach questions with the mindset of what potential sources might have the answer to this question rather than what I think is the answer to this question. Given this approach, the legal reference interview will generally provide more instruction on how to use and search the various sources, since ultimately it is up to the patron to determine what the answer to her question is.

THE PROCESS

The legal reference interview begins similarly to a regular reference interview in that you want to determine what a patron is looking for by asking open-ended questions. For example, which subject area does the legal question fall into? What information does the patron already have? What resources has the patron already used or contacted? For what purpose does the patron need the information? Is she appearing in court? And if so, which court? Does she have any citations? What deadline might the patron be up against? Our initial questioning will help lead us to the subject area that the patron needs information about. It can also give us clues about which jurisdiction to search and the purpose for which the patron needs the information.

After we have determined the general subject area, next we want to find the jurisdiction that the legal matter falls into. Is this something covered by local, state, or federal law? The reason why jurisdiction is important is that we need the authority, or laws, that the patron finds to be binding to the situation at hand. For example, if the patron pulls up laws pertaining to divorces in Nebraska but is filing for divorce in Colorado, the laws that he found do not apply to his case; they are not binding. Usually the subject area of the question can give you some clues about which jurisdiction will be the relevant one. In his work *Legal Reference for Librarians: How and Where to Find the Answers*, Paul Healey provides a helpful chart outlining some of the major legal topics encountered in libraries and their corresponding jurisdictions, as well as what types of law generally cover these areas (Healey 2014, 40). Generally, most legal questions that I field at the public library tend to be matters of state jurisdiction: topics such as divorce, landlord/tenant, and estate/probate. On occasion we receive questions regarding bankruptcy or employment discrimination, and these are usually matters of federal jurisdiction. Questions that involve local jurisdiction tend to be issues like dealing with noisy neighbors, building ordinances, and so on.

Another possible way to determine jurisdiction is to find out in which court the patron is required to appear. This does not always work if the patron is just starting her legal journey; however, if she already has been to court, then you can use this information to narrow down where you will begin searching. It is good to keep in mind that if you begin searching the laws of one jurisdiction and do not find anything, you can check other jurisdictions. For example, I had a patron ask me what laws the state of Colorado had about insurance requirements for contractors. The patron seemed knowledgeable in the area, and I had never researched this topic before, so naturally we began by seeing what laws we could find in the state statutes and regulations. We could not locate anything relevant to his question. So before assuming that there were no laws in this area, we next checked what local laws and agencies might regulate this area. And that is where we found our answer. Be thorough in your searching, but never be hesitant to switch gears if you keep turning up nothing.

Once you have determined where to search, the next step in the legal research process is to compile a list of key words for searching. Keep in mind that legal vocabulary can differ from day-to-day speech. A good legal dictionary, such as *Black's Law Dictionary*, or an online legal encyclopedia, like Cornell's Legal Information Institute's Wex, can be useful for figuring out the correct legal terminology. Often indexes will also provide cross-references to lead you to the correct term. In *Locating the Law*, Joan Allen-Hart provides some suggestions for brainstorming alternative terms. You can try to generate closely related words, substituting "motor vehicles" for "cars," for example. You can try either broader or narrower categories; or using synonyms and antonyms is another approach (Allen-Hart 2001, 5-5). Using a secondary source, one that explains the law, might also help you to better understand how things are described in legal terminology. However, from time to time you may encounter a library user who is not using the correct legal terminology for her situation. So if you are struggling to find anything with the terms that patron has given you, then it is time to either generate some synonyms or do some background research to better understand the legal topic and the terms used.

For example, I once worked with a patron who was looking for a form for a motion to change the judge who would hear her case. This seemed pretty straightforward. She was giving me what sounded like an official title, so I figured this would be a pretty easy known-item search. However, after we had searched through all of the motion forms on the court's website, it was clear that this was not what the form was called. After more research in the court rules and in a number of different secondary sources, she determined that the form was actually entitled "Post-Conviction Remedies"—nothing close to the terms with which we began. So just keep in mind that if nothing is coming up, it might be because that thing does not exist but it might also be because it is called something else. Also, if you hit what appears to be a dead end, and you have tried everything you and the patron can think of, this might be a good time to refer that patron to a law library to let her make the final determination that no such resource exists.

Once you have determined your subject area, jurisdiction, and a list of key search terms, it is time to demonstrate to the patron how to use the sources. Even if you have zero familiarity with the law, this next part is just basic-information literacy instruction. For online sources, point out how you can tell if a URL is from a government or an academic source. Show patrons how to evaluate a website. Demonstrate how to navigate a website and the web browser. Show them how to print. If it is a database that you are using, then demonstrate how to search the database, apply filters, and how to view records. Show patrons how to print and save results. Finally, if it is a print resource, demonstrate how the index and table of contents work. Do not assume that patrons will have those skills. Many legal sources in print also use two- or three-part numbering schemes to break apart various sections and laws, so you may also need to explain how those numbers work so patrons can locate the relevant sections.

So, to review the process, begin by determining the subject area of the question. Then use the subject area and other clues to figure out the jurisdiction where the legal matter is taking place. Next, brainstorm a list of key words to use when searching and do not be afraid to revise as you learn more about the matter. Finally, help the patron understand how to search for information in the applicable resources.

THE UNAUTHORIZED PRACTICE OF LAW

Something that all librarians who handle questions regarding legal matters should be aware of is the unauthorized practice of law. Most states have laws prohibiting people who are not licensed attorneys and who do not have an attorney–client relationship from offering legal advice. This is why it is important for librarians to offer only legal information and not to give legal interpretations or advice of any kind. While no librarian has been charged with the unauthorized practice of law and though most patrons realize that a librarian is not their attorney, this is still a healthy boundary to maintain (Allen-Hart 2001, 6-1; Healey 2014, 15). There are still many ways in which librarians can help patrons with legal questions without providing legal advice. In the next section of this chapter, I will try to clarify this delineation between legal information and legal advice.

One way to prevent you and your staff from offering legal advice and interpretations is to develop a legal reference policy. (For a longer discussion of legal reference policies, see Chapter 2.) Policies can be useful in that they articulate the difference between legal information and advice as well as give the reason why librarians cannot offer legal advice and interpretations. They make it clear to staff what kinds of help they can offer and make it clear to patrons what they can expect from library staff. Finally, for a staff member who has to deal with an irate and insistent patron, a policy supplies reasons why he cannot give into a patron's demands.

Even if the unauthorized practice of law was not something we had to worry about, there are other ethical and professional issues to consider when handling legal questions. For instance, there is the issue of liability for you, the library, and for the patron. Many librarians are hesitant to work with patrons who have legal questions because they fear being held liable for providing incorrect information. Our duty as librarians is to provide access to and assist patrons in finding information. We can be experts at finding information in a subject area without being experts in the subject itself. For example, I know how to find information in the automotive database AllData, yet I would never be able to fix my own car. I find myself being very blunt and upfront with patrons regarding the limits of my knowledge. At first, this can feel a bit uncomfortable, because I think that as librarians we like having the answers to things. However, we need to be truthful about when we do not know and when we cannot provide answers. Most patrons seem to appreciate honesty.

Further, I believe that in acknowledging the complexity of the law and the legal system we are doing our patrons a favor. Many people come in with the view that their legal problem is simple and can be easily solved in a short amount of time with limited effort. However, in many instances this is not the case. Some librarians worry that by encouraging self-represented litigants we are allowing them to be a liability to themselves and others. Misfiled court documents or a poorly drafted will can cause both problems and unneeded expense for the patron and his family. Librarians can sometimes provide a needed reality check to the patron by demonstrating how complex finding and digesting legal information can be. This, then, is our opportunity to connect patrons to legal experts through clinics and pro bono services to help them better navigate the legal system.

At the 2018 annual meeting for the American Association of Law Libraries, Pauline Afuso, Paul Healey, and Karen Westwood presented a session entitled "Uncertainty Management: A Tool to Assist Self-Represented Litigants." In this session they looked at how uncertainty can be a tool that librarians may leverage during the reference interview. Coming out of communications theory, uncertainty management examines how people balance uncertainty within their interactions. While generally I think a lot of people see uncertainty as a negative feeling, it does not always have to be. In some situations, uncertainty can increase hope. Either way, though, uncertainty is a concept that librarians can use during the reference interaction to demonstrate to patrons the complexity of the legal system and legal research.

LEGAL INFORMATION VERSUS LEGAL ADVICE

In navigating these issues of the unauthorized practice of law and liability, it helps to have a good working understanding of how legal information differs from legal advice. At times this distinction will not be very clear, and every librarian seems to have a slightly different interpretation of where the line between them lies. That being said, I would like to offer some of the distinctions that I use to help determine the difference between legal information and legal advice.

I would like to offer some commentary on Table 4.1. First, we never want to recommend specific forms to a patron; the act of selecting a specific form constitutes advice. Rather, we can show patrons where to find forms and how to search the resources for forms, but they must make their own selections. For example, if you have a patron who requests a form for divorce, you will find that multiple forms are needed when filing for divorce. A patron will

Table 4.1. Determining the Difference between Legal Information and Legal Advice

Legal Information	Legal Advice
Direct patrons to where they can find forms and instructions for forms.	Recommend a specific legal form; fill out a form; draft legal documents for a patron.
Suggest resources; locate an item or law using a citation.	Tell the patron this is the law he is looking for without him providing a citation.
Legal definitions; procedural definitions	Legal interpretations; procedural advice
Cites of statutes, court rules, and ordinances	Research of statutes, court rules, and ordinances
Options	Opinions
General referrals	Subjective or biased referrals

have to select forms based on a number of factors, such as if the couple has children. Depending on the state you reside in, there may be places to which you can direct patrons who are not sure which forms to select. In the state of Colorado, we have court employees called the Self-Represented Litigant Coordinators and the Family Court Facilitators who are allowed to help patrons determine what forms they need, but this may not be the case in your state. Check your state's judicial branch website to see if they offer any self-help services. Sometimes you may find that flowcharts or other tools to aid with selection are provided by the courts or legal aid organizations. These types of tools can help your patrons make determinations on their own. Or perhaps there are legal services organizations or clinics in the area that can assist patrons in selecting forms. When suggesting resources to a patron, I always like to offer options of what is available. Does she want to read the actual law itself? Or would she like to first look at a book that explains the law? Providing a range of options again places the onus of choice on the patron rather than the librarian. Even if you are relatively sure that a specific law pertains to the patron's situation, it is best to refrain from saying "Here is the exact law you need." A patron may have left out important pieces of information in your reference interview, so perhaps you do not know the full scope of the issue. I generally explain where to find the various types of laws that might apply, describe how to use and search within the source, but then leave it up to the patron to determine which laws apply.

In legal research, you will find secondary source materials extremely useful in helping patrons to find the laws they need. A good number of patrons want to dive right into the primary law, the law itself. However, using different types of secondary sources can assist the patron in finding the key laws and cases in a particular area of law. So while we as librarians might not be able to state directly what law covers that specific area, a secondary source may be able to provide that type of interpretation of the legal landscape for the patron. For example, if you encounter a library user with a specific citation or form number, it is fine to pull up what matches that citation. We can consider those known-item searches, and in that case you are not advising the patron or interpreting the law, you are just providing him with the information he requested.

On occasion you will encounter library users who are looking for attorney recommendations. Just as we would never recommend a specific doctor, so it is with attorneys. There are a number of different attorney directories, and some that provide reviews, and it is best to show patrons how to search those sources. A few places to look would be your state or local bar association; Martindale Hubbell, which is available as a print source but also online at martindale.com; or the website Avvo.com, to name two.

At times respecting the line between legal information and legal advice can feel like you are never providing direct answers, instead giving access to the information and then asking the patron to review and interpret the information on their own. This can feel a little odd at first, since I think we naturally want to get to the bottom of things and find answers for people. Also, patrons are sometimes taken aback because this is a different type of service than what they typically find at the library. For me, it helps to remember that we are offering not only access to legal information but instruction in important information literacy skills. Since most of us are not legal experts but rather experts in finding and assessing information, these are the skills and services that we can offer our patrons without any fear of liability.

ADDITIONAL THOUGHTS

I want to wrap up this chapter with just a few additional thoughts of points to consider when conducting a reference interview with patrons who have legal questions. The first thing is to never underestimate the power of listening. Many patrons with legal questions are going to feel overwhelmed and that they are not being heard. Providing people the opportunity to tell their story can be helpful by giving them the space to fully articulate and think about their situation. Some patrons you encounter will be fairly reticent; they may be embarrassed or want their privacy respected. However, more seem to be inclined to tell you everything. So there is a fine line between listening enough to give a person the space to tell his story and to get the information that you need to help him, and having him list every problem he is having beyond the issue at hand. Every transaction will be different, but it is best to try to be patient and give the patron the time to speak. Having this opportunity to articulate his situation can sometimes help him to fully think through the situation and weigh his options.

It is also good not to take things personally. Patrons who are navigating the legal system may not be at their best when you meet with them. Generally, dealing with the legal system is a stressful time for people. It is time-consuming, challenging, and expensive. There is a great deal of uncertainty, and people may be threatened by the loss of children, property, freedom, or status. Patrons may feel like they are getting the runaround because no one can offer them quick advice or direct answers to their questions. So naturally people are frustrated, and they may choose to take that frustration out on you. I would say that by and large most people are great to work with. They understand the limitations that librarians work under. However, every now and again you encounter someone who does not handle her situation gracefully. Maintaining an intellectual distance from these types of charged interactions may serve you well.

If a patron is in a protracted legal battle, chances are the process may take months or even years. You may have multiple interactions with the same person, so it is best to keep things professional at all times. One trick I use after any type of negative interaction with a patron is, when I see him next, I pretend I'm meeting him for the first time. That jettisons any negative emotional baggage from previous interactions and gives both of you the opportunity to make a better impression the second, or third, or fourth time around.

Since legal problems are complex and generally involve multiple steps, a lot of problems will not be solved after just one visit. I generally consider an interaction with a patron successful if I can move him one step forward. Perhaps I can show the library user where to find court forms, or give him the information for a legal clinic, or demonstrate how to search for statutes. These are all pieces of information that he will need to ultimately address the issue that he is facing. With a lot of other types of information and requests we have become accustomed to thinking that unless we answer a question right on the spot we have failed, but we need a different mindset when working with legal information where there are more limitations on the services we can provide and the nature of the process is lengthier. So after you start a patron on her journey, always invite her to come back as she moves through the process. As she pieces together more of the information on her own, there are still ways that we can assist as the situation develops.

Also remember that it is okay for you to take your time. Every now and again you encounter a patron who is in a rush. He may have procrastinated because he is overwhelmed by his situation and the paperwork needs to be filed at the courthouse immediately. This is unfortunate, but do not let the patron's franticness overwhelm you. You will think much more clearly if you do not allow yourself to be pulled into this frenzy.

Be comfortable making referrals. A lot of the work I do with legal reference questions is to provide referrals. I refer patrons to our court system's self-help offices when they need help selecting court forms. I refer patrons to legal clinics when they need help interpreting the law or are not sure where to start. I refer patrons to secondary source materials when they need to better understand the legal concepts in play. I refer patrons to other law libraries when we do not have the materials they need. Become familiar with the various legal resources in your community. What services might the court offer? Who provides pro bono help or legal clinics? Where is your closest law library? This is all good information to have on hand. (Referral resources are discussed in more detail in Chapter 2.)

Remember that sometimes there is no answer or that the answer is not the one that the patron wants. These questions are some of the most frustrating and time-consuming. I had a patron who was adamant that there were federal laws that regulated how security-camera footage must be stored and archived. First of all, federal law does not really address this matter. Any laws pertaining to security cameras that we found were all from state jurisdictions. Furthermore, in the state we were in, those laws only dictated that you had to notify the public that security cameras were in use. There was nothing regulating the storage of footage or archives. I finally had to confirm with our security team that there were no laws or regulations they had to follow with the security-camera footage our library generated. These questions with no answers, or answers that are different from what the patron expected, are always difficult, because you are never sure if there is something that was overlooked, or perhaps you were searching with the wrong terminology. I would recommend that if you find yourself in this situation and feel you have exhausted all the possible resources at your disposal, then refer the patron to a law library to verify that there are no pertinent laws he should be looking into.

REFERENCE SCENARIO

Patron: I need help with the law.
Librarian: Okay, we'll see what we can do. Can you tell me a little more?
Patron: Divorce laws.
Librarian: Are you looking for general information on divorce? Or how to file a divorce? And do you want that information for this state?
Patron: I need someone who is going to help me file for divorce.
Librarian: Are you looking to hire an attorney? Or did you want to see if there might be any legal aid services that you could apply for?
Patron: I don't think I can really afford an attorney, so it would be great if someone would do it for free.
Librarian: Okay, let me get you the information for the two organizations that offer legal aid services. Just so you are aware, they both have income requirements and there is no guarantee they will be able to take your case. While they do a lot of family law cases, they sometimes have to prioritize cases with domestic violence and things like that over a more straightforward divorce. I would reach out to both of them, though, to see if they can help at all. And if domestic violence is an issue, there is a separate organization that has attorneys available for that, so just let me know if you want their information. If you are unable to get legal aid, there are a number of free clinics that happen every month, so let me get you that calendar. If you are interested, I can also show you some general information about divorce and where to go on the court website for the forms and directions.
Patron: Yeah, I guess that would be a good idea in case the legal aid stuff doesn't work out.

Librarian: Sure, we have a few books that give a good overview of the process and what to expect. So let's grab those. And then, in our state they have a section on the court's website with the forms and some directions for divorce. So let's take a look at that.

Patron: There are so many forms! Which ones do I need?

Librarian: Unfortunately, I am not an attorney, so I don't know what are all of the forms you will need. You can either read through these questions that will guide you to the answer, or there is an office in the courthouse that helps people find the right paperwork for family law cases. They are not attorneys either, so they can't advise you, but they do have the authority to tell you what the correct forms are for your situation and to explain the process. Let me get you their flyer. If you visit them and they tell you what forms you need, you can always come back to the library to print them out, as it is a lot cheaper than buying the packet at the courthouse. I can help you with that once you know the exact forms you need.

Patron: Okay, that sounds good. I didn't realize it would be so much work.

Librarian: Yeah, legal problems can sometimes take a long time to solve and are often a lot of work. Let me give you my card so if you have any follow up questions you can reach me. I might not always know the answer, but I'll try my best to connect you with someone who does.

One of the main areas about which we receive questions is divorce. This is one topic area where it can be useful to know what resources are available in your community as well as if there are court forms that you can point people to. I try to give people reasonable expectations when contacting legal aid organizations. It is good to give them a heads-up that there are financial requirements and that they can't take every case. I still encourage people to reach out to them. As for forms, we can definitely show people where to find them, but we must refrain from helping them to select specific forms. Some states have court employees that can assist with that selection, but not all states do. It can be worth finding out if your state offers such a service. We make referrals all the time to our Family Court Facilitators and the Self-Represented Litigant Coordinators, as they can assist with form selection. In this particular situation, I tried to give the patron a range of options from general information to legal aid to court forms. Sometimes when people are first starting out on their legal journey they are not quite sure what they need. Always invite them back for more help, for legal problems usually have multiple steps and patrons may need help more than once.

CONCLUSION

To review, when working with a library user with a legal question our main goal is to assist the patron in finding binding primary authority for the question at hand. This means we want to assist the patron in locating the laws from the correct jurisdiction that apply to that subject area. During this process we want to refrain from offering advice or interpretations of the law so we are not committing the unauthorized practice of law. To do this, we begin by asking open-ended questions to find out more about the patrons needs and questions. This questioning can help us determine the subject area that the patron needs information about and potentially the jurisdiction that this matter is occurring in as well. After we have been able to determine those factors, then we want to brainstorm a list of key words to use while searching. Keep in mind that you may have to adjust this list. Lastly, we can then show the patron what potential sources might have the answers and then demonstrate how the patron can search and use those sources. We always want to be cognizant that we are not advising the patron or providing legal interpretations. However, we can still provide a great deal of help by giving the patron access to legal information.

REFERENCES

Afuso, Pauline, Paul Healey, and Karen Westwood. "Uncertainty Management: A Tool to Assist Self-Represented Litigants." Conference Presentation, AALL Annual Meeting and Conference, Baltimore, MD, July 15, 2018.

Allen-Hart, Joan. "Basic Legal Research Techniques." In *Locating the Law: A Handbook for Non-law Librarians with an Emphasis on California Law, Fourth Edition*, edited by Karla Castetter, 5-1—5-13. Los Angeles, CA: Southern California Association of Law Libraries, 2001.

Allen-Hart, Joan. "Legal Reference vs. Legal Advice." In *Locating the Law: A Handbook for Non-law Librarians with an Emphasis on California Law, Fourth Edition*, edited by Karla Castetter, 6-1—6-6. Los Angeles, CA: Southern California Association of Law Libraries, 2001.

Avvo. Accessed February 8, 2019. https://www.avvo.com/.

Garner, Bryan A., ed. *Black's Law Dictionary, 10th Edition*. Eagan, MN: Thomson West, 2014.

Healey, Paul D. *Legal Reference for Librarians: How and Where to Find the Answers*. Chicago: ALA Editions, 2014.

Martindale. Accessed February 8, 2019. https://www.martindale.com/.

Martindale Hubbell, Inc. *Martindale-Hubbell Law Directory*. Summitt, NJ: Martindale, 2018.

Wex, Cornell Law School Legal Information Institute. Accessed February 2, 2019. https://www.law.cornell.edu/wex.

FIVE

Legal Research Concepts

In this chapter I will discuss a number of concepts that come into play when delving into legal research questions. I will begin with a brief review of the structure of government and the different types of laws that are created. You will find more detailed descriptions of each branch of government, as well as where to find resources for each of those branches, in subsequent chapters. After reviewing the structure of government, we will take a look at the concept of jurisdiction and how it factors into legal research. A discussion of the different categories of law, authority, and currency follows. I conclude with a short explanation of the difference between official and unofficial publications, citation formats, and some brief remarks about where to look for materials. Having a working knowledge of these concepts can give you a sense of what types of law may be relevant, as well as what to look for when conducting legal research.

STRUCTURE OF GOVERNMENT AND TYPES OF LAW

The Federal Government

I begin this section by reviewing the structure of the federal government and the types of laws that are generated at this level. This will be followed by a similar discussion of state and local governments. As we know, the federal government is divided into three branches with distinct functions that provide a system of checks and balances. All three branches generate laws of some type (Table 5.1).

In the United States federal government, the Constitution is the overriding document that describes the powers of government and determines the scope of what laws can be created. It outlines the rights of the individual, and all laws created at the federal, state, and local levels must fall within its bounds.

Table 5.1. Federal Governmental Branches and the Types of Laws They Create

Branch of Government	Type of Law
Legislative	Slip laws
	Session laws
	Statutes
	Codes
Executive	Regulations
	Executive orders
Judicial	Case law
	Court rules

Laws created by state and local governments cannot contradict what is laid out the in the U.S. Constitution. The Constitution even sets limits on which areas of life the legislature can create laws about.

When most people think of laws, they tend to think of those which come out of the legislative branch, as generally that is where the process starts. Both houses of the legislature draft bills. If a bill is passed by both the House of Representatives and the Senate and then is signed into law by the president, it becomes what is known as a slip law. At the end of the legislative session, those slip laws are grouped together as session laws. At the end of the legislative session, these session laws are published as the *U.S. Statutes at Large* and are organized chronologically. Eventually the laws of a general and permanent nature are reorganized by topic in a process known as codification, after which they are known as the United States Code. A more thorough description of this process and where to find these laws in their various formats can be found in Chapter 7.

In the executive branch, most of the laws are created by the various government agencies. In order for those agencies to produce regulations, there must be some sort of statutory authority behind their creation. The legislative branch makes laws regarding what needs to be done, then the executive branch makes laws on how to do it. This process will be fully outlined in Chapter 9. Other laws originating in the executive branch that people may request are executive orders. Some federal agencies operate courts and produce rulings that also have the force of law. By and large, administrative law, or laws from the executive branch, are the types of laws for which I receive the fewest questions, even though many of them affect our daily lives.

Last are the laws that originate in the judicial branch. The task of the judiciary is to apply the laws created by the other branches of government. Laws from the judicial branch are comprised of opinions written by judges on the appellate and supreme courts. Case law consists of the cases that change legal precedent. Since the United States is what is referred to as a common-law system, this means that cases decided in appeals-level courts or higher provide a rule or guide for cases that go through the lower levels of the court. In other words, the lower courts must follow the precedent set by the cases in those higher-level courts of the same jurisdiction. The other type of law originating in the judicial branch are court rules. These rules outline how court procedures work. So patrons who are representing themselves in court will need to familiarize themselves with these laws in addition to the laws pertinent to the topic area of their case. More on the judicial branch in Chapter 8.

State and Local Governments

While state governments are completely separate entities from the federal government, they tend follow a three-part structure similar to that of the federal government and to create the same types of laws. State governments will have a legislative, executive, and judicial branch whose powers are all outlined by the state constitution. The state constitution will outline the areas the state is able to make laws about. There are some minor differences in structure that vary from state to state. Nebraska, for instance, is the only state currently that has a unicameral legislature with just has one house rather than two. Every state maintains a different legislative calendar for when the legislature is in session and voting on legislation. Some states hold legislative sessions only every other year. You will also find some differences in state governments with regard to the judiciary. States may have courts for specialized issues, depending upon the needs of the population. For example, Colorado has a water court, because water rights are an important and sometimes contested matter in an arid place. Overall, you will find state and federal legal research to be relatively similar in its sources and process, but the content will vary, since each jurisdiction has its own scope of what it can create laws about.

Local governments tend to be simpler in that you have fewer bodies creating laws, but they tend to vary more in their structures and powers. Some municipalities or counties may have a charter that has the same function as a constitution. Others may not have a charter, but rather their authority is limited by statute. Then either the city council or the county board of commissioners will pass ordinances. These ordinances will be organized by topic either as a code or sometimes as regulations. Because local governments vary so much we will not be able to address this area in as much detail. However, there are a couple of books that provide an overview of how local governments work: for instance, Sandra M. Stevenson's *Understanding Local*

Table 5.2. Hierarchy of Governments in the United States

United States Constitution—Establishes Federal System of Government

- United States Statutes
- Federal Agency Regulations and Rulings
- United States Supreme Court Cases
- United States Circuit Courts of Appeals Cases
- United States District Court Cases

State Constitution—Establishes State System of Government

- State Statutes
- State Agency Regulations and Rulings
- State Supreme Court or Court of Last Resort Cases
- State Appellate Courts Cases
- State District Court Cases

Government and David McCarthy's *Local Government Law in a Nutshell*. Many city codes are published by a handful of publishers, so you can see if the one you are looking for is available from Municode, Sterling Codifiers, American Legal Publishing, and/or General Code Publishers. You can also check the website for your city or county government to see if they provide access to the laws there.

The levels of government operate in a hierarchical fashion (Table 5.2). The United States Constitution is the highest law of the land, and everything subsequent to it is subject to its authority.

The focus of this book will primarily be on how to locate information for the federal and state governments. Other types of law that you may encounter would be territorial laws or tribal laws, depending on your location. For territorial laws, the Library of Congress Law Library maintains some excellent research guides on the various U.S. territories. For tribal law, you can find general information in William C. Canby Jr.'s *American Indian Law in Nutshell*, or the National Indian Law Library's website has some tribal law available online as well as a number of research guides.

JURISDICTION

Knowing the various levels of government helps us to understand the concept of jurisdiction. *Black's Law Dictionary* defines jurisdiction as

Table 5.3. Common Research Areas by Jurisdiction

Jurisdiction	Common Research Areas
Federal	Bankruptcy, copyright, immigration, employment discrimination, compliance with the Americans with Disabilities Act
State	Divorce, child custody, landlord–tenant, estate, probate, contract issues
Local	Building codes, neighbor disputes, property maintenance

"A government's general power to exercise authority over all persons and things within its territory." Different jurisdictions tend to make laws for different areas of our lives. The constitution for either the state or the federal government will outline what those areas are. Table 5.3 illustrates some common research areas broken down by the jurisdiction they fall into.

Most legal research questions that we field at the library where I work tend to be matters of state jurisdiction. Divorce and child custody issues are probably the topics we receive the most questions about, followed by estate/probate matters, then landlord–tenant issues. Common questions that involve federal jurisdiction tend to be about immigration, copyright, and some types of employment discrimination. Local matters will often relate to questions about building codes or property requirements as well as neighborly disputes like noise issues.

There are a few areas where you will find multiple jurisdictions involved. One example would be laws regarding Medicare. This is a federally created and funded program that is administered by the individual states. So there are federal statutes and regulations as well as state statutes and regulations all of which pertain to this one program. Knowing what jurisdiction covers which area of the law can be helpful in selecting materials. Usually, you deal with only one jurisdiction at a time; however, it can still be helpful to remember that there may be a few exceptions to this rule. So you may want to quickly check other jurisdictions to make sure nothing has been missed.

If you are unable to match the topic area with the jurisdiction, you may also be able to determine the jurisdiction if the patron has already visited a court to file or respond to paperwork. Courts will only hear cases on laws that fall within the jurisdiction of the system in which they are included; so a federal court would not allow you to file divorce papers, as divorce is a matter of state, not federal, jurisdiction. Knowing the court system that the patron is working with can help you determine which laws and court rules will be relevant. However, if the patron has yet to visit the court, and it is a topic area that you are not familiar with, the patron may need to search multiple jurisdictions to see where the matter is discussed in the law.

CATEGORIES OF LAW IN THE COURTS

There are a couple of broad categorizations of law that can also be helpful to know about when fielding patron questions. The first is the concept of public versus private law; the second is the division between civil, criminal, and regulatory law. In general, public laws are laws that are concerned with the relationship between the state and the individual. Public laws can cover the areas of criminal, constitutional, and administrative law. Generally, when researching questions regarding public law you may consult the constitution, statutes, and regulations.

Private laws generally tend to be about relationships between individuals. These laws can cover the areas of torts, contracts, and property. Torts deal with the areas of injury, negligence, and liability. A good deal of what constitutes private law will be dealt with in case law. These descriptions of public and private law are a bit oversimplified, but they should be enough to provide some guidance and working knowledge of where to start looking.

The other categorization to be familiar with is the notion of criminal, civil, and regulatory laws. In criminal cases the government is always the plaintiff, and these will be matters of public law. Generally, statutes will be the underlying law in criminal matters, and they can occur in federal, state, and local jurisdictions. Civil law is the broadest category of these three categories, and it generally concerns private laws. Disputes will be between two individuals or individual entities, such as businesses. In civil matters, case law is usually the underlying law. Regulatory cases generally deal with matters where the government again will be the plaintiff. These disputes will usually be based on regulations and their enabling statutes. The cases will be heard first in administrative courts, and will only be heard by courts of the judicial branch if the decision gets appealed.

Of these three categorizations, you will mostly encounter items that fall into civil law. If a person is involved with a criminal matter and cannot afford an attorney, she can be provided with a public defender. This right, which was established by the court case *Gideon v. Wainright*, gives one the right to an attorney if he cannot afford to hire one, but it applies only to criminal cases. If you are sued in a civil matter, you do not have an established right to an attorney if you cannot afford one. And as civil matters are the broadest area of law, this is another reason why at the library we encounter more people needing assistance in this area.

AUTHORITY

In legal research there are two notions of authority you want to be familiar with. They are primary and secondary authority, and binding and persuasive authority. Starting first with the concept of primary and secondary authority, primary authority is the law itself: statutes, regulations, case law, and other types of law are what make up primary authority. Secondary authority refers to sources that explain what the laws mean. This is similar to the division you find in historical research, where you have primary documents, the actual pieces of history itself, and secondary sources that describe and explain what those artifacts mean. The end goal of legal research is to locate the primary authority that applies to the situation at hand; but do not underestimate the usefulness of secondary sources in the process of locating primary authority. A good number of patrons whom I assist tend to want to jump right into the primary sources and look at the law itself. However, a bit of time using secondary sources when you start researching can save you a lot of time in the long run.

Secondary sources can take a variety of formats and will be discussed in more detail in Chapter 6. Some provide quick answers that clarify terms and concepts, such as legal dictionaries and encyclopedias. Others may give a slightly more thorough description of legal ideas but are geared toward a lay audience, such as the books published by Nolo or the Nutshell Series published by Thomson Reuters. Then, you have other materials like treatises and practice aids that are geared toward a specialized legal audience of judges, attorneys, and paralegals. These types of specialized sources can help lay out procedures, recommend strategies, interpret the laws, and provide the specific forms for particular legal actions. They may also identify the key cases and laws for a particular topic area. So while we are unable to interpret the law for a patron, or tell her that a specific law applies to her situation, a secondary source may be able to provide her that information.

The other concept of authority is the notion of binding versus persuasive. In order for authority to be binding it must be from the relevant jurisdiction. So, if I am in court for a landlord–tenant issue in the state of Idaho, then I want to be referencing Idaho laws and cases in order for the authority to be binding. If I cite cases from another jurisdiction, such as Oregon, those cases might be persuasive, but they will not be binding; meaning the court does not have to follow the precedent laid out in the decision from Oregon. Persuasive authority comes either from other jurisdictions or from lower-level courts in the relevant jurisdiction. Remember that the goal of the patron in doing legal research is to locate the binding primary authority—thus the laws from the jurisdiction in which the matter takes place.

CURRENCY

Because the law is continually changing, it is important to make sure that you are working with sources that are current and up-to-date. The one exception you may find is if you have a patron who is working on an appeal. However, generally you do not find too many pro se litigants who take on appeals, and usually by that point he will be familiar enough with legal research to ask for the version of the law from the year in question. Most of the freely available online sources that we will look at in subsequent chapters will keep things up-to-date, but there are a few that maintain separate historic collections should you need to view older laws. Nonetheless, it can still be useful to make sure what you are viewing online or in print is current.

In order to do this, it can be helpful to have a general sense of what your state's legislative session is. Most state legislatures meet for only a portion of the year. For example, the Colorado legislature meets from January to May. A few states—Montana, Nevada, North Dakota, and Texas—only meet every other year. In addition to a state's regular session, the governor may call a legislature to reconvene for a special session outside of their normal meeting time if need be. Generally, though, there will be a period of time when new laws that have been passed still need to be published. During this lag time, it can be useful to know how to look up session laws to make sure that what you are looking at has not been repealed or amended. You can generally find information about these session laws on the website for your state's legislature.

Another area of concern with regard to currency is the area of case law. When cases are published in print sources they just appear in chronological order. And when you find cases in a free online environment, it can also be difficult to tell what relevant cases came after the one you are viewing. In order to tell if a case has been overturned by a later decision, you will need to use a proprietary citator service. There are two major ones: the first is Shepard's Citations, which is owned by LexisNexis; and then there is KeyCite, which is a part of WestlawNext and owned by Thomson Reuters. A citator service will allow you to see if any subsequent cases have overturned or criticized the decision the patron is viewing. Generally, a person will need to contact or visit a law library in order to use one of these services, as they are a part of the databases LexisNexis and WestlawNext, which usually cannot be searched off-site unless you have a set of log-in credentials. If the patron has an exact citation he may be able to call or e-mail the law library to see if they would be willing to check the case, though not all law libraries may offer that service.

Print legal resources will be updated in a number of ways. Some sources will have you just paste new pages on top of the old ones. This is generally for brief updates that happen in between major publishing runs for the source.

Some print sources will issue new volumes with the updates. Others will use what are called pocket parts for the updates. Pocket parts are pamphlets inserted into the back of the book that will list which sections are updated and then will have the text of the update in the pocket part. If there are too many updates to be included in a pocket part, then the source may use supplemental volumes for their updates. If you are in doubt about the currency of something that a patron is using, this is another great time to reach out to a law librarian to verify what he has found.

OFFICIAL AND UNOFFICIAL PUBLICATIONS

When using legal research materials you will find what are known as official and unofficial publications. Official publications are the ones that are either created or sanctioned by the government entity. In the case of the federal government, the Government Publishing Office (GPO) is the official publisher. Most states and local entities hire an outside publisher to be their official publisher if they are unable to do it in house. So, for example, the official publisher for the Colorado Revised Statutes is LexisNexis. Unofficial publications will still have the exact same text of the law, however; they are also more likely to be annotated and oftentimes are available much more quickly than official publications. Annotations can provide useful cross-references and explanations; and you will find some official publications that include annotations as well.

To track down official publications, you can start with the website for the governmental body whose laws you are interested in viewing. The laws may either be available on that site or will lead you to where they are available. For federal documents and laws, the GPO houses all of those things on their website, Govinfo.gov. There are also a number of unofficial sites that make available law for all fifty states and the federal government—Legal Information Institute, Justia, and FindLaw for Legal Professionals to name a few. Both official and unofficial publications are okay to use, so don't be worried if you are consulting an unofficial source rather than an official one.

UNDERSTANDING CITATION FORMATS

Legal sources use their own method of citation. The authoritative source documenting all types of legal citation is *The Bluebook*. Each type of law will have its own citation format, but generally they are comprised of the same pieces, they may just appear in a different order. I have listed a few samples below, breaking them apart into their various pieces. You probably do not need to memorize these, but it is helpful to have a general sense of the different types of citation formats so you will be aware of what you are looking at should you have a patron arrive with a citation.

Citation Format for Statutes and Regulations

You will find some minor differences in how the citations for federal and state statutes are formatted. In the example for federal statutes (Table 5.4) there are a few things to note. First, when statutes are codified, they are organized into topics called titles; the word "title" just means the topic area. Then I listed three different code names. U.S.C. stands for the United States Code, and that is the official publication. U.S.C.A. is the United States Code Annotated, which is an unofficial version of the U.S. Code published by Thomson Reuters. U.S.C.S. is the United States Code Service, another unofficial version published by LexisNexis.

Citations for state statutes have the same pieces of information (Table 5.5), but in a slightly different order. Generally, the citations for state statutes will start with the abbreviation for the code. Each state uses a slightly different name for their statutes, and you will also find some official and unofficial titles in the table. C.R.S. stands for Colorado Revised Statutes; V.T.C.A. stands for Vernon's Texas States and Code Annotated; M.C.A. stands for Montana Code Annotated; and K.R.S. is for the Kentucky Revised Statutes. Most codes will use a two- or three-part numbering system. The first number is for the title or

Table 5.4. Examples of Federal Statutes

Title	Name of Code	Section	Year
42	U.S.C.	§12101	(1990)
12	U.S.C.A.	§2001	(2010)
31	U.S.C.S.	§5311	(2001)

Table 5.5. Examples of State Statutes

Name of Code	Section	Year
C.R.S.	18-1-704	(2000)
V.T.C.A.	§15.101	(2011)
M.C.A.	15-1-704	(1947)
K.R.S.	§241.090	(2017)

topic area. The year may or may not appear in the citation. Generally, if no year is listed it is referring you to the most recent version of the law.

Citations for regulations pretty much follow the same structure as citations for statutes. For federal regulations, which are published in the Code of Federal Regulations, a citation would look like this: 38 C.F.R. §10.16. That first number is for the title where the regulation can be found. Then you have an abbreviation for the name of the source, which is followed by a section number. For example, a regulation for something published in the Colorado Code of Regulations would look like this: 8 C.C.R. 1511-1.8.00.

Citation Formats for Cases

Citations for court decisions include a little more information than statutes, but there are some similar elements (Table 5.6). Case citations always begin with the parties' names. The plaintiff, the party bringing the suit, is always listed first and the defendant's name is second. After the listing of the parties comes the portion that bears some similarities to the statute citations and will tell you in what reporter the case was published. Reporters are the sets of books where cases are published. Cases may be published in more than one reporter set, so you may find cases with what are called parallel citations. The volume number for the reporter will be listed first, it is then followed by an abbreviation of the name of the reporter, and the page number will be listed last. After the reporter information you may find the name of the court that heard the case along with the year. Often you may have just a portion of the complete citation. But the reporter information will always lead you directly to the document itself, so that is really the only part of the citation that you need.

Table 5.6. Citation Formats for Court Decisions

Party Names	Reporter Information	Jurisdiction and Year
[Plaintiff]v. [Defendant]	[Vol.] [Reporter] [Page Number]	([Court] [Year])
Gideon v. Wainright	83 S. Ct. 792	(U.S. Supreme Court 1963)
Archuleta v. Gomez	140 P. 3d 281	(Colorado Court of Appeals 2006)
Player v. Bassford	172 Ga. App. 135	(Court of Georgia Appeals 1984)

WHERE TO LOOK

This section will provide a brief overview of locating sources; please see subsequent chapters for a more thorough discussion and listing of sources. If you are looking for print resources, many public libraries may carry books by Nolo, a copy of their state's statutes, their city code, and possibly a copy of *Black's Law Dictionary*. Other places to look for legal materials in print would be courthouse law libraries and law school libraries. If an institution is publicly funded, it will have a mission to serve the public; but if an institution is private, make sure that their collection is open to the public before making referrals. On occasion, you may also find some legal research materials in college and university libraries, but currency can sometimes be an issue with those collections, as they may not have the budget to keep up law subscriptions.

Many sources are also available online. If you are looking for court forms, check first on court websites. Generally, court forms will be housed in a section labeled "Self-help" or "Forms," though keep in mind that not all courts will make their forms available in this way, nor will all court systems use the same forms in all of their courts. A number of subscription databases also provide access to legal forms, such as Gale Legal Forms or Nuwav Legal Documents, to name two. There are also a number of primary laws available online from both official and unofficial publishers. Govinfo.gov will have primary law for the federal government, and you can check on the website for your state or city government to see if they have their laws available online. Unofficial sources for primary law include Legal Information Institute, Findlaw for Legal Professionals, and Justia, to name a few. You can also find secondary source materials from Nolo websites, Legal Information Institute, and Justia. We will look more in depth at where specifically to locate the different types of laws in upcoming chapters.

REFERENCE SCENARIO

Patron: I need a Power of Attorney form.

Librarian: Okay, we subscribe to a database, Gale Legal Forms, that has a number of different types of Power of Attorney forms available. Do you know what type that you need?

Patron: What do you mean?

Librarian: Well, there are different types. Some cover just financial matters, some are for health decisions, there are durable Power of Attorney forms, and so on.

Patron: Oh, I thought there would just be one. I want one for financial matters.

> **Librarian:** Okay, let's take a look in the database and see what choices you have. It looks like there are still several to choose from for financial matters. Do you want the power of attorney to take effect immediately or upon disability?
>
> **Patron:** I'm not sure, what do you think is best?
>
> **Librarian:** I really can't say, as I am not an attorney and I don't know what is going to be best for your situation.
>
> **Patron:** Well, I really thought you would know.
>
> **Librarian:** I am an information professional, not a legal professional. So I don't want to tell you something and then have it be the wrong form. That could put you in a really bad position. How about this? I will print out the examples for the financial Power of Attorney forms and here is a copy of the free legal clinic calendar. I would recommend you read through the forms and then take them to talk with an attorney to see which one you should use. These are pretty serious forms, so you really want to make sure you have the one that is going to do what you need it to do.

We get a lot of requests for Power of Attorney forms. Patrons generally know enough to ask for one by name, but then, when it gets to the specific form they need they are generally less sure of what they want. So while we might be able to help narrow it down with a few questions, we still don't want to recommend a specific form for them, because doing so would constitute legal advice. If you have a subscription to a legal forms database like Gale Legal Forms, or Nuwav, or something similar, you should have access to many different kinds of Power of Attorney forms. If your library does not have a legal forms database, you can find many of these documents online. However, that usually demands a fee, so providing a patron with multiple options can get expensive, particularly if she is not sure what she really needs. This is a situation where, if you have a legal clinic or other free legal service, you can send patrons there with their questions so they can ultimately choose the right form for their situation.

CONCLUSION

Understanding the structure of our government helps us find what types of laws are available. Laws are created by all three branches of government at the federal, state, and local levels. Knowing the different levels of government tells us which jurisdiction we should refer to. Beyond jurisdiction, laws are categorized in a number of ways. We have public and private laws; and we also have criminal, civil, and regulatory laws. These distinctions can help you to identify whether statutes, cases, or regulations might be relevant.

In legal research we must concern ourselves with two types of authority: primary/secondary and binding/persuasive. While ultimately we want to locate binding, primary authority, secondary sources and persuasive authority can still be useful in tracking down those materials. You will want to make sure that the sources you are using are current, as laws do change and new cases will overturn older ones. Law will be printed by both official and unofficial publishers. While there will be no difference in the text of a law, you may find different annotations in the various sources, so if you are able to check both kinds of publications you can potentially find more relevant sources for your research. Last, having a basic understanding of citation formats can be useful, though you don't necessarily need to memorize all of the abbreviated titles and formats. But a basic understanding means that when a patron does come in with citations you will at least know what kinds of sources to direct him to first.

REFERENCES

American Legal Publishing. Accessed March 7, 2019. http://www.amlegal.com/.

Canby, William C., Jr. *American Indian Law in a Nutshell*. St. Paul, MN: Thomson/West, 2009.

FindLaw for Legal Professionals. Accessed March 7, 2019. https://lp.findlaw.com/.

Garner, Bryan A., ed. *Black's Law Dictionary, 10th Edition*. Eagan, MN: Thomson/West, 2014.

General Code. Accessed March 7, 2019. https://www.generalcode.com/.

Gideon v. Wainwright, 372 U.S. 335 (1963).

Govinfo. Accessed March 8, 2019. https://www.govinfo.gov/.

Justia. Accessed March 7, 2019. https://www.justia.com/.

Legal Information Institute. Accessed March 7, 2019. https://www.law.cornell.edu/.

Library of Congress. "U.S. States and Territories." Accessed March 7, 2019. https://www.loc.gov/law/help/guide/states.php.

McCarthy, David J. *Local Government Law in a Nutshell*. St. Paul, MN: Thomson/West, 2003.

Miles Prince, Mary, ed. *The Bluebook: A Uniform System of Citation*. Cambridge, MA: Harvard Law Review Association, 2016.

Municode. Accessed March 7, 2019. https://www.municode.com/.

National Indian Law Library. Accessed March 7, 2019. https://narf.org/nill/.

Sterling Codifiers. Accessed March 7, 2019. https://www.sterlingcodifiers.com/.

Stevenson, Sandra M. *Understanding Local Government*. Newark, NJ: LexisNexis, 2009.

SIX

Secondary Sources

Secondary source materials are an excellent way to understand and access the law. In this chapter, I will begin by reviewing what secondary sources are and how they fit into legal research. Next I will outline the various types of secondary sources. This will be followed by a discussion of how secondary sources are useful in legal research and why you would want to consult them. Then I will provide a list of freely available online secondary sources, and will conclude with some purchase considerations should you wish to add any print secondary sources to your collection.

In Chapter 5, one of the legal research concepts we addressed was the idea of primary and secondary authority. Primary authority describes the actual laws themselves; secondary authority comes from sources that explain the law and are excellent tools for determining the correct primary authority for the situation at hand. These sources can also provide context and explanation of the law, as well as information about legal strategies and procedures. Secondary sources can take some of the guesswork out of legal research and assure you that you have located the correct primary authority. They can help you to define legal terms and understand legal concepts. As we will see in the listing below, secondary sources come in a variety of formats and are geared toward multiple audiences. Some may provide more of a basic overview for a lay audience, whereas others will be highly technical and geared toward an expert audience.

TYPES OF SECONDARY SOURCES

In this listing, I will attempt to move through the types of sources, starting with the ones that give more of a basic overview to a lay audience and moving to the ones that are more technical and designed for an expert audience.

Dictionaries

Legal dictionaries define terms used in the law and can explain the meaning of language that may be different in a legal context than in common usage. There are number of different legal dictionaries out there both in print and online, but the one that patrons seem to ask for by name is *Black's Law Dictionary*, and so it tends to be the industry standard.

Encyclopedias

Legal encyclopedias are similar to general encyclopedias in that they provide short articles that briefly explain a legal concept or area. *Nolo's Encyclopedia of Everyday Law* offers this type of resource for a lay audience. For something a bit more technical, the two main, long-standing legal encyclopedia sets are *American Jurisprudence* (AmJur) and *Corpus Juris Secundum* (CJS). In these sets, you will find references to other sources as well, so they do a nice job of showing you where to look in other secondary source sets for more information.

Nolo and Nutshell Series

These two sets of books are great because they are really geared toward a lay audience. Nolo books describe books published by the company Nolo. And Nutshell refers to the books that are part of the "In a Nutshell" series by West Academic Publishing. Nolo and Nutshell both give a good overview of the legal topic area that the specific volume is addressing. Both series cover a wide range of legal topic areas. Nolo has some books that are more practically focused, such as how to start a nonprofit or how to write your own will. Nutshell is slightly more advanced in its language and description, but tends to be more of an overview rather than a practical description. One thing to note about each of these types of sources is that they will not reference individual state laws. However, they are great for helping people to get a basic understanding of many different legal topics and issues. They also tend to be moderately priced.

Legal Periodicals

There are a variety of types of legal periodicals, and these can be a great way to find information on a specific legal issue. These are written for different types of audiences and will range in their depth and specificity. One type of legal periodical are law review articles. They are typically produced by law schools, many of which will sometimes have more than one review that focuses on a specific area of law. These articles are usually written for an expert audience, but they can be a great way to get a quick overview of a legal issue, and they can also point you to the key laws and cases. While many of these reviews are only available through subscription, there are a few places where you can find some for free, which I will discuss later.

Another type of legal periodical are professional magazines. These are usually published by bar associations. While not as formal as law reviews, these articles still are geared toward practitioners. However, again, these articles can be a great way to get a quick synopsis and information about what the key laws and cases are in the particular area. These sources are harder to find and use without a subscription.

The last type of periodical I want to touch on in this section is not a periodical in the traditional sense, but it can provide the same type of information and is usually geared toward a lay audience. A number of attorneys will maintain blogs on their websites. On these blogs, you will find short articles for a specific topic, and they will generally point you to key statutes in a particular area. A couple of notes of caution here: generally these blogs are tied to the attorneys selling their services, so they can be a great place to start your research, but it is not where I would finish. I try to find a few articles from different sites that say the same thing. Once you start seeing the same statute or case mentioned, then you have found a good lead. Also, specify the jurisdiction in your search, because you want to find a blog that references laws binding to your jurisdiction.

Treatises

Treatises are books or sets of books that examine a specific area of law in depth and are geared toward a more expert audience. Examples include *Couch on Insurance* or *Corbin on Contracts*. Treatises are updated as laws change. So generally, if you invest in a set you will have to pay for subscription updates. You may occasionally hear the term "hornbook" too. Hornbooks are similar to treatises in that they focus on one area of law in depth. Hornbooks are usually just a single volume, not a multivolume set, and are generally written for law school students rather than practicing attorneys.

Practice Aids

Another type of material geared toward attorneys are referred to as practice aids. These types of materials come in a variety of formats from multivolume sets covering a variety of topics for a specific jurisdiction to loose-leaf binders of continuing legal education materials on a particular legal topic. Practice aids can provide many kinds of useful information. They may identify the key laws and cases in a particular topic area, so they are great for identifying primary authority. They may also describe strategies and tactics for how to proceed with a specific legal action. Some of them will also provide legal forms, and also the context or history of a particular area of law.

American Law Reports

These last two types of secondary sources are, again, for a more expert audience, but they can be very useful in understanding a specific point of law and determining the legal precedent that makes up that law. *American Law Reports* (ALR) is a unique secondary source. It began as a reporter for U.S. Supreme Court cases. The cases were followed by what is called an annotation. This annotation is different from the annotations that may be found in other sources. ALR annotations are really an in-depth report that analyzes the law for the case reported and that covers every relevant precedent for almost every jurisdiction in that particular area of law. Now ALR just specializes in producing these annotations and not in reporting cases. If you can find an ALR annotation on the area of law you are researching, it can be a treasure trove of information, in that it gives you the history and context for that point of law as well as references to the primary authorities in that area.

Restatements of the Law

Restatements of the Law is a unique secondary source, as it attempts to come to a consensus of multiple jurisdictions' common law. Since each state and the federal judicial system follows its own legal precedent, *Restatements* has examined these and then attempted to draft what the most common position is on a matter. This set has multiple volumes and each volume takes on a different type of law, so you have *Restatements on Torts, Restatements on Contracts*, and so on. Each volume is made up of articles that begin by restating the law with the common principle found from looking at all the jurisdictions and then following that principle or restatement of the law with a discussion. While many judges may cite *Restatements* in their decisions, please remember that because this is a secondary source it has persuasive authority but is not binding.

THE PURPOSE OF USING SECONDARY SOURCES

Using secondary sources in legal research yields many distinct benefits. Secondary sources help to clarify legal terms and concepts. This can be done briefly or in-depth. As legal terms are sometimes used differently from everyday language, it can be helpful to consult a legal dictionary or encyclopedia when first encountering a concept. Even just a brief consultation with these types of sources can help you generate search terms to use when looking for primary sources. Sources that have a more in-depth discussion can help the reader to better understand a particular area of the law. Because as librarians we are forbidden to offer our interpretation of the law to patrons, certain types of secondary sources can help explain the intricacies of the law to patrons.

Another distinct benefit of using secondary sources is that they may point you to the key cases and laws that cover a particular area. Sometimes locating a law in primary sources is straightforward; however, many times it is not. Additionally, secondary sources may point out any other relevant cases and statutes that you may also need to be aware of. Often patrons will come in and ask broad questions like "I need to see the law on school accountability." There may be multiple laws on school accountability and you may find them in the statutes, regulations, and possibly even in cases. And with this particular example, you may find things in both federal and state sources. A secondary source might alert you that you need to be looking in multiple places to find what the patron needs. Secondary sources may also help to put the information you find into context. Since law is not a static entity, understanding the development of legislation or how a case moved through the courts may help the patron to better understand the law as it exists today. These sources help you make complete sense of the full legal landscape of an issue by letting you know all of the statutes, regulations, and cases that apply.

Some of the more advanced secondary sources may also offer practical advice and tactical suggestions to the reader. While generally there is a huge learning curve for self-represented litigants as they work their way through the legal system, having access to this information gives them an understanding of what issues attorneys consider when they are trying cases. This type of information can assist a patron in better representing herself, as she will have a foundational understanding of procedures and strategies.

Overall, secondary sources will save the researcher time. This does not mean you have to read a treatise set cover to cover, but consulting secondary sources at some level will help you to search primary sources with a better understanding of what you are looking for and where to find it. The vast majority of patrons I work with are mostly interested in jumping straight into searching primary sources. However, if you can find the correct citation for a law in a secondary source, you have eliminated a lot of the uncertainty of

legal research. Since we are not legal experts, we can use the work of secondary source authors to help us.

WHERE TO FIND FREE SECONDARY SOURCES

There are a few places where you can locate free secondary source material on the Web. These free sources are generally going to be shorter and less
in-depth than what you find in the subscription sources geared for an expert
audience. However, they can still help clarify concepts, define terms, and
locate key laws. For defining terms, U.S. Legal has a good free legal dictionary on its website. Nolo also maintains a website that defines legal terms. If
you are looking for a legal encyclopedia, Cornell's Legal Information Institute
has an excellent one on their website called Wex. Nolo also has a website with
longer, encyclopedia-like-type articles.

Then there are a number of places to look for articles that discuss things in
slightly more depth than an encyclopedia. On their websites, Justia and Find-
Law both maintain large sets of articles that cover a wide range of legal topics. Another place to look for this type of information are bar association
websites. The American Bar Association does have some information geared
toward the public, and what you find on state bar association websites will
vary, but look to see if there is a section labeled for the public, and that is
generally where those sources will be. You can also find free access to some
law reviews through Justia and the Law Review Commons. When trying to
track down citations for laws at a state level is a time when you may want to
consult attorney blogs. Just make sure to specify the jurisdiction that you are
interested in when searching, and I also would make sure you verify that
information by looking at multiple sources. On occasion, I have used Wikipe-
dia to find the citation information for a federal law. This can sometimes be
useful for queries like "I want to read the American with Disabilities Act."
For major pieces of federal legislation there are usually fairly decent Wikipe-
dia pages that will give you the correct citation as well as the history and
some discussion of that law. You can then use that citation to find the full text
of the law.

PURCHASE CONSIDERATIONS

While many secondary sources are expensive to buy and require subscriptions to maintain, there are some that are affordable or worth the expense.
Black's Law Dictionary can be a useful source for defining legal terms, and
also for getting ideas for synonyms to use in searches. While initially a little

costly—*Black's* runs around $80–$90—it does not get updated too frequently, so one purchase should last you a while.

Nolo titles are also a good investment, as they do a great job of helping to make legal concepts easier to understand. The books are relatively inexpensive. The only drawback is that they are more general and will not cite specific state laws. You may also find Nolo titles as eBooks in the EBSCO database Legal Information Reference Center. That database sometimes will be lumped in with EBSCO packages, so check to see if your library already subscribes. The Nutshell Series books are a little denser, but are still a good choice for a public library audience. They tend to be priced similarly to Nolos, but may be slightly more expensive on average. You can also find many of the Nutshell titles as eBooks in Overdrive.

You might also see if your state bar association produces any publications. The Colorado State Bar Association publishes a series of books that, while they are geared toward attorneys, are a bit more affordable than those produced by the major legal publishers. The other advantage is that they will have citations for the relevant state laws in them. And finally, if you have a flush collection development budget, the last item I would recommend is to see if your state has an attorney practice series available. Not all states do, but many of these sets contain a lot of useful information. In Colorado, we have the *Colorado Practice Series*. It is a multivolume set with an expensive initial cost, and it must be maintained by subscription. Sometimes publishers will offer these sets at a monthly subscription price; or they will allow you to purchase only the volumes and updates that you are interested in. So, for example, you could just buy the volumes concerning family law if that is what most of your law questions were about. While these sets are geared toward an attorney audience, they can still be of use to those who are acting as their own attorney. The set can identify the key statutes and cases; they may also give procedural recommendations, trial tactics, and more.

REFERENCE SCENARIO

Patron: I am helping my mom put together her will. She has one from before that I think we can update. A friend told me we would just need to add a codicil. What is that?

Librarian: Ah, yes, I have heard the term "codicil"—I think it is like an amendment to a will. Let's look it up, though, to get the exact definition and see what the requirements are for adding one to an existing document.

Patron: Great, that sounds good.

Librarian: Okay, here are a couple of definitions. The first is from the Legal Definitions section of our Legal Forms database. Then there is also a definition of what a codicil is from this online legal encyclopedia from Nolo. They both explain what the codicil is, and it looks like you will need some witnesses to sign as well. Another question, when the original will was written, was your mom living here in the same state?

Patron: I think so, why?

Librarian: The reason I ask is that estate laws vary from state to state. So if it was written by an attorney from another state and was based on those state laws, then you may want to have an attorney here review it so there are not any surprises. There a few free clinics where you could ask an attorney any questions you have about the will and codicil. Also, we have a few books on wills and estates that I could show you. The books may also help you learn what to ask if you go to the clinic.

Patron: Yeah, that would probably be good. All of these legal terms are so confusing. I just don't want to mess this up.

Librarian: Totally, a will is a pretty important document. So let's go pull those books, and I can get you a clinic calendar. Also, here is my card, so if the attorney tells you to look into anything else, I can help you track it down.

Occasionally we will get questions that seem pretty straightforward, as the patron might be asking for the definition of a legal term. In those instances it is good to know where to look those things up quickly. Nolo has a good free legal encyclopedia. You can also use Wex, another free online source. Gale Legal Forms, which is a subscription database, also has a list of legal definitions available. However, also keep in mind that there may still be other issues at play. In this instance, jurisdiction might also be an issue and other sections of the will might need to be revised. With questions on estate planning I still always encourage people to touch base with an attorney if they can. A good number of people try to draw up these types of documents for themselves, but there can be serious repercussions if they are done incorrectly.

CONCLUSION

As we have seen, secondary sources cover a wide range of materials that vary in their levels of depth, specificity, and their target audience. They range in price from very expensive subscription sets to freely available online sources. Each type of secondary source can assist with the legal research process in different ways. Dictionaries and encyclopedias can give you a basic familiarity with legal terms and concepts. They are also great tools for finding words and synonyms to use when searching. Shorter works, like Nolo and

Nutshell, are excellent for bringing a lay researcher quickly up to speed in language that is easy to understand. Legal periodicals can give you a more in-depth look at specific legal topics and can sometimes supply you with useful citations so you will know where to find the primary authority. Treatises and practice aids are great for also providing citations, procedural strategies, and more in-depth discussion of a legal area.

Remember that secondary sources are your friends. They can save you time and bring certainty to the legal research process. If you find that you are struggling to locate a particular law, there may be a secondary source that can help you with that search. Further, since we as librarians must avoid giving legal interpretations or advice, many of these sources can provide that type of information to our patrons.

REFERENCES

American Bar Association. Accessed May 17, 2019. https://www.americanbar.org/.

American Law Book Company. *Corpus Juris Secundum*. St. Paul, MN: West Publishing Co., 1936.

Colorado Practice. St. Paul, MN: West Publishing Co., 1983.

FindLaw. Accessed May 17, 2019. https://www.findlaw.com/.

Garner, Bryan A., ed. *Black's Law Dictionary, 10th Edition*. Eagan, MN: Thomson West, 2014.

Irving, Shae. *Nolo's Encyclopedia of Everyday Law: Answers to Your Most Frequently Asked Legal Questions*. Berkeley, CA: Nolo, 2017.

Justia. Accessed March 7, 2019. https://www.justia.com/.

Law Review Commons. Accessed May 17, 2019. https://lawreviewcommons.com/.

Lawyer's Co-operative Publishing Company. *American Jurisprudence*. 2nd ed. Rochester, NY: Lawyer's Co-operative Publishing Company, 1975.

Legal Definitions and Legal Terms Defined, U.S. Legal. Accessed May 17, 2019. https://definitions.uslegal.com/.

Legal Topics, Nolo. Accessed May 17, 2019. https://www.nolo.com/legal-encyclopedia.

Nolo's Free Dictionary of Law Terms and Legal Definitions, Nolo. Accessed May 17, 2019. https://www.nolo.com/dictionary.

Wex, Cornell Law School Legal Information Institute. Accessed February 2, 2019. https://www.law.cornell.edu/wex.

SEVEN

Laws from the Legislative Branch

Article I of the United States Constitution outlines the powers of the legislative branch. The Constitution gives the legislative branch the ability to enact laws, declare war, approve many presidential appointments, and levy taxes—among other things. Since the process of creating laws begins with the legislative branch, and it is the only branch of government that can issue new laws, the statutes and codes it generates are what most people think of when they think of laws. In my work, statutes tend to be the often most requested type of law that patrons want to see. Statutes are important because they lay the groundwork for many of the other types of laws created by the other branches of government. For example, government agencies cannot make regulations unless there is an enabling statute, and most case law is based on the courts applying the statutes to real-life disputes.

At the federal level, the legislative branch is made up of the Senate and the House of Representatives. State governments follow a similar structure and process, with the exception of Nebraska, which just has a senate. In this chapter we will look, first, at how constitutions set up the government and where to locate those documents. Second, I discuss the legislative process and the various types of documents and laws that are created within the legislative branch. Third will follow a discussion of which documents get published or released and how to find and search those sources, both in print and online. Last, I address a couple of tangential topics—namely, court rules and uniform laws.

CONSTITUTIONS

A constitution is the foundational document for federal and state governments. Constitutions set up the form of government and enumerate the powers of each branch. In addition these documents establish and enumerate the rights of citizens. Constitutions outline those civil rights citizens have that the government cannot infringe upon. Federal and state laws generally cover different areas of life, but when they do come into conflict, federal law will have supremacy. For example, a state constitution may not contradict or limit the rights of citizens that the federal constitution guarantees. However, a state may offer additional protections beyond what the federal constitution provides. Constitutions are drafted and adopted by a constitutional convention. All other laws created will have to stay within the bounds the constitution allows.

You can locate the U.S. Constitution in a number of places. In the print environment, it will be published with the United States Code. If you are looking for your state's constitution, you will also be able to find it published with your state's code. In the online environment, the U.S. Constitution is in several locations. Many of the sites that have primary law also have the Constitution—for instance, Govinfo.gov, Legal Information Institute, Justia, and FindLaw for Legal Professionals. The Library of Congress also maintains a site called "Constitution Annotated" that has many useful secondary resources that better explain the document. The National Archives and Records Administration's website "America's Founding Documents" has a copy of the Constitution, the Declaration of Independence, and the Bill of Rights. Online access to state constitutions can usually be found on whatever site hosts your state's code. Legal Information Institute, FindLaw for Legal Professionals, and Justia also will connect you to any state's constitution.

THE LEGISLATIVE PROCESS

For the sake of simplicity, in this section I will outline the federal legislative process. This process follows a similar trajectory at the state level. Legislation may be introduced in either house of the legislature. Several types of documents may be presented on the floor of the legislature that accomplish different things. We are most familiar with bills, as these generally become law. Another type of document, less frequently used, is a joint resolution. These are similar to a bills in that they may become law. You also have resolutions, sometimes referred to as simple resolutions, which do not become law but, rather, deal with matters concerning one of the chambers. Oftentimes they are used to establish consensus on an issue, or the state house will also use them to establish rules for debate. Last, you may also find concurrent resolutions that concern both chambers and do not become law.

Below, I will focus on the path that a bill takes through the legislative branch. Although the legislative branch creates many other documentation and rules, most library patrons are going to be concerned with the laws that impact their lives. The bills that eventually make up the statutes and codes are all laws that are of a general and permanent nature. Occasionally, you may have a patron ask for a government budget, or something of that kind, but most people seem more concerned with laws that have more immediate implications for them. Table 7.1 gives a basic overview of the legislative process. In the next couple of sections I will discuss the process in more depth along with some commentary about how to access the various types of documents created in the process.

BILLS

Bills can be written by anyone, but they must be introduced by a representative or senator—depending on the body hearing it. After the introduction, the bill moves into committee. It will first be considered and investigated by the appropriate subcommittee based on the topic of the bill. There the bill can be accepted, amended, or rejected. If the bill is accepted or amended, then it will be heard by the full committee under which the subcommittee falls. Then the process is repeated, and the committee can accept, amend, or reject the bill. If the bill makes it through the committee's review, then it will be reported to the floor of the House or the Senate, where the majority leadership will decide whether it gets added to the calendar or not.

Table 7.1. The Federal Legislative Process

Bill is introduced and given a number

Referred to a committee or subcommittee

Committee makes changes

Voted on by committee

Committee Reports and bill are put on the calendar.

Reading and floor debate; amendments may be made

Full vote by chamber

If passed, the bill moves to the other chamber and the process is repeated.

Any differences in the house and senate bills are reconciled.

Sent to president, who may sign or veto

If signed into law, the bill is assigned a Public Law Number and is now known as a session law.

Published in the *U.S. Statutes at Large*

Laws of a general and permanent nature are organized by topic (codified) and published in the United State Code.

If the bill is heard, each chamber has its own process for debate. The House limits the time for the debate and the number and type of amendments that can be made. The Senate has no limits on the length of debate, and any type of amendment can be introduced. After the debate is completed, the bill is voted on, and a simple majority is required for the bill to pass. At that point, bills that originated in the Senate move to the House to repeat the process; and bills that originated in the House move to the Senate. The bill must pass both houses in order to be sent to the president. Before the bill is sent to the executive branch, a conference committee will meet to make sure that the wording of both the House bill and the Senate bill is the same. Both the Senate and the House vote on the conference committee report, and now the bill is ready to move along to the president.

Once the president has received the bill, there are several paths the legislation may take. If the president approves of the bill and signs it, then the bill becomes a law. It is now known as a public law and will be a part of the session laws and the *U.S. Statutes at Large.* These public laws will be assigned a number that looks like this: Pub.L. 115-3. If the president disapproves of the bill, then he may veto it. The Congress can override that veto with a two-thirds vote in each chamber, which will then make the bill a law. If Congress is in session and the president takes no action within ten days, then the bill will become a law. Or if the president takes no action, but Congress adjourns before the ten days pass, then the bill does not become a law, and that is what is known as a pocket veto.

While the bill moves through the process of becoming a law, a number of types of documents are created that may be of use to researchers. By and large, most patrons will be primarily interested in the final products, which are usually referred to as statutes or codes. However, from time to time you will have researchers who want to know the history of a piece of legislation. In those instances, it is helpful to know about the original wording of a piece of legislation or the various documents that are created during the process. I will try to be brief in my remarks here, as this generally is not an area in which we field many questions at our library. The Library of Congress has a good online guide that discusses where to start when compiling a federal legislative history if you need more information. Another helpful source in this area is *Mastering United States Government Information: Sources and Services* by Christopher C. Brown.

When a bill is first introduced, it is assigned a number that will indicate if the bill began in the Senate or the House of Representatives. If it originated in the Senate, the number will be preceded by S., and if it began in the House of Representatives, by H.R. Most states will follow a similar format, though in some states you may see S.B. (for senate bill) and H.B. (for house bill).

Knowing the bill number will be critical for finding not only the original text of the legislation but also information and documentation regarding the history of the bill. If you need to obtain the bill number, most legislative bodies will have a way to search for that information on their websites. In that instance, it is helpful to know what year the piece of legislation was introduced and who may have sponsored the bill.

If you are looking for the text of a federal bill, it is best to start on the website Congress.gov. Each chamber has its own website. Senate.gov does have bills and other pieces of legislation available, but House.gov will just direct you to the Congress.gov website if you search for a bill number. On Congress .gov, you will find materials going back to 1974. You can find legislation, reports, and other types of communications. The Senate.gov and House.gov websites are good sources of information for the current session's day-to-day activities and members. For state legislation, most states will have just one website for their legislative branch. How much documentation those sites contain and the coverage of years will vary.

Once a bill enters committee, there will be additional materials created in the forms of committee reports, hearings, and committee prints. Committee reports can be a very useful source when compiling a legislative history, as these reports may lay out in detail the purpose of the bill, any relevant history of the legislation, or why something may be worded in a particular way. Keep in mind that multiple committees and subcommittees may generate reports on a piece of legislation. Sometimes the multiple reports remain individual entities, sometimes they are merged into one. These reports can be located on Congress .gov. Hearings can be more difficult to track down, as not all hearings are published and they are not necessarily verbatim transcripts. The Government Publishing Office's website, Govinfo.gov, is a good place to start when looking for different types of committee documentation. You can also find committee prints at Govinfo.gov. The content of the committee prints will vary depending on the nature of the legislation being discussed. They can include statistical materials, investigative reports, studies, and many other things.

If a bill makes it out of committee and onto the floor, then you may also be able to find transcripts of the floor debate in the *Congressional Record*, which is available on the Congress.gov website. The voting record for how each member of congress voted on the bill can be located on the website for the legislative body in question. After a bill makes it through both chambers, and if it gets signed into law, it is now known as a session law. Session laws will be organized chronologically, and they are generally published at the conclusion of the legislative session. It can be useful to have a vague notion of your state's legislative session so you will know when to be on the lookout for new laws and can then know when to look for updates. The federal session laws are also sometimes referred to as the *U.S. Statutes at Large* and can be located on the Govinfo.gov website.

STATUTES AND CODES

After the new laws are published as session laws or in the *U.S. Statutes at Large*, they will eventually go through the codification process so they can be integrated into the topical organization of the United States Code (U.S.C.). State codes will also be organized by topic, and you will notice that states use slightly different terminology, as some will be referred to as code while others may be called revised statutes or something similar.

The U.S.C. is organized in fifty-four titles. "Title" is just another term for topic area: for example, all the criminal laws are a part of Title 18. A citation for a federal statute will generally follow a format like this: 18 U.S.C. § 201. The first number indicates the title number, U.S.C. is an abbreviation for United States Code, and the last number indicates the specific section within the title where you will find the law in question. State citations will sometimes have a three-part number instead and might look something like: C.R.S. 14-1-101. In this example, C.R.S. is the abbreviation for the Colorado Revised Statutes. The number 14 indicates the title, the number 1 is the article, and 101 is the section.

Before we look at where to find codes and statutes I want to make a few remarks about the difference between official and unofficial publications. The official publication is the one produced by the governmental entity. Some governments publish their own laws, but a number of states and smaller entities will use a commercial publisher, like LexisNexis, to produce their state's laws for them. The text of the law in the official and unofficial publications will be identical. What will differ will be any annotations or editorial notes. The publications will also have slightly different titles. For example, the *United States Code* is the official publication produced by the Government Publishing Office. The *United States Code Annotated* is the version published by Thomson Reuters West; and the *United States Code Service* is the version published by LexisNexis. A thorough researcher might search out both official and unofficial publications in order to compare those annotations and editorial notes.

The United States Code can be found for free in a number of places online. The first is through the Government Publishing Office (GPO), which again is the official publisher. The GPO has a website called Govinfo.gov that is a great place to locate many different types of laws and governmental documents. Given the large quantity of documents that you can access through that site, I would recommend using the advanced search feature to select just the U.S.C., then you only have to look through results from one document collection. You can also find unofficial copies of the U.S.C. online for free through the following websites: The Office of Law Revision Counsel, Legal Information Institute, Justia, and Findlaw for Legal Professionals, to name a few. Most of these sites will have limited ways to find things. Generally, you will only be able to browse through and drill down into the titles, or you can conduct a full text search across everything. If you are looking for your state's laws, a good place to start is the American Association of Law Libraries, Public Library Toolkit. On this site, they will have links for each state and will offer information about where to find state laws in print and online.

The print environment contains additional types of finding aids. Print sets will include an index for locating laws within the source. Indexes can be useful due to "see also" notes. Often the common language used to describe something is not the legal language, so an index can point you to the correct term. In the U.S.C. you will find tables that will help you to connect the *U.S. Statutes at Large* to the U.S.C. There you can look up a law by its Pub.L. number and it will point you to the correct section of the code. Also, there is an *Index and Finding Aids for the Code of Federal Regulations.* You can use this volume to locate any corresponding regulations by looking up a section of the U.S.C. as well as find regulations by an index. You will also find what are known as popular name tables. This can be useful if you know the everyday name for the law rather than its actual title. So, for example, in Colorado you can use the popular name table to locate the "Hannah Montana" law or the "Make My Day" law without knowing the official title of that piece of legislation. There may also be tables for "Words and Phrases" in state codes. These tables help you to locate where particular terms get defined within the law.

Different patrons will have different preferences for which type of format they prefer to use. While most statutes and codes are easily accessible online, you will still have some patrons who prefer to use print sources. If your library can afford a print copy of your state's statutes, you may want to consider purchasing a set. However, keep in mind when budgeting that the set will need to be updated every or every other year (depending on your state's legislative session). At our library, our set of the Colorado Revised Statutes is our most used print legal resource. Compared to any other legal resource, it gets five times as much use. So while it requires a cost investment, people do want to see those statutes in print.

COURT RULES

Another area of law that will appear with the statutes both in print as well as online are the court rules. While court rules are technically a type of administrative law, I am going to discuss them in this section as you will find them published with the statutes. The court rules are the laws that outline the procedures of the courts. These laws are created through a different process that varies from jurisdiction to jurisdiction and usually involves both the legislature and the judiciary. Court rules will lay out timelines, spell out which forms are required, and explain the procedural workings of the judicial system. Each type of court will have its own set of rules. So you will have rules for civil, criminal, probate, juvenile, and so on.

In addition to these separate volumes of court rules, you may also find parts of the statutes that cover the workings of the courts. For example, in the U.S.C., Title 28 covers the judiciary and judicial procedure. Court rules are a good place to start when patrons have questions related to court procedures such as what forms to file, or how long they have to respond to a lawsuit, and so on.

UNIFORM LAWS

Uniform laws are created by the Uniform Law Commission, a body made up of legal experts appointed by each state. The Uniform Law Commission creates potential or suggested legislation that can be adopted and used by each state. The purpose of uniform laws is to help prevent conflicts between state laws. For example, this can be particularly useful in the area of commerce since lots of commerce happens across state lines. States can amend uniform laws to suit their specific needs, but by and large uniform laws enable states to work more easily together. One of the better-known uniform laws is the Uniform Commercial Code. A version of this law is in effect in all fifty states. It can be difficult to track these laws down in print outside of a law library. You can learn about what laws the Uniform Law Commission has drafted and where they are in effect through their website. The Legal Information Institute also has the most commonly used version of the Uniform Commercial Code available on their website.

REFERENCE SCENARIO

Patron: There's a big leak in the ceiling of my apartment and my landlord refuses to fix it. I don't think I should have to pay rent, as the place is dangerous to live in, and I want to see what the laws say. What do you think I should do?

Librarian: Oh wow, I'm sorry that is happening to you. I am not sure what the best course of action is, and you want to be careful about withholding rent, as there are usually certain procedures you should follow, though I am not sure how that all works so I can't really advise you. Let's see what we can find in the state laws about that. We also have some general books on landlord–tenant law that might also help explain things. Have you recently read through your lease to see if it addresses anything like that?

Patron: No, to be honest, I haven't read the lease. It's so long.

Librarian: I know, they are long, but since it is a contract you signed it might tell you more about what the landlord has to do and what could happen to you if you withhold any rent, so you may want to go back and read through it all to see what is there. As for the laws, though, you live here in town?

Patron: Yes, I do.

Librarian: Okay, so let's take a look at the state laws. We can use the index to see what is there for landlord and tenant. There is also a free copy of the state laws online as well that I can show you, so if you need to read any of this while you are not at the library you can do that as these books don't check out.

We also have these Nolo books that do check out. They are helpful because they are a bit easier to read than the law itself. They won't specifically reference our state laws, but they can help you better understand some of the concepts. We have a few different ones on renter's rights, so let's take a look at those too.

Then if you want to talk with an attorney for free, I can grab you a copy of the legal clinics calendar. An attorney is better equipped to explain what your options would be in this situation and if you can withhold rent until your landlord makes repairs.

While it might be tempting, we never want to advise patrons what to do in their legal situation, even if we have experienced something similar ourselves. You can, however, encourage them to read through their lease or to look at various sources or to reach out to an attorney. It is also okay to acknowledge that they are in a tough situation, as that can help to build rapport with the patron.

When patrons ask to read the law itself, I also try to give them some secondary source options as well. The actual law may be difficult to understand, and certain secondary sources, like Nolo books, can help them parse what they read in the law. The one thing to note about Nolo books, is that they will not be specific to your state's laws, so I always try to tell them that. When showing patrons the law, you may also want to explain how the sources work. It's okay to demonstrate how the index works and how the numbering schemes operate. Or, if you are using an online source you can show a patron what the various search and browse options are.

CONCLUSION

The legislative process creates many documents. Most library patrons will be concerned with the finished products known as statutes or codes. I have found that the most requested resource in our legal collection are our state statutes. If you only have time to familiarize yourself with one area of law, this is where you should begin. Similarly, if you can only afford one legal publication, this should be a set you consider purchasing and maintaining. Also, it is worth spending some time familiarizing yourself with your state's court rules. Court rules can be an important resource for people representing themselves in court, as it is these laws that lay out the procedures they will need to follow.

Govinfo.gov is a great online resource for finding documents created throughout the federal legislative process. From committee documentation to the finished code and court rules, you can find most federal legislative materials on their website. Again, if you are looking for your state resources be sure to check out the Public Library Toolkit from the American Association of Law Libraries. These guides will point you to the correct websites for each state.

REFERENCES

America's Founding Documents, National Archives and Records Administration. Accessed December 17, 2019. https://www.archives.gov/founding-docs.

Brown, Christopher C. *Mastering United States Government Information: Sources and Services.* Santa Barbara, CA: Libraries Unlimited, 2020.

Constitution Annotated, Library of Congress. Accessed December 17, 2019. https://constitution.congress.gov/.

Court Rules, Duke Law. Accessed September 30, 2019. https://law.duke.edu/lib/research guides/courtr/.

Federal Legislative History: Initial Steps, Library of Congress. Accessed September 30, 2019. https://www.loc.gov/law/help/leghist.php.

Findlaw for Legal Professionals. Accessed August 21, 2019. https://lp.findlaw.com/.

Govinfo. Accessed September 30, 2019. https://www.govinfo.gov/.

Justia. Accessed August 21, 2019. https://www.justia.com/.

Legal Information Institute. Accessed December 17, 2019. https://www.law.cornell.edu/.

Office of Law Revision Counsel, United States Code. Accessed August 21, 2019. https://uscode.house.gov/.

Public Library Toolkit, American Association of Law Libraries. Accessed October 14, 2019. https://www.aallnet.org/lispsis/resources-publications/public-library-toolkit/.

Uniform Commercial Code, Legal Information Institute. Accessed October 10, 2019. https://www.law.cornell.edu/ucc/index.html.

Uniform Law Commission. Accessed October 10, 2019. https://www.uniformlaws.org/home.

EIGHT

Laws from the Judicial Branch and Court Forms

In this chapter we are going to look at two different sets of resources: case law and court forms. Case law, also known as opinions or decisions, consists of the documents that make up the law generated in the judicial branch of government. I will begin by taking a look at this type of law more in depth and will discuss what it encompasses and how it is generated. That will be followed with a discussion of how case law is published and accessed. Case law presents some unique challenges and is the most difficult of the types of primary laws to research without the aid of commercial resources. Most patrons who are seeking case law will likely need to visit a law library in order to use those specialized resources.

After my examination of case law, I will spend a little time looking at where to find court forms and other types of legal forms and documents. A good number of patrons visit our library in search of court forms and other types of legal document templates. While we can show patrons where to look for forms and other documents, we want to refrain from recommending specific forms and documents to a patron, as that can be construed as the unauthorized practice of law. Still, there are ways in which you can assist patrons, and some of those strategies are discussed in the section below.

CASE LAW

Case law is the body of law that is created within the judicial branch. Other terms that you may hear from people looking for this type of law are opinions, decisions, or common law. Case law encompasses the judicial decisions written by judges at the appellate level and higher that change legal precedent. Not all court cases make up what is known as case law. In order to better understand this, let us take a look at how the courts are set up.

In most states and in the federal government the courts are broken into three levels. You have the trial level (also referred to as "district court"), the appellate level, and then the court of last resort, or the Supreme Court. At the trial-court level, courts will hear disputes and the decisions are binding only to the parties involved, so these cases do not make up what is known as case law as the decisions only affect those who were a part of that case. These trial-level cases are not published, and you will need to reach out to the court that heard the case to see what is publicly available. The federal courts have an online system, PACER (Public Access to Court Electronic Records), that will allow you to retrieve case and docket information for federal district, appellate, and bankruptcy courts. Users will have to set up an account with PACER, and there are fees to retrieve documents using the system. Some states may also allow you to request documents online rather than having to visit the court in person. Generally, the court will charge you for any of these documents that you request online or in person.

Appellate courts hear cases where one of the parties wishes to appeal the decision of a lower court. The appellate court will look at how the initial case was adjudicated. So an appeal is not a retrial of the original case; rather, it is an investigation of how the case was handled by the trial court. This means that you cannot appeal a case just because you did not like the outcome, you need to find some sort of legal evidence that the case was mishandled. Usually, most cases end at this level unless the case is sent back to the lower court to be reheard or if a party appeals again to the Supreme Court level. The Supreme Court will generally hear only a fraction of the cases that request this level of appeal. So then, case law and the decisions that are published are decisions from the appellate and supreme courts, as these cases instruct the courts on how to handle similar cases.

Another important step toward understanding how case law works is jurisdiction. (We examined jurisdiction more closely in Chapter 5.) Courts are tied to a particular jurisdiction whether it is a county, state, or the federal government. Federal courts will generally only hear cases that regard federal laws, and state courts will only hear cases that involve state laws. Case law will only be binding in the jurisdiction that produces it. So, for example, a decision that comes from the 10th Judicial District of the federal courts is binding only for that district and does not apply to other federal judicial districts. Or a decision from the courts in the state of California will not be considered binding in the state of Oregon because they are separate jurisdictions and each state has its own set of laws. For this reason, it is important to make sure you are searching the correct jurisdiction when researching case law.

A second important concept for understanding case law is the idea of precedent. Precedent is defined as "an action or official decision that can be used as support for later actions or decisions" (Garner 2019, 1424). If a decision is considered legal precedent, then it is binding for the jurisdiction that produced it. Case law usually covers two areas, in that it helps to interpret or apply the statutes and then creates what is known as "common law" for areas that are not covered by the statutes. We have inherited a common-law tradition from England. Generally, common law covers areas of private law—laws that cover relations between individual people. These laws generally tend to be in the realms of torts, contracts, and property issues.

ACCESSING CASE LAW

Researching case law is challenging for a number of reasons. The two main difficulties are finding cases by topic area and making sure that a case has not been overturned by a later case. In this section, I want to begin by discussing the difference between unofficial and official sources. Then we will look at how case law is accessed in the print environment. That will be followed with a discussion of accessing case law with subscription databases. And last, we will look at what can be done with free online sources in this area. However, there are some risks to using free online sources in this area of legal research, as I will explain.

Similarly to other areas of legal publishing, we have what are known as official and unofficial publications. An official publication is created by a governmental entity and is often contracted out to a commercial publisher. An unofficial publication is one that is not created by a governmental entity; the text of the decision will be the same in official and unofficial publications but any editorial commentary or annotations may differ.

Researching Cases in Print

In the realm of researching case law in print there are three types of sources: reporters, digests, and citators. Reporters are the sources where the actual cases are published. The reporters will usually collect cases for a jurisdiction or region, and then the cases are published in chronological order. As the new cases are published in reporters, no adjustments are made to the older volumes to let you know if a case has been overturned by a newer case. Citations for cases in printed reporters will usually look something like this:

Masterpiece Cakeshop, Ltd. v. Colorado Civil Rights Comm'n, 138 S. Ct. 1719 (2018). In this example, we start with the parties' names. The plaintiff (the party bringing the lawsuit) is always listed first, the defendant second. Then, in the coded part, 138 is the volume number for the reporter set in which the case is available. S. Ct. is an abbreviation for the title of the reporter set. So in this example the case is available in the *Supreme Court Reporter.* The number after the reporter title, 1719, is the page number where the case begins. And the last piece of information is the year the decision is from. Often, if a patron comes in with a citation, it might be just a portion of what is listed here. Patrons may just have the party names and year, or what court the case was heard in. Or they may just have 138 S. Ct. 1719. Usually, that will be enough to track the case down.

One last thing to keep in mind is the issue of what are known as parallel citations. Since we have both official and unofficial reporters, if a case is printed in multiple reporters you will have what are known as parallel citations, which point to the exact same case. From the example above, you can also use this citation to find the Masterpiece Cakeshop case: 201 L.Ed.2d. 35. In this citation, 201 is the volume number, L.Ed.2d stands for the *Lawyer's Edition for U.S. Supreme Court Reports, Second Series*, and the case can be found on page 35.

Digests are tools you can use in the print environment to find cases by a specific topic or area of the law. Digests are sources that index points of law. Each appellate case covers a range of legal issues, and a single case may contain legal precedent in a number of different topic areas. The points of law in each case are mapped out by what are known as headnotes. The broader headnotes are then matched to specific Key Numbers. The Key Number System is a hierarchal system of subject headings for case law. The Key Numbers are grouped by large topics that get broken into more specific topics. It is a system that was developed by West Publishing and makes it possible to find cases by specific topic area.

The final tool one would use in conducting case-law research in the print environment is a citator. The best-known print citator tool is Shepard's Citations, which is now owned by LexisNexis. Lexis has an online version of Shepard's that is built into its legal research database, and Westlaw's citator is known as KeyCite. Citators allow you to research whether a case has been overturned by a later decision. So using a citator is key to case-law research because it allows you to know if you are citing timely legal precedent. When using a citator tool, you may find several different outcomes for cases; these outcomes are referred to as "treatment." Negative treatment can include a case that has been reversed by a higher court, overruled at a later date, superseded by a statute, or criticized without being overruled. Also keep in mind that, since a case deals with multiple points of law, not all points of law will be overruled in a case, but you will want to proceed with caution if you see that a case has negative treatment. In addition to validating whether a case is still good law, citators also help you to locate other decisions and secondary sources that may cite that particular case. This can be tremendously useful when conducting case-law research, because if you find one case that is on point, these citing references can lead you to more cases that cover the same area.

Researching Cases with Commercial Databases

There are a few commercial databases that allow you to research case law in a more streamlined fashion than how it works in the print environment. The two major ones are WestlawNext and LexisNexis' Lexis Advance. There are also databases available from Bloomberg Law, Fastcase, Ross Intelligence, Casemaker, and a few others, but I will focus my discussion here on WestlawNext and Lexis Advance. What is nice about using a database is that all three sources (reporters, digests, and citators) work together at once. When working in a database you can begin with searching a specific citation, or you can search using natural language. In WestlawNext, you can also start by searching just the Key Number index as a way to find cases by topic.

While WestlawNext and Lexis Advance display information in a different fashion, they have many of the same tools embedded in their records. Each case will start with a synopsis of the case written by an editor. The synopsis will then be followed by a section that lists and explains the headnotes that are addressed in the case. WestlawNext takes an additional step by mapping each headnote onto any relevant Key Numbers. In both databases, the headnotes are hyperlinked, so you can find any other cases in the jurisdiction you are searching that match that headnote. And then, in WestlawNext, the Key Numbers are hyperlinked so you can see any other cases indexed under that number.

In Lexis Advance, they will have the Shepard's citation information to the right of the case. Shepard's uses a system of symbols to indicate what type of treatment a case has received, which can range from positive to questioned to negative. You will see that symbol in the records list, so it is easy to identify any cases that have received negative treatment. In the case on the right in the Shepard's area, you can see the history of the case and if it has any negative treatment, then you can also access citing references and authorities. WestlawNext's KeyCite uses a simpler flag system to indicate if cases have had negative treatment: a red flag notes cases that have been overturned, and a yellow flag indicates cases that have been criticized. Then, in the case, West-lawNext places its KeyCite information in tabs along the top of the case. There you can find the history of the case, filings, negative treatment, citing references, and a table of authorities. Both databases will hyperlink any cases, statutes, or court rules referred to in the decision, so it is easy to view those other documents.

Citing references and authorities can be another way for researchers to find more useful cases and other documents within the subject area they are searching. Citing references will be the cases and other document types that cite that particular case. Authorities are the cases and other documents that the case in question uses for its arguments. So if you find a relevant case, you will want to look through the headnotes, Key Numbers, citing references, and authorities for more relevant content. These built-in tools really streamline the case-law research process in that you can easily locate cases by topic area and quickly tell whether or not those cases are still good law. Further, having hyperlinked headnotes, citing references, and authorities makes it easy to find additional content in the same area.

Researching Cases Online

Finally, I want to discuss searching for cases in the free online environment. This is probably the most difficult way to find cases by topic, and it is also risky as there is not a free citator service that will let you know whether or not a case has been overturned by a later decision. There are a number of places where you can locate cases for free on the open Web. A number of the courts will list decisions on their websites. Usually, these lists will not be a comprehensive list of every case decided by the court but cases from a given period of time or cases of note.

U.S. Supreme Court cases can be found for free in a number of places. On the U.S. Supreme Court website you can find decisions dating back to 1992. This site also has files of some oral arguments that you can listen to. Justia, in their Supreme Court Center, has a complete listing of all U.S. Supreme Court cases, including cases that were heard even before the Supreme Court was officially established. You can also find Supreme Court cases on the Legal Information Institute website, and they have a feature that allows you to search by topic area. The Oyez project will also let you search by issue on their site; they will just provide you with a synopsis of the case, but then they will link you to Justia's site to read the decision. Oyez also provides some recordings of oral arguments. Findlaw for Legal Professionals also has a complete listing of Supreme Court cases, and they allow you to browse by year and also to search across the documents in a number of ways, including a free text search.

For federal cases, you will want to look at the website for the district court for your region, as the U.S. Courts' website will point you to PACER, which is a fee-based service. You can also locate federal cases on the Govinfo.gov website. The coverage will vary district by district: some will only go back to the early 2000s, and others may go back to the late 1980s. Findlaw for Legal Professionals also has some federal cases available. Most districts seem to have coverage back through the mid-1990s, and again you can search across case collections in a number of different ways.

For cases from a state jurisdiction, you can see if any are published on that state judicial branch's website. Findlaw for Legal Professionals has pretty good coverage of state cases. Justia is another place to look. You can also find cases for state and federal jurisdictions through Google Scholar. Another place that covers multiple jurisdictions is PlainSite. PlainSite will allow you to find information about court cases, such as the filings. You can search by topic area or jurisdiction.

There are two sites both of which have good coverage and will allow you to see citing references for each case. Google Scholar has an option to search case law and will allow you to select a specific jurisdiction. In the results list you will see options to see who the case is cited by and how it is cited. The other site, Court Listener, will allow you to see citing references and authorities for each case. Having the option to see the citing references and authorities is very helpful, but still, neither has a tool that will quickly tell you if a case has had negative treatment.

When using any of these free online services to research case law you will want to use caution. While it is possible to find most cases online if you have a citation, there is no free citator service that will allow you to tell if a decision has been overturned or reversed. Also, as the tools to search by topic area are limited, if you are searching for cases without a citation, it can be difficult to know if you are finding the key cases in a particular topic area or jurisdiction. I would recommend either sending patrons with case-law research needs to a law library, or contacting a law library with the citations in question to verify if they are still good law.

COURT FORMS

A good number of patrons visit our library looking to access court forms and other types of legal documents. This section will cover how to find forms that get filed with a court as well as other legal forms and templates. Depending on your jurisdiction, some court forms are available for free online, but some jurisdictions may require you to purchase the forms from the courthouse. Other legal documents can be obtained through subscription databases or for a fee on the Web.

Helping patrons locate forms can be tricky, as they often do not know what specific form they need. If your court has any sort of self-help resources, there may be court employees who can help patrons to determine the correct form. In general, I show patrons where to locate forms and other documents, but I refrain from making recommendations, for if I am wrong and they pay to file the incorrect form, they won't be able to get their money back. Similarly, with other legal documents there can be serious ramifications if someone is using the incorrect type of document. If I am able to, I will show people the range of possibilities, print out their options, and then direct them to a legal clinic where they can discuss the specific forms with an attorney.

First, I will address finding forms for federal courts. A discussion about locating forms for state courts will follow. After I discuss forms that are filed with the courts, I will turn to locating other types of legal documents that are considered forms. I will conclude with some suggestions of outside resources that can assist people in determining the correct form for their needs.

Federal Court Forms

There are a number of forms available for the Federal Court System on the U.S. Courts website. Once you are on that page, look for the section labeled "Services and Forms." In general, I get very few patrons who are representing themselves in federal court, but it is still good to know about this resource. The one area in which I do occasionally receive requests is bankruptcy matters. U.S. Courts has several useful pages in this "Services and Forms" section that explain the various types of bankruptcy and provides the forms for people wishing to file for bankruptcy.

In addition to looking on the U.S. Courts' website, you should consult the website for the Federal Judicial District that you are in. Each website has a different layout, but look for a section labeled "forms." Please consult Table 8.1 to determine which federal judicial district your state falls in.

Another resource to consult when searching for federal court forms would be the Federal Court Rules, which are part of the United States Code. The court rules are broken down for each type of court—civil, criminal, appellate, and so on—so make sure you are consulting the correct area. In addition to finding out what forms may be needed for a particular action, the court rules will also provide information on court procedures. If patrons have access to a

Table 8.1. Federal Judicial Districts by State

District	States
First	Maine, Massachusetts, New Hampshire, Puerto Rico, and Rhode Island
Second	Connecticut, New York, and Vermont
Third	Delaware, New Jersey, Pennsylvania, and U.S. Virgin Islands
Fourth	Maryland, North Carolina, South Carolina, Virginia, and West Virginia
Fifth	Louisiana, Mississippi, and Texas
Sixth	Kentucky, Michigan, Ohio, and Tennessee
Seventh	Illinois, Indiana, and Wisconsin
Eighth	Arkansas, Iowa, Minnesota, Missouri, Nebraska, North Dakota, and South Dakota
Ninth	Alaska, Arizona, California, Guam, Hawaii, Idaho, Montana, Nevada, Northern Mariana Islands, Oregon, and Washington
Tenth	Colorado, Kansas, New Mexico, Oklahoma, Utah, and Wyoming
Eleventh	Alabama, Florida, and Georgia

law library, they may also be able to find information about federal court forms in *Federal Practice and Procedure*.

State Court Forms

Every state judicial branch is set up differently, and the ability to access forms will vary from state to state. Some states have what are known as unified forms, meaning that the same forms can be used in courts throughout the state; what form is accepted in other states may vary from court to court. A good place to start with locating your state's court forms is the website for the National Center for State Courts; under "Access and Fairness" you will find a page called "Self-Representation" that has an area for links for each state. You can also look up your state's judicial branch website to see if they have a section for either self-help or forms. Or, if your state has a state law library (not every state does), it may also have information about where to find state court forms on its website.

Additionally, you can consult your state's court rules, which again will be a part of your state's statutes. The court rules will have information about court forms and procedures. Sometimes you can also find information about state court forms in practice manuals or continuing legal education materials for your particular state. However, those types of resources will generally be held only by a law library.

Other Legal Forms and Documents

There are a wide range of other legal forms and documents that do not get filed with a court. These might be documents like power of attorney forms, a last will and testament, a lease, or a partnership agreement. Keep in mind that not all legal forms are necessarily fillable forms. A fillable form is one where the form asks for a piece of information and you just simply fill it in the space provided. Some types of legal forms are really just document templates. The form will tell you what content needs to be included and the order the information needs to be in, but the patron will actually have to draft the document.

There are a number of databases libraries can subscribe to in order to provide access to these types of forms and documents. Our library subscribes to Gale Legal Forms, and I know of a number of other libraries that subscribe to Nuwav. You will also find other vendors selling legal forms on the web: Rocket Lawyer, Law Depot, USLegal, and Legal Zoom, just to name a few. Legal forms can be pricey to purchase online, so it may be risky for a patron to purchase an expensive form if he isn't sure it is the correct document he needs.

Strategies for Helping Patrons

As I mentioned earlier, we want to refrain from selecting forms for patrons as this can be construed as providing legal advice. Nor do we want to be responsible for patrons paying to file an incorrect form or drafting a legal document that could ultimately do them harm. Nevertheless, there are still ways we can assist patrons in this area. We can show them where to locate materials and how to access those forms and documents. We can refer them to self-help centers in the courts (if they exist in your area), or we can refer them to legal clinics where they can discuss various options with trained legal professionals. A number of jurisdictions have created flowcharts for common areas like divorce that will tell a patron what form they need based on their situation. Check with your local courts to find if these resources exist in your area. Also, the court rules and other practice aids can also provide patrons guidance about what forms they need for a particular action.

REFERENCE SCENARIO

Patron: I need some cases to cite in my brief.

Librarian: Okay, great, can you tell me a little more about it? What's the subject area, and which court are you submitting your brief to?

Patron: It's about parental visitation rights, and I am submitting it to the district court here in town.

Librarian: Have you found any other useful cases yet, or do you have a particular statute that applies to the situation?

Patron: I have a couple of cases that I found on Google, but I am not sure if they are okay to use.

Librarian: At our library we have a subscription to Westlaw, which is going to be the easiest for us to use to find cases. We can search just the jurisdiction you need and can also tell if a case has been overruled. We can also take a look at the cases you found to see if they are still good law and if they are from the same jurisdiction.

Patron: Why is the jurisdiction so important?

Librarian: Great question, what we are ultimately looking for are cases that will be considered binding, primary authority. That means cases that are in the same jurisdiction as where you are filing your brief. Judges are supposed to follow the precedent that has been set in their jurisdiction. Cases from a different jurisdiction might be persuasive to a judge, but he doesn't necessarily have to follow it.

Patron: Well, here are the cases I found. It looks like they are from another state. So is that outside of our jurisdiction?

Librarian: Unfortunately, yes. But I bet we can find some Colorado cases that would apply to your situation. So there are a few ways we can use Westlaw to locate cases. We can always search the cases in our jurisdiction using this search bar that is kind of like Google. We can look through this subject heading list called Key Numbers to see if there is a good match for the subject area. Or, if you have a statute or case, we can locate that and see if any of the annotations or citations lead us to any cases. Sometimes you might not find what you are looking for right away, so it can help to have a few different ways to look for things. Let's start with the search bar and see what we can find. First, we want to make sure we have the jurisdiction set to Colorado, and then you can type in some words or a phrase that describes the subject.

Patron: [Runs search for "parental visitation rights."]

Librarian: Okay, there are a few things I want to explain before you start reading through the cases. First, you want to be on the lookout for these red and yellow flags next to the entries. The flags are part of a feature called KeyCite. Treat the red flag like a stop sign; it means the case has been overturned and is no longer good law, so you don't want to use it. The yellow flag is like a yellow light: proceed with caution. The decision has been criticized, so you want to be careful.

Then let's open up a case and I will show you a few more things. On the main document page is where you will find the text of the decision. However, first there will be an abstract explaining what the case is about. Next you will have this section called Headnotes. Each case will usually touch on multiple points of law; they are called headnotes and are labeled with numbers. You will see these numbers as you read through the judge's decision so it's easier to find where a particular topic is being discussed. Then, each of the headnotes maps onto what are called Key Numbers, which are like subjects. If you see a Key Number that looks like it is on-topic for you, you can click on it; and that will bring up any other case that has the same topic covered in it. So the Key Numbers can really help you find more on-point cases. After the headnote section, you'll see the parties listed, who they were represented by, and then finally the judge's decision. Any other cases or laws that are referred to will be hyperlinked so you can read them if you like, then at the bottom you may find additional references or citations. So that's the layout of the decision.

Next let's look at some of these tabs along the top. There is one called Negative Treatment. If a case has a red or yellow flag next to it, then you can use this tab to see which decisions either criticized or overturned the case we are looking at. There is a history tab, so if a case had multiple appeals, you can see how it moved through the courts. Next there is a tab called Citing References. This one can be pretty useful if you have found a good case for your issue. Under Citing References you will find cases and other sources that came after this case but cited it as an example. And then, last, there is a tab called Table of Authorities. On this tab you will see the cases that the case we are looking at has cited. So, again, it can be another quick way to find more cases on your topic.

So that is how the database works. You can e-mail copies of the cases or the results to yourself by clicking on this little envelope icon. I will let you start sifting through some of the results. And here is my card should you want to meet again or have any more questions.

When helping a patron find cases, there are two important things to remember. First, the case needs to come from the same jurisdiction where the patron is appearing in court. Second, you have to have a way to verify if the case is still good law, meaning that it has not been overturned by a later case. The first is relatively easy to do using free case-law research sources. Google Scholar will let you select the jurisdiction you want to search, and FindLaw for Legal Professional has a limited number of jurisdictions that you can easily search. The second task of telling if a case is still good law is much more difficult to accomplish with free sources. Google Scholar does have a "how cited" feature that will show you which cases cite the one you are looking at as well as snippets of the case that cites it, but it does not clearly spell out whether it is a negative citation. My recommendation is that you refer a patron who needs to know if a case is still good law or not to a law library to verify any cases she has found.

CONCLUSION

As we have seen, case-law research presents a number of unique challenges that may be more easily met through the use of commercial resources. If you live in proximity to a law library, case law is an area where it may be best to refer patrons to it. Commercial databases make it easier to find cases by topic and to quickly reveal if a case is still good law. Even if you do not live near a law library, it still might be worthwhile contacting it via phone or e-mail to check any citations for cases you find to make sure those cases are still legal precedent. Remember, however, that not all court cases will be published and accessible through a law library. Published cases come only from appellate courts and higher, and in some jurisdictions they will only publish those cases that actually change legal precedent. When searching out case law be sure you are looking at the correct jurisdiction to find precedent that is binding.

With regard to forms, what you find in each jurisdiction will vary. Check to see if there are any self-help offices for your jurisdiction, as these resources can sometimes be useful for patrons who are trying to determine what court forms they need. Again, we want to refrain from selecting forms for patrons ourselves, or from helping them draft any type of legal document. In these situations, it can be useful to know of any legal clinics in your area to which you can refer patrons for help with those questions.

REFERENCES

Court Listener. Accessed April 2, 2020. https://www.courtlistener.com/.

FindLaw for Legal Professionals. Accessed December 9, 2019. https://lp.findlaw.com/.

Garner, Bryan A., ed. *Black's Law Dictionary, 11th Edition*. Eagan, MN: Thomson West, 2019.

Google Scholar. Accessed December 9, 2019. https://scholar.google.com/.

Govinfo. Accessed December 9, 2019. https://www.govinfo.gov/.

Justia. Accessed March 7, 2019. https://www.justia.com/.

National Center for State Courts. "Self-Representation State Links." Accessed December 6, 2019. https://www.ncsc.org/Topics/Access-and-Fairness/Self-Representation/State-Links.aspx.

Oyez. Accessed December 9, 2019. https://www.oyez.org/.

PlainSite. Accessed December 9, 2019. https://www.plainsite.org/.

Public Access Court Electronic Records. Accessed December 6, 2019. https://www.pacer
    .gov/.

Supreme Court of the United States. Accessed December 9, 2019. https://www.supreme
    court.gov/.

United State Courts. Accessed December 6, 2019. https://www.uscourts.gov/.

Wright, Charles, and Arthur Miller. *Federal Practice and Procedure*. Eagan, MN: Thom-
    son West, 2019.

NINE

Laws from the Executive Branch

The executive branch of government produces a wide range of information. Our discussion in this chapter will focus primarily on those documents that are considered laws. To begin, I first offer a quick overview of the range of information produced by the executive branch. This will be followed by a review of executive orders that carry the force of law and how to locate them. Next I will delve into the regulatory process and how to locate regulations and rules. I will also look at other types of administrative legal sources and the administrative courts. And last, I will briefly discuss how to locate state regulatory sources.

OVERVIEW OF EXECUTIVE SOURCES

A wide range of information sources are produced by the various agencies that make up the executive branch of government. As this book focuses on laws and legal issues, I will limit my discussion to those areas. However, it can still be useful to have a broad familiarity with some of the different government sources. Christopher C. Brown offers a thorough overview of these sources in his work *Mastering United States Government Information: Sources and Services.*

Among the few executive branch sources that I have encountered while working with patrons the first would be the budget for the United States Government. While Congress controls the pursestrings and how funds are allocated, the United States Budget and its analysis can be found in a number of places: The Office of Management and Budget of the White House, The Congressional Budget Office, and on Govinfo.gov. The Census Bureau, part of the

Department of Commerce, has a wealth of demographic information that patrons may want to access. The Center for Disease Control and Prevention also maintains a range of demographic information on their pages for vital statistics.

Other useful sources of information include EDGAR from the U.S. Securities and Exchange Commission, where patrons can find financial information for public businesses; Grants.gov, where patrons can locate and apply for federal grants; and Huduser.gov, where patrons can find data on housing and community development. A general familiarity with the services available on the website for the U.S. Patent and Trademark Office is also useful as on this site patrons can search and apply for patents. And though it is not technically a part of the executive branch because it falls under the direction of the Library of Congress, the U.S. Copyright Office also has a helpful website that explains copyright law as well as how to register a copyright. These are just a few examples of the plethora of resources available from federal government agencies.

EXECUTIVE ORDERS

Executive orders are presidential issuances that carry the force of law. These orders can be used for a variety of purposes. They can establish new policies or be used to change current regulations, to alter the interpretation of current legislation, or to outline how legislation should go into effect. Executive orders can also be used to reorganize government agencies. And last, they can be used to declare a national emergency.

There are a number of places where you can access executive orders. If you are looking for recent orders first check on the Federal Register website hosted by the National Archives; they should have documents dating back to 1994. For older orders you can access the Federal Register through 1936 on Govinfo .gov. Executive orders will also appear in the Compilation of Presidential Documents that is available on Govinfo.gov. You can also find executive orders in Title 3 of the Code of Federal Regulations.

If you are trying to determine where executive orders are integrated into the United States Code, you can use Table IV, which is a part of the print set. Or you can access Table IV of the United State Code on the Office of Law Revision Counsel's website that hosts the code; just look in the section labeled "Popular Names and Tables." Another useful tool that will tell you which executive orders are still in effect are the Disposition Tables that are available on the National Archives' website. There you can search by each year of an administration to see the status of each order.

REGULATIONS AND RULES

Regulations and rules are two terms that can be used interchangeably to describe laws that are generated by the various government agencies. Government agencies cannot issue these rules on their own; they need an enabling statute from the legislative branch in order to create a rule. Congress gives this rule-making authority to the agencies as they usually employ experts in those specific areas. The legislative branch will decide what needs to be done and then the executive branch will determine how to do it. The rules and regulations created by agencies will carry the full force of the law. Although regulations and rules are the types of laws that most often shape our day-to-day lives, they are rarely requested by patrons. Below I will outline the process for how regulations are created, and while it is complicated, I still feel that regulations tend to be a more nimble type of law than statutes. Many times, if a patron is looking for information such as Medicaid income limits, information that might change more rapidly based on economic trends, this type of law seems to be more likely found in regulations rather than statutes.

The modern process to make regulations did not really fall into place until 1936 with the first publication of the Federal Register. You can find the entire rule-making process mapped out on the Reg Map, which is available through the Reginfo.gov website. The process in broad strokes goes as follows. First the enabling legislation is created and passed. Then the appropriate agency will begin internally drafting the regulation. The proposed rule is first published in the Federal Register. After the initial publication, there is a period for public comment on the proposed rule. Those comments are considered, and then the rule is revised and published a second time in the Federal Register in its final form. Then last, most rules will be codified and organized by topic in the Code of Federal Regulations.

When researching regulations there are three useful main sources: the Federal Register, the Unified Agenda, and the Code of Federal Regulations (CFR). The Federal Register is good for finding proposed and newly passed rules. The Unified Agenda is a semiannual report that requires the agencies to report on any regulatory actions that are in a stage of development or that have been recently completed. The CFR contains the finalized rules organized by title, which makes it the easiest to search for something by topic. Most of the questions I have fielded that pertain to regulations could be answered by referring to the CFR. However, if you are searching for new or proposed regulations then the Federal Register and the Unified Agenda are the sources you want to consult.

The Federal Register is published daily and can be found online in a number of places, for instance, Federalregister.gov and Govinfo.gov. The Federal Register contains the following: notice of proposed rules and information on how the public can submit comments; the final rules that will be codified in the CFR; which parts of the CFR are affected by the new rules; presidential documents such as executive orders, proclamations, and administrative orders; and a reader's aid. On their website the National Archives provide a helpful tutorial on using the Federal Register.

The Unified Agenda is published twice a year. It can be accessed on Reginfo.gov, the website for the Office of Information and Regulatory Affairs, which is part of the Office of Management and Budget. The Unified Agenda can also be found on Govinfo.gov. On the Reginfo.gov site, it is easy to search for regulatory information by agency. In the Unified Agenda you will also find information about proposed and recently passed regulations; and then the site will link you to the rules in the Federal Register as published on the Govinfo.gov site. If patrons are looking to comment on proposed rules, then they will want to visit Regulations.gov. This site also has access to the Unified Agenda.

Once rules are finalized, they are published in the Code of Federal Regulations. The CFR is going to contain most finalized rules; however, regulations of a temporary nature, such as those created for emergencies and rules that do not have broad applicability, will not be included. The CFR is broken up into fifty titles. These titles are not quite parallel to the titles in the U.S. Code. Sections of the CFR are updated quarterly. Titles 1–16 are updated in January; titles 17–27 are updated in April; titles 28–41 are updated in July; and titles 42–50 are updated in October. Each title describes a broad topic. The individual agencies that have rules within this topic area will have chapters under the title. The part subdivision will be used for programs from the agency. The parts are divided into sections that explain the provisions of the program. The sections are then divided into paragraphs. While there is an attempt at a standardized numbering scheme in the CFR, you still may find some gaps in numbering. This happens when sections or parts are removed, or when agencies reserve numbers for anticipated regulations. As long as the numbers within the title continue to grow larger, it is okay to ignore gaps in the numbering.

The CFR is available from a number of sources: in print; on Govinfo.gov; on sites like Legal Information Institute, Justia, and Findlaw for Legal Professionals; and on the site eCFR. Within the CFR, Title 3 will contain presidential documents. In the print version, these volumes will be compiled and not replaced like the others. If you need to check to make sure a regulation in print is up-to-date, there is a process to correlate. First consult the CFR for the latest annual version of the regulation. Then, in the reader's aids for the Federal Register, check the cumulative list of parts affected for the CFR. Next, check the latest monthly List of Sections Affected in the Federal Register. And then, lastly, examine each daily Federal Register issue on the topic. This process is quite lengthy. An easier way to correlate would be to consult the eCFR website.

The eCFR website is updated daily. While it is not technically the official version of the CFR, it is still the easiest place to see the most current version of the CFR without going through the lengthy correlation process on your own. The website will clearly tell you the date the CFR is current through. The eCFR can also show you what regulations were in force to any prior date going back to January 1, 2015. The eCFR page defaults to browsing, but there is also a simple search feature that will allow you to search across the entire code or just within a specific title.

One final resource to be aware of in the CFR is the Parallel Table of Authorities and Rules. This table will help you locate which section in the CFR correlates to parts of the U.S. Code, the *U.S. Statutes at Large*, Public Laws, and a range of presidential documents. This table can be found in the Index volume of the print CFR, and also be found on Govinfo.gov under "CFR Index and Finding Aids." In the left-hand column of the table you will find listings for the various titles and sections of the U.S. Code, the *U.S. Statutes at Large*, the Public Laws, and presidential documents. In the right-hand column you will see which sections of the CFR correspond to those various laws. This can be helpful in order to find if there are any regulations that pertain to a particular law. Or if you are trying to locate the enabling statute for a part of the CFR, you can open the PDF version of the table on Govinfo.gov and do a CTRL+F search for the regulation in question.

ADMINISTRATIVE LEGAL RESOURCES

There are a group of agencies that are known as Independent Regulatory Agencies. What this means is that these agencies do not serve at the pleasure of the president and their rules are not reviewed by the Office of Management and Budget. Most other agencies fall under the direction of one of the cabinets. These Independent Regulatory Agencies are usually created by statute with the goal of their remaining nonpartisan from administration to administration. Many of these agencies are run by a board or commission rather than by a single director. Presidents will be able to appoint members to the board or commission; however, the terms are staggered and often run longer than four years, which limits the amount of control any one administration can have on the makeup of the group. The Independent Regulatory Agencies include the following and any other agency that has been designated by statute:

- Board of Governors of the Federal Reserve System
- Bureau of Consumer Financial Protection

- Commodity Future Trading Commission
- Consumer Product Safety Commission
- Federal Communications Commission
- Federal Deposit Insurance Corporation
- Federal Energy Regulatory Commission
- Federal Housing Finance Agency
- Federal Maritime Commission
- Federal Trade Commission
- Interstate Commerce Commission
- Mine Enforcement Safety and Health Review Commission
- National Labor Relations Board
- Nuclear Regulatory Commission
- Occupational Safety and Health Review Commission
- Office of Financial Research
- Officer of the Comptroller of the Currency
- Postal Regulatory Commission
- Securities and Exchange Commission

The regulations from these agencies do not get published in the Federal Register. You can find them on the various agency websites and in the CFR. These agencies still follow a fairly similar rule-making process that considers public comment. It is good to know these agencies exist, for if you are searching the Federal Register and can't find something, you can check the agency websites or the CFR for these rules.

ADMINISTRATIVE COURTS

Some government agencies are granted the ability to adjudicate their own rules. This allows individuals and the agencies themselves to resolve disputes outside of district courts. These administrative courts will have an appeals process; however, some decisions can be appealed to a district court if need be. In my position, I have not dealt with any federal administrative courts. What I have seen a bit of that falls into this realm is people appealing a worker's compensation decision that came from the state Department of Labor.

Every state will have a different method for this appeals process, so it is best for patrons to consult your state's Department of Labor for the forms and procedures. In handling these issues it is probably best to start with the website for the agency in question to see what resources are available regarding appealing administrative decisions. Then, depending on the jurisdiction, you may also be able to find information in the state or federal statutes about when and how an administrative court decision can be appealed to district court.

STATE REGULATORY SOURCES

While there is not the space here to provide information on how to locate and use all fifty states' regulations, I do want to make a few general comments regarding state regulatory resources. Most states will follow a process similar to the federal process, where proposed rules are published in a document usually called a register or a bulletin along with information about how the public can comment. After public comment is collected and considered, finalized rules of a general and permanent nature will be codified. First thing to note is that states will publish their registers less frequently than the federal government. In Colorado, our state register is published twice a month as opposed to daily. The second thing to note is that public comment will be collected differently from the electronic system used by the federal government. Again, if you look at the Colorado Register, it will list the hearing times for when the public can provide comment on a proposed rule.

In searching for your state's regulations, you may try one of the following phrases with the name of your state: Code of Regulations, Administrative Code, or Administrative Rules. A number of states will have their codified regulations and the register available on their secretary of state's website, so you may want to check there. You can also locate state codified regulations on Findlaw for Legal Professionals and the Legal Information Institute website.

REFERENCE SCENARIO

Patron: I need to appeal the decision on my worker's compensation claim.
Librarian: Okay, let's see what we can find that might help you. Where did you file the claim? Was it here, in this state?
Patron: It was here.
Librarian: Did you get any paperwork from the decision with any directions for an appeal?
Patron: I think so, but I left it at home.
Librarian: Okay, you may want to take a look at that paperwork once you are back home. It might have important information about how to appeal the decision. But for now, let's see if maybe the

Department of Labor has any information on its website. And if we don't find anything there, maybe we can see if there is a page for administrative courts in our state.

Patron: Oh, here is a section for Worker's Compensation on the Department of Labor website, should I look in there?

Librarian: Yes, let's start there and see what it says.

Patron: There is a section called "Review a Decision," and it has a bunch of forms, do I need them all?

Librarian: You know, I am not sure. We can print all of them out, just in case. When you are reviewing your paperwork at home, see if they mention any of these forms by name. Then here is a copy of the legal clinic calendar. You might want to go speak with an attorney for free to see if he might be able to answer that question. I would bring along all of the forms and any paperwork you have on the matter. Then, if you have any follow-up questions after talking with the attorney, here is my card so you know how to reach me.

For certain types of legal questions relating to executive matters, it can sometimes be easiest to start with the website for the particular executive agency in question. If you do not find what you need there, then you might also see if your state has a website for an office of administrative courts. With regard to forms, we always want to refrain from selecting specific forms for patrons. I always err on the side of giving patrons more forms than they need rather than trying to determine which is the correct form, sometimes printing them out for free if the situation warrants it. Then I encourage the patron to try to speak with an attorney if that is an option. Last, in this situation it is always important to remind patrons to read carefully through any paperwork they have received on the matter, as that may tell them what procedures they need to follow, which are the relevant forms, and what the pertinent laws are.

CONCLUSION

An often overlooked source of law, regulations and rules are important legal sources to be familiar with. These laws can flesh out the specifics for legislation created by statute. While the process and the number of sources that can be used to access this information are a bit overwhelming, remember that a good number of patron questions relating to regulations can be accessed through the CFR. In addition to regulations and rules, remember that executive orders will also carry the force of law. Finally, having a broad understanding of the range of information resources created by the executive branch of government can be useful in answering a variety of patron questions, both those that are related to legal matters and those that are not.

REFERENCES

Brown, Christopher C. *Mastering United States Government Information: Sources and Services*. Santa Barbara, CA: Libraries Unlimited, 2020.

Compilation of Presidential Documents, U.S. Government Publishing Office. Accessed December 31, 2019. https://www.govinfo.gov/app/collection/CPD.

Congressional Budget Office. Accessed December 31, 2019. https://www.cbo.gov/.

EDGAR, U.S. Securities and Exchange Commission. Accessed December 31, 2019. https://www.sec.gov/edgar.shtml.

Electronic Code of Federal Regulations (eCFR). Accessed January 9, 2020. https://gov.ecfr.io/cgi-bin/ECFR?page=browse.

Executive Orders Disposition Tables Index, National Archives. Accessed December 31, 2019. https://www.archives.gov/federal-register/executive-orders/disposition.

Federal Register, National Archives. Accessed December 31, 2019. https://www.federalregister.gov/.

Federal Register, U.S. Government Publishing Office. Accessed December 31, 2019. https://www.govinfo.gov/app/collection/fr.

Federal Register Tutorial, National Archives. Accessed January 2, 2020. https://www.archives.gov/federal-register/tutorial.

Findlaw for Legal Professionals. Accessed January 9, 2020. https://lp.findlaw.com/.

Govinfo. Accessed December 31, 2019. https://www.govinfo.gov/.

Grants.gov. Accessed December 31, 2019. https://www.grants.gov/.

HUD User. Accessed December 31, 2019. https://www.huduser.gov/portal/home.html.

Justia. Accessed January 9, 2020. https://www.justia.com/.

Legal Information Institute. Accessed January 9, 2020. https://www.law.cornell.edu/.

National Center for Health Statistics, Centers for Disease Control and Prevention. Accessed December 31, 2019. https://www.cdc.gov/nchs/nvss/index.htm.

Office of Management and Budget, White House. Accessed December 31, 2019. https://www.whitehouse.gov/omb/.

Reg Map, Office of Information and Regulatory Affairs. Accessed December 31, 2019. https://www.reginfo.gov/public/reginfo/Regmap/index.myjsp.

Regulations.gov. Accessed January 9, 2020. https://www.regulations.gov/.

Unified Agenda, Office of Information and Regulatory Affairs. Accessed January 8, 2020. https://www.reginfo.gov/public/do/eAgendaMain.

United States Census Bureau. Accessed December 31, 2019. https://www.census.gov/.

United States Code, Office of Law Revision Counsel. Accessed December 31, 2019. https://uscode.house.gov/browse.xhtml.

United States Copyright Office. Accessed January 7, 2020. https://www.copyright.gov/.

United States Patent and Trademark Office. Accessed January 7, 2020. https://www.uspto.gov/.

TEN

Conclusion

When I took my position at Pikes Peak Library District in 2014, it was the first time I had ever worked with a legal collection or assisted patrons with legal reference questions. I tell you this so you will understand that it is possible to approach the law as part of library work as you would any other subject area in which you are not an expert. I have taught myself enough about the law that I now understand the sources at play and where to look for things, but I am not in a position where I would ever feel comfortable advising someone about the law. Over time I have become familiar with the legal community in my area, so I know where to make referrals and what services are available. I have found partners in the community who can offer their expertise through classes and legal clinics. Law librarianship is still librarianship. Do not let the subject area intimidate you; you already have skills and resources you can apply to this area. In this last chapter, I would like to offer a few reflections and things I have learned about the subject area and how to offer services to patrons with legal questions.

THE IMPORTANCE OF SERVING THIS POPULATION

Providing access to laws and legal information helps make our judicial system more equitable. Libraries can play a huge role in closing the justice gap and providing equal access for all. It is important to remember whom you are serving and what may be at stake for them. Patrons with legal questions may be facing the loss of their home, their children, their money or health benefits, or worse. Legal problems can create a great deal of stress for these patrons, so they may not always be at their best. Patrons with legal issues tend to get the runaround, as very few people can actually provide them with legal advice. So, naturally, when you encounter them they may be frustrated. Try to remain patient with folks as they work through these issues. By and large most patrons are going to be appreciative of your assistance, even if it is limited. While we might not be experts in the law, we are experts in helping people find things, and most people can recognize when you are sincerely trying to help them.

Sometimes just listening may be a more important service than you realize. Because of this, it is important to employ active listening skills. Ask clarifying questions, try to paraphrase to check your understanding, and be aware of what you are communicating nonverbally. Giving a patron time to explain her issue will better help you to understand her situation and what she is seeking, but it will also give the patron time to fully think through what she is facing and what she needs. And while you may not be able to solve her problem for her, giving her the opportunity to be heard can be empowering for her. Showing a patron empathy for her situation does not mean you have to agree with or advise her, but it can help you to build a relationship so you can better serve her in her quest for information. Also keep in mind the idea of uncertainty management; we want to help patrons understand the entire scope of their situation and what obstacles they may face. Giving people the opportunity to fully articulate their situation and have it heard by someone else can help them come to terms with what they are dealing with.

Remember that legal problems are usually process oriented; they are rarely solved by taking just one step or action. I consider my reference interactions a success if I can move the patron at least one step forward on her journey. If I can connect a patron with a legal clinic, or show her where to find and print out forms, or how to look up court rules—all of these steps will ultimately help the patron in the process of addressing her issue. I try to approach questions by thinking about what source might have an answer for the question rather than what the answer to the question is. This helps me to stay focused on providing information rather than advising the patron. In addition, it places the onus of finding the answer back on the patron where it belongs.

Also keep in mind that many legal problems, particularly if the patron is going to court, take time to solve. So expect patrons to return with more requests. This is why it is important to try to maintain healthy relationships with patrons. If I have had a particularly rough interaction with a patron here is one trick I use: the next time I see him, I pretend I am meeting him for the first time. I try to refrain from letting baggage from our last interaction interfere with my ability to work with him on his next request. Obviously, you do not want to tolerate abusive patrons, but try to extend grace to them when possible.

Last, it can be tempting to judge a patron for her legal issue. Or you might wonder, is this person just trying to sue everyone around her? This is a trap you should try not to fall into. Just as we would never judge a patron by a book she requests, the same goes for legal information. Try to remain focused on helping the patron to locate the information being requested without imposing any of your own judgments on her or her situation. We want to treat all patrons equally and to honor every request for information.

FOCUS ON WHAT YOUR LIBRARY DOES ALREADY

Taking on an entirely new subject area can be overwhelming. Try to remember all of the services and resources that you are already comfortable offering and then see how they can be applied to the area of law. As librarians we do not need to master a subject area in order to help with it. Remember that we are just providing access to legal information, not interpreting the law or advising patrons about the law. In fact, it is better not to be an expert, for then you might be tempted to advise patrons. This is also where a clear legal reference policy can be useful. It can let both staff and patrons know what is the scope of services that the library can provide in the area of law. A good policy will empower staff to help connect patrons with information while protecting them from the unauthorized practice of law.

I think that, as librarians, we love knowing the answers and helping people with their problems. However, it is also okay to let a patron know when you do *not* know the answer. This is a good time to demonstrate how to search for things and develop information literacy skills, which will serve your patrons better, as they can begin to build skills in researching and identifying the credibility of sources. Legal reference work involves a great deal of information literacy and research methods instruction because the patron is responsible for determining his own answer. Remember that the goal for patrons is to locate binding primary authority, meaning laws from the relevant jurisdiction. So while we cannot determine the exact law that might apply, we can show patrons where they can find primary laws in local, state, and federal jurisdictions. We can also explain to them why jurisdiction is important to them in their research.

It is also okay to tell people no when you cannot do something for them. While a patron may think that she wants you to fill out her court paperwork for her, in fact that serves no one's interests. Try to stay focused on what you can do rather than what you cannot. Patrons will sometimes accuse me of "not wanting to help them" because I am not doing the specific task they asked me to do. In reality, though, if I were to do a patron's paperwork, I would be committing the unauthorized practice of law, and chances are I would also not complete the paperwork correctly, which would do him more harm than good. So in those situations I always try to reframe with what I as a librarian can do and then try to refer him to people who can help him with the paperwork or whatever specific task he is trying to perform. It is always better to be honest and up front about the limitations to our services and then to focus on the areas in which we can provide help. While you may get some resistance, most patrons seem to understand and appreciate your honesty. And most will also appreciate your taking the time to listen and work with them.

Along with a policy, thorough training can help staff to feel more comfortable working with patrons with legal questions. Again, staff will just need to be familiar with which resources are available, not what they mean or how they apply to a patron's situation. When staff understand the difference between legal information and legal advice, it can empower them to assist patrons. Even if all that staff know is where to point people in the community for free and low-cost legal services, that is an important service.

Remember that it may take time to set up the services and collection that will be of most help to your patrons. Be aware of which areas of law you are getting questions in so you can then tailor your collection and programming to those areas. When designing classes and programs, give yourself some flexibility. Things may not work out as you hoped the first time, but be okay with failure and willing to learn from it. Give yourself permission to try new things and different approaches; what works and what does not can sometimes be surprising.

FINDING AND WORKING WITH PARTNERS

Developing partnerships with outside organizations can take time, so be patient with yourself. Sometimes it is just a matter of finding the right person in an organization whom you can work with, so be persistent. Do not immediately give up on an organization if you do not get the initial response you wanted. It is good if you can demonstrate what resources the library can bring to their organization and the people they serve. For example, libraries have free space for use; free access to technology and the Internet; and low-cost printing. These are all things that can help legal organizations to better serve those with whom they are working. Keep in mind that many organizations providing legal assistance are overwhelmed, so point out to them the valuable services the library can offer them and their clients.

Community referrals are key, and they end up being a large component of the work librarians do with patrons with legal questions. Find out what the best ways are to refer people to these organizations. Some places do not want phone calls; others want only phone calls. Find out what specific services they offer so you will be sure to send people to the correct organization; it is less frustrating for both organizations and patrons if you send referrals to the right place. Also, let organizations know what services the library offers so they can refer people to you. If you can find an existing list of legal aid providers or free legal clinics, this is a tremendous resource to have ready for patrons. If one does not exist, it will be worth taking the time and effort to create and maintain one.

THE LAW ITSELF

A few final thoughts on the subject area. Different types of laws accomplish different things. Statutes and codes provide higher-level guidance on how society should operate. They tend to be less specific and do not always address every aspect of a situation. Sometimes we think there might be a statute on something but there is not. Regulations will tend to be more specific than statutes, as they can really delve into how things are done. Case law tends to focus more on the areas of the law where there are disputes in how the law should be applied. Cases can fill in some of those gray areas. Most importantly though, cases give judges guidance in how they should rule and apply the law. Always remember the importance of jurisdiction and currency when researching laws. The patron's goal is to find primary binding authority for their particular legal issue.

Always remember, too, that secondary sources are your friends. These invaluable resources can save you time and uncertainty. They can lead you to the key statutes, regulations, and cases. They can be the expert guidance you need to be assured that you are searching in the right place. In addition, because we are limited in the type of help we can offer patrons, secondary sources can do some of that work for us. They can provide interpretations of the law, explain procedures, and reassure patrons that they are following the right path. Nonetheless, you may need to demonstrate the value of secondary sources to patrons. Often patrons want to jump straight into the law itself without realizing how secondary sources can help them understand and navigate it. While some of the more technical secondary sources are expensive to purchase and maintain, Nolo provides affordable secondary sources in the area of law.

Law is not the most accessible subject area. The terminology is confusing and the process complex. The numbering and citation formats may also seem foreign. Keep this in mind, as patrons may not always use the correct terms or know what it is they are really looking for. If you find you keep reaching a dead end, it may mean that you need to revise your terms, check a different jurisdiction, or try a different type of law. Generally, a good number of patron questions may start with state statutes, but if you are not finding what you need there, it might be a regulation or a case, or it might be a matter of federal or local jurisdiction. Also remember that not every topic has legislation or regulations about it.

It is a good idea to know where your closest law library is. Then you can refer patrons who have more in-depth questions or patrons who need to do case-law research. Even if the law library is physically far away it still may have e-mail or phone reference services that patrons can take advantage of.

As you are learning more about the various sources of law, the two areas I would encourage you to focus on first are your state's statutes and the court forms for your state courts. These are the two most requested sources at our library. Your library may differ, but most of our patrons are dealing with matters that fall under state jurisdiction—namely, divorce, landlord–tenant issues, and estates.

If you have the budget to maintain a print copy of your state's statutes, I would advise you to consider making the purchase. While it is easy to find state statutes online for free, the print sources may have an index that is helpful in searching. Additionally, some of the published statutes include annotations that can direct you to additional resources when researching.

Access to court forms will vary from state to state. In some states, all courts will use the same forms, which makes things easier. In other states the forms may vary from district to district. Start by checking the judicial branch website for your state. See if there is a page for self-help or for forms. If you don't find resources there, then check at the clerk's office in your local state district court to see how they recommend that people obtain the forms.

Approach the law the way you would any other subject area in which you are not an expert. Every question can be a learning opportunity. Soon you will have more familiarity with the terms and sources involved. I have found that the longer I have done this work, the easier it gets. And while I am still asked questions about issues I have never heard of, I am smarter about where to start looking for answers to them.

Appendix

Online Resources

In this appendix, I have attempted to gather useful online resources to assist you in your research. In the first section, labeled "Access to Justice Resources," you will find not only resources and organizations that will help you understand the scope of the justice gap but also resources to help connect patrons with legal services. The next section, labeled "Multi-Jurisdiction Resources," list those resources that generally include information for all fifty states and the federal government. Next is a section that contains information on federal resources, followed by resources for all fifty states. As with any list of online resources, please keep in mind that URLs change over time and sometimes resources disappear or are merged. If you find a link that no longer works, try searching by the title of the source or using one of the multi-jurisdictional resources to help you find the updated resource.

CONTENTS

Each state (listed alphabetically) includes its resources in this order: Legal Aid and Self-Help Resources, Law Libraries, Legislative Resources, Judicial Resources, Executive Resources, and Research Resources.

ACCESS TO JUSTICE RESOURCES

This section will cover resources with information and statistics regarding Access to Justice issues.

Groups Working on Access to Justice Issues

American Bar Association, Resource Center for Access to Justice Initiatives, https://www
.americanbar.org/groups/legal_aid_indigent_defendants/resource_center_for
_access_to_justice/
The Justice Index, https://justiceindex.org/
National Center for State Courts, Access to Justice Commissions, https://www.ncsc.org
/microsites/access-to-justice/home/Topics/Access-to-Justice-Commissions.aspx
National Center for State Courts, Self-Representation, State Links, https://www.ncsc.org
/Topics/Access-and-Fairness/Self-Representation/State-Links.aspx
Self-Represented Litigation Network, https://www.srln.org/

Legal Aid Services

LawHelp.org, https://www.lawhelp.org/
Legal Services Corporation, https://www.lsc.gov/
National Center for State Courts, Legal Aid/Pro Bono Guide, https://www.ncsc.org
/Topics/Legal-Services/Legal-Aid-Pro-Bono/Resource-Guide.aspx
Pro Bono Net, https://www.probono.net/

TRAINING RESOURCES

Civil Legal Justice: The Crucial Role of Libraries, WebJunction, https://learn.webjunction
.org/enrol/index.php?id=474
Creating Pathways to Civil Legal Justice, WebJunction, https://learn.webjunction.org
/course/view.php?id=471
FDLP Academy, Federal Deposit Library Program, https://www.fdlp.gov/about-the-fdlp
/fdlp-academy
Federal Register Tutorial, National Archives and Records Administration, https://www
.archives.gov/federal-register/tutorial
Helping Patrons with Legal Questions, Part 1, Legal Research Basics, CSL in Session,
https://cslinsession.cvlsites.org/past/helping-patrons-with-legal-questions-part-1
-legal-research-basics/
Helping Patrons with Legal Questions, Part 2, Researching State and Local Laws, CSL in
Session, https://cslinsession.cvlsites.org/past/helping-patrons-with-legal-questions
-part-2-researching-state-and-local-laws/
Helping Patrons with Legal Questions, Part 3, Federal Laws and Secondary Sources, CSL
in Session, https://cslinsession.cvlsites.org/past/helping-patrons-with-legal-questions
-part-3-federal-laws-and-secondary-sources/
Improving Access to Civil Legal Justice through Public Libraries, WebJunction, https://
www.webjunction.org/explore-topics/access-civil-legal-justice.html
Legal Information vs. Legal Advice, WebJunction, https://www.webjunction.org/news
/webjunction/legal-information-vs-legal-advice.html

Legal Reference at the Library, Building Skill through Practice, WebJunction, https://www.webjunction.org/news/webjunction/legal-reference-at-the-library.html

Legal Reference at the Library, Financial Information to Empower Patron Decision-making, WebJunction, https://www.webjunction.org/explore-topics/access-civil-legal-justice.html

Libraries Prepare to Answer Civil Legal Questions in Times of Crisis, WebJunction, https://www.webjunction.org/events/webjunction/libraries-prepare-to-answer-civil-legal-questions.html?_ga=2.119849162.314641133.1591392620-1894186140.1591392620

Rural Libraries Connect Communities to Legal Aid, WebJunction, https://www.webjunction.org/news/webjunction/rura-libraries-connect-communities-to-legal-aid.html

Tutorials, Wisconsin State Law Library, https://wilawlibrary.gov/learn/tutorials/index.html

MULTI-JURISDICTION RESOURCES

Below you will find a list of resources that provide information for multiple jurisdictions.

Legal Resource Aggregators

FindLaw, https://www.findlaw.com/
FindLaw for Legal Professionals, https://lp.findlaw.com/
Justia, https://www.justia.com/
Legal Information Institute, Cornell Law School, https://www.law.cornell.edu/
The Public Library of Law, Fastcase, http://www.plol.org/Pages/Search.aspx

Research Guides

American Association of Law Libraries, Public Library Toolkit, https://www.aallnet.org/lispsis/resources-publications/public-library-toolkit/

Georgetown Law Library, Research Guides, Treatise Finders, and Tutorials, http://guides.ll.georgetown.edu/home

Library of Congress, Law Library, Research Guides, https://www.loc.gov/law/help/how-find.php

Library of Congress, Law Library, Guide to Law Online, https://www.loc.gov/law/help/guide.php

Library of Congress, Law Library, Guide to Law Online: U.S. States and Territories, https://www.loc.gov/law/help/guide/states.php

Legislative Resources

Free Advice Legal, State Law and Code Links, https://www.freeadvice.com/resources/statecodes.htm

Indiana University School of Law, State Legislative History Research Guides Inventory: Introduction, https://law.indiana.libguides.com/state-legislative-history-guides

National Conference of State Legislatures, https://www.ncsl.org/

Nolo Civil Statute of Limitations Chart for 50 States, https://www.nolo.com/legal-encyclo
pedia/statute-of-limitations-state-laws-chart-29941.html
Uniform Law Commission, https://www.uniformlaws.org/home

Judicial Resources

Court Reference, Court Records Directory, https://www.courtreference.com/
CourtListener, https://www.courtlistener.com/
Google Scholar, https://scholar.google.com/
LLRX, Court Rules, Forms, and Dockets, https://www.llrx.com/courtrules/
National Center for State Courts, https://www.ncsc.org/
PlainSite, https://www.plainsite.org/

Executive Resources

Administrative Codes and Registers Section of National Association of Secretaries of
State, Administrative Rules, http://www.administrativerules.org/administrative
-rules/
ALA Government Documents Roundtable, State Agency Databases, https://godort.lib
guides.com/statedatabases

Municipal Resources

Code Publishing Co., Customers by Municipality, https://www.codebook.com/listing/#ID
Coded Systems, Code Library, http://www.codedsystems.com/codelibrary.html
General Code, Code Library, https://www.generalcode.com/library/
Municode, Code Library, https://library.municode.com/
National Association of Counties, https://www.naco.org/
National League of Cities, https://www.nlc.org/
Sterling Codifiers, Codes, https://www.sterlingcodifiers.com/#codes

Secondary Sources

American Association of Law Libraries, How to Research a Legal Problem: A Guide for
Non-Lawyers, https://www.aallnet.org/wp-content/uploads/2018/01/HowToRe
searchLegalProblemFinal_2014.pdf
American Bar Association, Legal Resources for the Public, https://www.americanbar.org
/about_the_aba/aba_public_resources/
Law Review Commons, https://lawreviewcommons.com/
Law Technology Today, Free Full Text Online Law Review/Journal Search, https://www
.lawtechnologytoday.org/free-full-text-online-law-review-journal-search/
Legal Information Institute, Wex, https://www.law.cornell.edu/wex
Nolo's Free Dictionary of Law Terms and Legal Definitions, https://www.nolo.com
/dictionary
Nolo's Legal Encyclopedia, https://www.nolo.com/legal-encyclopedia
U.S. Legal, Legal Definitions and Legal Terms Defined, https://definitions.uslegal.com/

FEDERAL RESOURCES

Legislative Resources

Congress.gov, https://www.congress.gov/

Govinfo, https://www.govinfo.gov/

Law Librarians' Society of Washington D.C., Federal Legislative History Research, https://www.llsdc.org/federal-legislative-history-guide

Library of Congress, Constitution Annotated, https://constitution.congress.gov/

Library of Congress, Law Library, Federal Legislative History: Initial Steps, https://www.loc.gov/law/help/leghist.php

Library of Congress, Law Library, Guide to Law Online: U.S. Constitution, https://www.loc.gov/law/help/guide/federal/usconst.php

Library of Congress, Law Library, Guide to Law Online: U.S. Laws, https://www.loc.gov/law/help/guide/federal/uscode.php

Library of Congress, Law Library, Guide to Law Online: U.S. Legislative, https://www.loc.gov/law/help/guide/federal/uscong.php

National Archives and Records Administration, America's Founding Documents, https://www.archives.gov/founding-docs

Office of Law Revision Counsel, United States Code, https://uscode.house.gov/

United States House of Representatives, https://www.house.gov/

United States Senate, https://www.senate.gov/

Judicial Resources

Duke Law, Court Rules, https://law.duke.edu/lib/researchguides/courtr/

Govinfo, https://www.govinfo.gov/

Library of Congress, Law Library, Guide to Law Online: U.S. Judiciary, https://www.loc.gov/law/help/guide/federal/usjudic.php

Oyez, https://www.oyez.org/

Public Access to Court Electronic Records [fee based], https://www.pacer.gov/

United States Courts, https://www.uscourts.gov/

United States Courts, Court Website Links, https://www.uscourts.gov/about-federal-courts/federal-courts-public/court-website-links

United States Supreme Court, https://www.supremecourt.gov/

Executive Resources

Electronic Code of Federal Regulations (eCFR), https://gov.ecfr.io/cgi-bin/ECFR?page=browse

Govinfo, https://www.govinfo.gov/

Library of Congress, Law Library, Guide to Law Online: U.S. Executive, https://www.loc.gov/law/help/guide/federal/usexec.php

National Archives and Records Administration, Executive Orders Disposition Tables Index, https://www.archives.gov/federal-register/executive-orders/disposition

National Archives and Records Administration, Federal Register, https://www.federalregister.gov/

National Archives and Records Administration, Federal Register Tutorial, https://www.archives.gov/federal-register/tutorial

Office of Information and Regulatory Affairs, Reg Map, https://www.reginfo.gov/public
    /reginfo/Regmap/index.myjsp
Office of Information and Regulatory Affairs, Unified Agenda, https://www.reginfo.gov
    /public/do/eAgendaMain
Regulations.gov, https://www.regulations.gov/
USA.gov, https://www.usa.gov/
The White House, https://www.whitehouse.gov/
The White House, Office of Management and Budget, https://www.whitehouse.gov
    /omb/

STATE RESOURCES

In this section you will find information on the following: legal aid services and self-help resources; law libraries; state legislative resources; state judicial resources; state executive resources; and state research guides. A few notes about what is included and what is not. I have attempted to locate law libraries that are open to the public; however, this list is not comprehensive. Some county law libraries, may not have websites. In a couple of instances I found law libraries that charge a small fee (usually $5.00) for use by the public. I included those in the list. I would encourage you to look at the access policy for any law library before referring patrons to visit it. A good number of the university law libraries that are open to the public may have restricted hours or may require identification to enter. In the area of judicial resources, I have usually included just the main state court website. Some states may have separate websites for each judicial district, and each of those websites may have links to forms and other resources that pertain to that judicial district. Generally, if you start out at the main state court website and look under courts, you can find the information for your judicial district. For legal aid listings, again this may not be comprehensive. I would also check on Findlaw, Justia, and the Lawhelp websites to see if there are any additional resources for your area. In the area of executive resources, I have included information about administrative codes and registers, office of the governor, executive orders, and state agencies. Some states may refer to their register as a bulletin. And if you are looking for items like attorney general opinions, you can either visit the website for your state's attorney general, or look at the Library of Congress research guide for your state.

Alabama

Legal Aid and Self-Help Resources

Alabama Legal Help, https://www.alabamalegalhelp.org/
Legal Services Alabama, https://legalservicesalabama.org/
South Alabama Volunteer Lawyers Program, http://www.savlp.org/

Law Libraries

Bounds Law Library, Alabama Law, University of Alabama, http://library.law.ua.edu/
Faulkner Law Library, Faulkner Law, Thomas Goode Jones School of Law, http://libguides
    .faulkner.edu/jones-library
Jefferson County Law Library, https://lawlib.jccal.org/

Lucille Stewart Beeson Law Library, Cumberland School of Law, Samford University, https://www.samford.edu/cumberlandlaw/library/

Supreme Court and State Law Library, Alabama Judicial System, https://judicial.alabama .gov/library/index

United States Court of Appeals for the Eleventh Circuit Libraries, https://www.ca11 .uscourts.gov/eleventh-circuit-library

Legislative Resources

The Alabama Legislature, http://www.legislature.state.al.us/aliswww/default.aspx

Bills, The Alabama Legislature, http://alisondb.legislature.state.al.us/alison/Splash_Bills .aspx

The Code of Alabama, 1975, http://alisondb.legislature.state.al.us/alison/CodeOfAlabama /1975/Coatoc.htm

The Constitution of Alabama, 1901, http://alisondb.legislature.state.al.us/alison/CodeOf Alabama/Constitution/1901/Constitution1901_toc.htm

Legislative Acts, Alabama Secretary of State, https://www.sos.alabama.gov/government -records/legislative-acts

Legislative Acts, Journals, and Constitutions, Alabama Department of Archives and History, http://digital.archives.alabama.gov/cdm/landingpage/collection/legislature

Judicial Resources

Alabama Administrative Office of Courts, https://www.alacourt.gov/

Alabama Judicial System, https://judicial.alabama.gov/

Civil Decisions and Opinions, Alabama Judicial System, https://judicial.alabama.gov /decision/civildecisions

Criminal Decisions and Opinions, Alabama Judicial System, https://judicial.alabama.gov /decision/criminaldecisions

Supreme Court Decisions and Opinions, Alabama Judicial System, https://judicial.alabama .gov/decision/supremecourtdecisions

Executive Resources

Alabama Administrative Code, http://www.alabamaadministrativecode.state.al.us/

Alabama Administrative Monthly, http://www.alabamaadministrativecode.state.al.us /monthly.html

Atlas Alabama, State Agencies and Departments, https://atlasalabama.gov/state-agencies -departments/

The Office of the Alabama Governor, https://governor.alabama.gov/

The Official Website of the State of Alabama, https://www.alabama.gov/

Research Resources

American Association of Law Libraries, Public Library Toolkit: Alabama, https://www .aallnet.org/lispsis/wp-content/uploads/sites/11/2019/12/LISPSIS-PLToolkit -Alabama.pdf

Library of Congress Guide to Law Online, Alabama, http://www.loc.gov/law/help/guide
/states/us-al.php

Alaska

Legal Aid and Self-Help Resources

Alaska Law Help, https://alaskalawhelp.org/
Alaska Court System, Self-Help Services, http://courts.alaska.gov/shc/representing-yours
elf.htm
Alaska Legal Services Corporation, https://www.alsc-law.org/
Alaska Network on Domestic Violence and Sexual Assault, https://andvsa.org/

Law Libraries

Alaska State Court Law Library, http://courts.alaska.gov/library/

Legislative Resources

Alaska Legislative History Online, Alaska State Court System, https://public.courts
.alaska.gov/web/library/docs/akleghistory.pdf
Alaska State Legislature, https://akleg.gov/
Alaska Statutes, Bills, Journals, and Session Laws, http://www.legis.state.ak.us/basis
/folio.asp
The Constitution of the State of Alaska, https://ltgov.alaska.gov/information/alaskas
-constitution/
Legal Resources, Alaska, Alaska Court System, http://courts.alaska.gov/library/aklegal.htm
United States Courts for the Ninth Circuit Library, https://www.ca9.uscourts.gov/library
/directory/

Judicial Resources

Alaska Case Law Service, https://govt.westlaw.com/akcases/Index?__lrTS=20200525024
341162
Alaska Court System, http://courts.alaska.gov/home.htm
Court Rules, Alaska Court System, http://courts.alaska.gov/rules/index.htm#rules
Criminal Pattern Jury Instructions, Alaska Court System, http://courts.alaska.gov/rules
/crimins.htm
Forms, Alaska Court System, http://courts.alaska.gov/forms/index.htm
Legal Resources, Alaska, Alaska Court System, http://courts.alaska.gov/library/aklegal.htm
Supreme Court Orders, Alaska Court System, http://www.courts.alaska.gov/sco/index.htm

Executive Resources

Administrative Agencies and Departments, The State of Alaska, http://alaska.gov/akdirl.html
Alaska Administrative Code, Alaska State Legislature, http://www.legis.state.ak.us/basis
/aac.asp

Alaska Executive Orders, http://www.legis.state.ak.us/basis/folioproxy.asp?url=http://wwwjnu01.legis.state.ak.us/cgi-bin/folioisa.dll/exor

Legal Resources, Alaska, Alaska Court System, http://courts.alaska.gov/library/aklegal.htm

Online Public Notices, State of Alaska, https://aws.state.ak.us/OnlinePublicNotices/default.aspx

Research Resources

American Association of Law Libraries, Public Library Toolkit: Alaska, https://www.aallnet.org/lispsis/wp-content/uploads/sites/11/2018/03/LISPSIS-PLToolkit-Alaska-2018.pdf

Library of Congress Guide to Law Online, Alaska, http://www.loc.gov/law/help/guide/states/us-ak.php

Arizona

Legal Aid and Self-Help Resources

Arizona Bar Association, Legal Help and Education, https://www2.azbar.org/LegalHelpandEducation

Arizona Justice Center, https://www.azjusticecenter.org/

Arizona Self-Service Centers, https://www.azcourts.gov/selfservicecenter

AZ Law Help, https://www.azlawhelp.org/

Community Legal Services, https://clsaz.org/

DNA Legal Services, https://dnalegalservices.org/

Morris Institute for Justice, https://morrisinstituteforjustice.org/

Southern Arizona Legal Aid, https://www.sazlegalaid.org/

Superior Court of Maricopa County, Self-Help Resources: https://superiorcourt.maricopa.gov/llrc/self-help-resources/

Law Libraries

Arizona State Library, Archives, and Public Records, https://azlibrary.gov/

Daniel F. Cracchiolo Law Library, James E. Rogers College of Law, The University of Arizona, http://lawlibrary.arizona.edu/

Maricopa County Law Library, https://superiorcourt.maricopa.gov/llrc/law-library/

Pima County Law Library, https://www.sc.pima.gov/default.aspx?tabid=60

Ross-Blakely Law Library, Sandra Day O'Connor College of Law, Arizona State University, https://lawlib.asu.edu/

United States Courts for the Ninth Circuit Library, https://www.ca9.uscourts.gov/library/directory/

Legislative Resources

Arizona Revised Statutes, https://www.azleg.gov/arstitle/

Arizona State Constitution, https://www.azleg.gov/constitution/

Arizona State Legislature, https://www.azleg.gov/

Introduced Bills, Arizona State Legislature, https://www.azleg.gov/bills/
Session Laws, Arizona State Legislature, https://www.azleg.gov/sessionlaws/

Judicial Resources

Arizona Court Rules, https://govt.westlaw.com/azrules/Index?__lrTS=202005252047283
56&transitionType=Default&contextData=%28sc.Default%29
Arizona Judicial Branch, https://www.azcourts.gov/
Arizona Office of Administrative Hearings, https://www.azoah.com/
Decisions, Arizona Court of Appeals Division One, https://www.azcourts.gov/coa1/Deci
sions/DecisionsoftheCourt
Decisions, Arizona Court of Appeals Division Two, https://www.appeals2.az.gov/ODSPlus
/recentdecisions.cfm
Forms, Arizona Judicial Branch, https://www.azcourts.gov/selfservicecenter/Forms
Opinions and Memorandum Decisions, Arizona Supreme Court, http://www.azcourts.gov
/opinions/

Executive Resources

Agencies, AZ Direct, https://azdirect.az.gov/agencies
Arizona Administrative Code, https://azsos.gov/rules/arizona-administrative-code
Arizona Administrative Register, https://azsos.gov/rules/arizona-administrative-register
Office of the Governor, https://azgovernor.gov/

Research Resources

American Association of Law Libraries, Public Library Toolkit: Arizona, https://www
.aallnet.org/lispsis/wp-content/uploads/sites/11/2018/01/LISPSIS-PLToolkit
-Arizona.pdf
Arizona Law, Legislative History, Ross-Blakely Law Library, http://libguides.law.asu.edu
/ArizonaLaw/legislativehistory
Library of Congress Guide to Law Online, Arizona, http://www.loc.gov/law/help/guide
/states/us-az.php
Roadmap to Legislative Research, Arizona State Library, Archives, and Public Records,
https://azlibrary.gov/branches/state-arizona-research-library/legislative-assistance
-and-resources/guide-arizona

Arkansas

Legal Aid and Self-Help Resources

Arkansas Judiciary, Self-Help Resources, https://www.arcourts.gov/directories/resources
Arkansas Legal Services Online, Court Help, http://www.arlegalservices.org/courthelp
Arkansas Legal Services Online, Pro Bono Portal, http://www.arlegalservices.org/ProBono
Legal Aid of Arkansas, https://arlegalaid.org/

Law Libraries

Arkansas Supreme Court Library, https://www.arcourts.gov/courts/supreme-court
/library

Craighead County Law Library, https://craighead-county-law-library.business.site/

Sebastian County Fort Smith District Law Library, https://scfsdlawlibrary.org/

U.S. Courts Library for the 8th Circuit, https://www.lb8.uscourts.gov:444/index1.htm

Washington County Public Law Library, http://wcpll.org/

William H. Bowen School of Law Library, University of Arkansas Little Rock, https://
ualr.edu/lawlibrary/

Young Law Library, School of Law, University of Arkansas, https://law.uark.edu
/library/

Legislative Resources

Acts, Arkansas State Legislature, https://www.arkleg.state.ar.us/Acts/Search

Arkansas State Legislature, https://www.arkleg.state.ar.us/

Bills, Arkansas State Legislature, https://www.arkleg.state.ar.us/Bills/Search

Code of Arkansas, https://advance.lexis.com/container?config=00JAA3ZTU0NTIzYy0z
ZDEyLTRhYmQtYmRmMS1iMWIxNDgxYWMxZTQKAFBvZENhdGFsb2
cubRW4ifTiwi5vLw6cI1uX&crid=a2bab119-26c3-4e02-8a7c-7680bbdcb540

Constitution of the State of Arkansas of 1874, https://advance.lexis.com/container?config
=0145JAA3MTdkMDQ2Mi01Yjg3LTQ5YjUtOTM2NS05MzE5ZjhjNGY5N2M
KAFBvZENhdGFsb2cWtateMur7cOlHYN8TgmNk&crid=d854f347-13b1-432c
-a838-28c219605933

Judicial Resources

Arkansas Judiciary, https://www.arcourts.gov/

Arkansas Judiciary, Information for the Public, https://www.arcourts.gov/public

Court Forms, Arkansas Judiciary, https://www.arcourts.gov/forms-and-publications/court
-forms

Court Rules, Arkansas Judiciary, https://opinions.arcourts.gov/ark/cr/en/nav_date.do

Opinions, Arkansas Judiciary, https://opinions.arcourts.gov/ark/en/nav.do

Self-Help Forms, Arkansas Legal Services Online, http://www.arlegalservices.org/node
/1041/self-help-forms

Executive Resources

Agencies, Arkansas.gov, https://portal.arkansas.gov/agencies/

Arkansas Administrative Rules, https://www.sos.arkansas.gov/rules_and_regs/index.php
/rules/search/new

Arkansas Governor, https://governor.arkansas.gov/

Arkansas Register, https://www.sos.arkansas.gov/rules-regulations/arkansas-register/

Executive Order, Arkansas Governor, https://governor.arkansas.gov/our-office/executive
-orders/

Research Resources

American Association of Law Libraries, Public Library Toolkit: Arkansas, https://www
.aallnet.org/lispsis/wp-content/uploads/sites/11/2018/01/LISPSIS-PLToolkit
-Arizona.pdf
Library of Congress Guide to Law Online, Arkansas, http://www.loc.gov/law/help/guide
/states/us-ar.php

California

Legal Aid and Self-Help Resources

Bay Area Legal Aid, https://baylegal.org/
Bet Tzdek, Free Legal Services, http://www.bettzedek.org/
California Courts, Family Law Facilitators, https://www.courts.ca.gov/selfhelp-facilita
tors.htm
California Courts, Self-Help Center, https://www.courts.ca.gov/selfhelp.htm
California Indian Legal Services, https://www.calindian.org/
California Rural Legal Aid Foundation, https://es.crlaf.org/
California Rural Legal Assistance, http://www.crla.org/
Central California Legal Services, https://www.centralcallegal.org/
Chapman University's Fowler School of Law Clinics, https://www.chapman.edu/law/legal
-clinics/index.aspx
Community Legal Aid SoCal, https://www.communitylegalsocal.org/
Greater Bakersfield Legal Assistance, https://www.gbla.org/
Harriet Buhai Center for Family Law, https://www.hbcfl.org/
LawHelpCA, https://www.lawhelpca.org/
Legal Aid at Work, https://legalaidatwork.org/
Legal Aid Foundation of Los Angeles, https://lafla.org/
Legal Aid Foundation of Santa Barbara County, http://www.lafsbc.org/
Legal Aid Society of San Diego, https://www.lassd.org/
Legal Aid Society of San Mateo County, https://www.legalaidsmc.org/
Legal Services of Northern California, https://www.lsnc.net/
Neighborhood Legal Services of Los Angeles County, https://www.nlsla.org/
OneJustice, https://onejustice.org/

Law Libraries

California's County Law Libraries, Locating the Law, https://www.aallnet.org/lispsis/wp
-content/uploads/sites/11/2019/01/Locating-the-Law-Sixth-Edition.pdf
Darling Law Library, UCLA Law, https://www.law.ucla.edu/library/
Jerene Appleby Harnish Law Library, Caruso School of Law, Pepperdine University,
https://law.pepperdine.edu/library/
Law Library, Berkeley Law, University of California, https://www.law.berkeley.edu/library/
Mabie Law Library, UCDavis School of Law, https://law.ucdavis.edu/library/
Pardee Legal Research Center, School of Law, University of San Diego, https://www
.sandiego.edu/law/library/
UCI Law Library, https://www.law.uci.edu/library/

United States Courts for the Ninth Circuit Law Library, https://www.ca9.uscourts.gov
/library/

Legislative Resources

Bills, California State Legislature, http://leginfo.legislature.ca.gov/faces/billSearchClient
.xhtml
California Code, http://leginfo.legislature.ca.gov/faces/codes.xhtml
California Constitution, http://leginfo.legislature.ca.gov/faces/codesTOCSelected.xhtml
?tocCode=CONS&tocTitle=+California+Constitution+-+CONS
California State Legislature, http://www.legislature.ca.gov/

Judicial Resources

California Courts, https://www.courts.ca.gov/
California Official Reports, https://www.courts.ca.gov/opinions.htm
Forms, California Courts, https://www.courts.ca.gov/forms.htm
Opinions, California Courts, https://www.courts.ca.gov/opinions.htm
Rules of Court, California Courts, https://www.courts.ca.gov/rules.htm

Executive Resources

California Code of Regulations, https://govt.westlaw.com/calregs/Index?transitionType
=Default&contextData=%28sc.Default%29
California Regulatory Notice Register, https://oal.ca.gov/publications/notice_register/
Office of Administrative Hearings, https://www.dgs.ca.gov/oah/
Office of Administrative Law, https://oal.ca.gov/
Office of Governor, https://www.gov.ca.gov/
State Agency Listing, https://www.ca.gov/agenciesall/

Research Resources

American Association of Law Libraries, Public Library Toolkit: California, Locating the
Law, https://www.aallnet.org/lispsis/wp-content/uploads/sites/11/2019/01/Locating
-the-Law-Sixth-Edition.pdf
Library of Congress Guide to Law Online, California, http://www.loc.gov/law/help/guide
/states/us-ca.php

Colorado

Legal Aid and Self-Help Resources

Colorado Checkerboard, http://www.checkerboard.co/
Colorado Judicial Branch, Self-Help and Forms, https://www.courts.state.co.us/Self_Help
/Index.cfm
Colorado Legal Services, https://www.coloradolegalservices.org/

Colorado Resource Network, https://www.coloradoresourcenetwork.com/
Denver Bar Association, Metro Volunteer Lawyers, https://www.denbar.org/mvl
The Justice Center, https://www.justicecentercos.org/

Law Libraries

Colorado Supreme Court Library, https://cscl.colibraries.org/colorado-judicial-branch
Pikes Peak Library District, Law Collection, https://research.ppld.org/lawandlegal
    resources
The United States Court of Appeals for the Tenth Circuit Law Library, https://www.ca10
    .uscourts.gov/library
William A. Wise Law Library, Colorado Law, University of Colorado Boulder, http://law
    library.colorado.edu/

Legislative Resources

Bills, Resolutions, and Memorials, Colorado General Assembly, http://leg.colorado.gov
    /bills
Colorado Constitution, https://leg.colorado.gov/colorado-constitution
Colorado General Assembly, https://leg.colorado.gov/
Colorado Revised Statutes, https://leg.colorado.gov/colorado-revised-statutes
Legislative Council, Colorado General Assembly, http://leg.colorado.gov/agencies/legislative
    -council-staff
Legislative Records, Colorado State Archives, https://www.colorado.gov/pacific/archives
    /legislative-records
Session Laws, Colorado General Assembly, http://leg.colorado.gov/session-laws?field
    _sessions_target_id=64656&sort_bef_combine=field_page_value%20ASC
Session Laws Archive, Office of Legislative Legal Services, https://leg.colorado.gov
    /agencies/office-legislative-legal-services/session-laws-archive

Judicial Resources

Colorado Judicial Branch, https://www.courts.state.co.us/
Court of Appeals Case Announcements, https://www.courts.state.co.us/Courts/Court_
    Of_Appeals/Case_Announcements/Index.cfm
Court Rules, https://advance.lexis.com/container?config=00JABiMzRkN2Q5Ny1iMGZi
    LTQwYWYtOGEyMC0xNGIyNDAyMTViOTTcKAFBvZENhdGFsb2dTqXrsE
    3Hsqu82D2r8ESV5&crid=94336635-3c2c-4aa6-bbd6-4cf0d340cf02
Forms, Colorado Judicial Branch, https://www.courts.state.co.us/Self_Help/Index.cfm
Supreme Court Case Announcements, https://www.courts.state.co.us/Courts/Supreme
    _Court/Case_Announcements/Index.cfm

Executive Resources

Colorado Code of Regulations, https://www.sos.state.co.us/CCR/Welcome.do
Colorado Register, https://www.sos.state.co.us/CCR/RegisterHome.do

Office of the Governor, https://www.colorado.gov/governor/
State Agencies, https://www.colorado.gov/state-agencies

Research Resources

American Association of Law Libraries, Public Library Toolkit: Colorado, https://www
.aallnet.org/lispsis/wp-content/uploads/sites/11/2020/04/LISPSIS-PLToolkit
-Colorado.pdf
Colorado Law Project, Sturm College of Law, University of Denver, https://www.law.du
.edu/the-colorado-law-project
Library of Congress Guide to Law Online, Colorado, http://www.loc.gov/law/help/guide
/states/us-co.php

Connecticut

Legal Aid and Self-Help Resources

Connecticut Legal Services, https://ctlegal.org/
CTLawHelp, https://ctlawhelp.org/en/home
Greater Hartford Legal Aid, https://www.ghla.org/
New Haven Legal Assistance Association, https://nhlegal.org/
State of Connecticut Judicial Branch, Court Service Centers, https://www.jud.ct.gov/csc/
State of Connecticut Judicial Branch, Representing Yourself, https://www.jud.ct.gov
/lawlib/SRP/default.htm
State of Connecticut Judicial Branch, Self-Help Section, https://www.jud.ct.gov/selfhelp
.htm
Statewide Legal Services of Connecticut, https://www.slsct.org/

Law Libraries

Legislative Library, Office of Legislative Research, https://wp.cga.ct.gov/lib/
Lynne L. Pantalena Law Library, Quinnipiac University School of Law, https://www
.qu.edu/on-campus/our-campus/libraries.html#lynnelpantalenalawlibrary
information
State of Connecticut Judicial Branch, Law Library Services, https://jud.ct.gov/lawlib
/index.asp
Thomas J. Meskill Law Library, School of Law, University of Connecticut, https://library
.law.uconn.edu/

Legislative Resources

Advanced Legislative Document Search, https://search.cga.state.ct.us/r/adv/
Basic Legislative Document Search, https://search.cga.state.ct.us/r/basic/
Connecticut General Assembly, https://www.cga.ct.gov/
Constitutions/Historical References, https://www.cga.ct.gov/asp/Content/constitutions.asp
General Statutes of Connecticut (browse), https://www.cga.ct.gov/current/pub/titles.htm
General Statutes of Connecticut (search), https://search.cga.state.ct.us/r/statute/

Judicial Resources

Connecticut Practice Book and Court Rules, https://www.jud.ct.gov/pb.htm
Official Court Webforms, https://www.jud.ct.gov/webforms/
Opinions, State of Connecticut Judicial Branch, https://www.jud.ct.gov/opinions.htm
State of Connecticut Judicial Branch, https://jud.ct.gov/
State of Connecticut Judicial Branch, Frequently Asked Questions, https://www.jud.ct.gov /faq/
State of Connecticut Judicial Branch, Publications and Videos, https://www.jud.ct.gov /pub.htm

Executive Resources

Connecticut eRegulations System: Portal to Connecticut Regulations, https://eregulations .ct.gov/eRegsPortal/Browse/RCSA
Connecticut State Register and Manual, https://portal.ct.gov/SOTS/Register-Manual /Register-Manual/Connecticut-State-Register—Manual
Departments and Agencies, https://portal.ct.gov/Government/Departments-and-Agencies
Governor's Actions, https://portal.ct.gov/Office-of-the-Governor/Governors-Actions /Governors-Actions-Main
Office of the Governor, https://portal.ct.gov/Office-of-the-Governor

Research Resources

American Association of Law Libraries, Public Library Toolkit: Connecticut, https://www .aallnet.org/lispsis/wp-content/uploads/sites/11/2019/10/LISPSIS-PLToolkit -Connecticut-2019.pdf
Connecticut Law by Subject, Connecticut Judicial Branch Law Libraries, https://www.jud .ct.gov/lawlib/law/
Law and Legislation Reference Services, Connecticut State Library, http://libguides .ctstatelibrary.org/law
Library of Congress Guide to Law Online, Connecticut, http://www.loc.gov/law/help/guide /states/us-ct.php

Delaware

Legal Aid and Self-Help Resources

Community Legal Aid Society, http://www.declasi.org/
Delaware Legal Help Link, https://delegalhelplink.org/
Delaware State Courts, Self-Help, https://courts.delaware.gov/help/
Legal Services Corporation of Delaware, https://www.lscd.com/

Law Libraries

Delaware Law School Library, Widener University, https://delawarelaw.widener.edu/current -students/library/

Judicial Law Libraries, Delaware State Courts, https://courts.delaware.gov/lawlibraries/

Legislative Library, Delaware General Assembly, https://legis.delaware.gov/Offices/Division
OfResearch/LegislativeLibrary

United States Court of Appeals for the Third Circuit Library, https://www.ca3.uscourts
.gov/circuit-libraries

Legislative Resources

All Legislation, Delaware General Assembly, https://legis.delaware.gov/AllLegislation

The Delaware Code Online, https://delcode.delaware.gov/

The Delaware Constitution of 1897 as Amended, https://delcode.delaware.gov/constitution
/index.shtml

Delaware General Assembly, https://legis.delaware.gov/

Session Laws, The Laws of the State of Delaware, https://delcode.delaware.gov/session
laws/

Judicial Resources

Civil Pattern Jury Instructions, Delaware State Courts, https://courts.delaware.gov/superior
/pattern/

Criminal Pattern Jury Instructions, Delaware State Courts, https://courts.delaware.gov
/superior/pattern/pattern_criminal.aspx

Delaware State Courts, https://courts.delaware.gov/

Forms, Delaware State Courts, https://courts.delaware.gov/forms/

Opinions and Orders, Delaware State Courts, https://courts.delaware.gov/opinions/

Rules of the Delaware State Courts, Delaware State Courts, https://courts.delaware.gov
/rules/

Executive Resources

Delaware's Administrative Code, https://regulations.delaware.gov/AdminCode/

Delaware Regulations, https://regulations.delaware.gov/index.shtml

Executive Orders, https://governor.delaware.gov/executive-orders/

Office of the Governor, https://governor.delaware.gov/

State Directory, https://alpha.delaware.gov/state-directory

Research Resources

American Association of Law Libraries, Public Library Toolkit: Delaware, http://libguides
.law.widener.edu/c.php?g=772866

Delaware Legislative History, Delaware Law School, Widener University, http://libguides
.law.widener.edu/c.php?g=772871

Library of Congress Guide to Law Online, Delaware, http://www.loc.gov/law/help/guide
/states/us-de.php

District of Columbia

Legal Aid and Self-Help Resources

Children's Law Center, https://www.childrenslawcenter.org/
D.C. Bar Pro Bono Center, https://www.dcbar.org/pro-bono/index.cfm
District of Columbia Courts, If Representing Yourself, https://www.dccourts.gov/services
    /represent-yourself
District of Columbia Courts, Self-Help Center, https://www.dccourts.gov/services/family
    -matters/self-help-center
LawHelp.org D.C., https://www.lawhelp.org/DC/
Legal Aid Society of the District of Columbia, https://www.legalaiddc.org/
Neighborhood Legal Services Program, http://www.nlsp.org/
Washington Lawyer's Committee, https://www.washlaw.org/
Whitman Walker Legal Services, https://www.whitman-walker.org/legal-services

Law Libraries

The Judge Kathryn J. DuFour Law Library, Columbus School of Law, The Catholic University of America, https://www.law.edu/about-us/law-library/index.html
Law Library, David A. Clarke School of Law, University of the District of Columbia, https://udclaw.libguides.com/home
Law Library, Howard University School of Law, http://library.law.howard.edu/index
Pence Law Library, Washington College of Law, American University, https://www.wcl.american.edu/impact/library/

Legislative Resources

Council of the District of Columbia, https://dccouncil.us/
D.C. Code, Council of the District of Columbia, https://code.dccouncil.us/
District of Columbia Home Rule Act, https://dccouncil.us/dc-home-rule/
District of Columbia Official Code, https://advance.lexis.com/container?config=014FJAB
    mNTMyNmZlNy00N2U5LTRmNDktYmI0YS1jMzc4ZjNkNDcwZWUKAFB-
    vZENhdGFsb2dWztW4MDtB3pBcSj7lPd0T&crid=d9bf93b7-a906-4eef-bd64
    -21ebadc4fcf7
Legislation and Laws, Council of the District of Columbia, https://dccouncil.us/legislation/
Legislative Information Management System, Council of the District of Columbia, https://lims.dccouncil.us/

Judicial Resources

D.C. Court of Appeals Opinions and Memorandum of Judgements, http://www.dccourts.gov/court-of-appeals/opinions-memorandum-of-judgments
District of Columbia Courts, https://www.dccourts.gov/
Forms Help Online, District of Columbia Courts, https://www.probono.net/dccourts/

Executive Resources

Agency Directory, DC.gov, https://dc.gov/directory
District of Columbia Municipal Regulations and District of Columbia Register, https://www.dcregs.dc.gov/
Office of the Mayor, https://mayor.dc.gov/

Research Resources

American Association of Law Libraries, Public Library Toolkit: District of Columbia, https://www.aallnet.org/lispsis/wp-content/uploads/sites/11/2018/01/LISPSIS-PLToolkit-DC.pdf
Library of Congress Guide to Law Online, District of Columbia, http://www.loc.gov/law/help/guide/states/us-dc.php

Florida

Legal Aid and Self-Help Resources

Bay Area Legal Services, https://bals.org/
Community Legal Services of Mid-Florida, https://www.clsmf.org/
Florida Courts, Family Law Self-Help Information, https://www.flcourts.org/Resources-Services/Court-Improvement/Family-Courts/Family-Law-Self-Help-Information
Florida Courts, Self-Help Centers, https://www.flcourts.org/Resources-Services/Court-Improvement/Self-Help-Information/Self-Help-Centers-Near-You
Florida Law Help, https://www.floridalawhelp.org/
Florida Legal Services, http://www.floridalegal.org/
Gulf Coast Legal Services, https://gulfcoastlegal.org/
Jacksonville Area Legal Aid, https://www.jaxlegalaid.org/
Legal Aid Society of Palm Beach County, https://legalaidpbc.org/
Legal Services of Greater Miami, https://www.legalservicesmiami.org/
Legal Services of North Florida, https://www.lsnf.org/

Law Libraries

Ave Maria School of Law Library, https://www.avemarialaw.edu/library/
College of Law Research Center, Florida State University, https://law.fiu.edu/library/
Florida A&M University Law Library, http://library.famu.edu/c.php?g=276137&p=1841476
Florida International University Law Library, https://law.fiu.edu/library/
Florida Supreme Court Law Library, https://www.floridasupremecourt.org/Law-Library
Law Libraries, Florida Courts Help, https://help.flcourts.org/law-libraries/
Lawton Chiles Legal Information Center, Levin College of Law, University of Florida, https://www.law.ufl.edu/library
United States Court of Appeals for the Eleventh Circuit Libraries, https://www.ca11.uscourts.gov/eleventh-circuit-library
University of Miami School of Law Library, https://www.law.miami.edu/iml/library?op=0

Legislative Resources

Bills, Florida House of Representatives, https://www.myfloridahouse.gov/Sections/Bills
/bills.aspx
Bills, Florida Senate, https://www.flsenate.gov/Session/Bills/2020
Constitution of the State of Florida, http://www.leg.state.fl.us/Statutes/index.cfm?Mode
=Constitution&Submenu=3&Tab=statutes
Florida Legislature, http://www.leg.state.fl.us/Welcome/index.cfm?CFID=101086131&C
FTOKEN=84c460b4f05c472d-042136E9-5056-B837-1A97E1251FBD2E13
Florida Statutes, http://www.leg.state.fl.us/statutes/index.cfm?
Session Laws, http://laws.flrules.org/

Judicial Resources

Case Law Updates, Florida Courts, https://www.flcourts.org/Resources-Services/Court
-Improvement/Case-Law-Updates
Family Law Forms, Florida Courts, https://www.flcourts.org/Resources-Services/Court
-Improvement/Family-Courts/Family-Law-Self-Help-Information/Family-Law
-Forms
Family Court Opinions, Florida Courts, https://www.flcourts.org/Resources-Services
/Court-Improvement/Family-Courts
Florida Courts, https://www.flcourts.org/
Florida Rules of Court Procedure, The Florida Bar, https://www.floridabar.org/rules
/ctproc/
Florida Standard Jury Instructions, Florida Courts, https://jury.flcourts.org/
Florida Supreme Court Opinions, https://www.floridasupremecourt.org/Opinions?qf
=&sort=attr_disposition_date_dt%20desc,%20attr_type_s%20desc,%20attr
_case_number_s%20asc&type=written&view=embed_custom&searchtype
=opinions&recent_only=1&hide_search=1&hide_filters=1&limit=25&offset=0
Landlord Tenant and Living Will Forms, The Florida Association, https://www.floridabar
.org/public/consumer/#1497360078847-4056c593-37bc
Opinions, Florida 1st District Court of Appeal, https://www.1dca.org/Opinions
Opinions, Florida 2nd District Court of Appeal, https://www.2dca.org/Opinions
Opinions, Florida 3rd District Court of Appeal, https://www.3dca.flcourts.org/Opinions
Opinions, Florida 4th District Court of Appeal, https://www.4dca.org/Opinions
Opinions, Florida 5th District Court of Appeal, https://www.5dca.org/Opinions

Executive Resources

Executive Orders, Office of the Governor, https://www.flgov.com/executive-orders
-desantis/
Florida Administrative Code and Florida Administrative Register, https://www.flrules
.org/default.asp
Office of the Governor, https://www.flgov.com/
State Agency Homepages, https://dos.myflorida.com/library-archives/research/florida
-information/government/state-resources/state-agency-homepages/
State of Florida Divisions of Administrative Hearings, https://www.doah.state.fl.us/ALJ/

Research Resources

American Association of Law Libraries, Public Library Toolkit: Florida, https://www
.aallnet.org/lispsis/wp-content/uploads/sites/11/2018/01/LISPSIS-PLToolkit
-Florida.pdf

Florida Legislative History, University of Florida, https://guides.uflib.ufl.edu/c.php?g
=147438&p=970113

Library of Congress Guide to Law Online, Florida, http://www.loc.gov/law/help/guide
/states/us-fl.php

Georgia

Legal Aid and Self-Help Resources

Appalachian Family Law Center, https://www.appflic.org/

The Council of Superior Court Judges, Appalachian Judicial Circuit Superior Courts, Self-
Represented Litigants, http://www.cscj.org/circuits/appalachian/Self-Represented
+Litigants

Family Law Resource Center, Chatham County Superior Court, https://courts.chatham
countyga.gov/Superior/FamilyLawResourceCenter

Family Law Information Center, Fulton County Superior Court, https://www.fultoncourt
.org/family/family-flic.php

Georgia Court Self-Help Centers, https://www.georgialegalaid.org/court-info

Georgia Legal Aid, https://www.georgialegalaid.org/

Georgia Legal Services Program, https://www.glsp.org/

Legal Aid Atlanta, https://atlantalegalaid.org/

Pauper's Affidavit, Court of Appeals Georgia, https://www.gaappeals.us/pauper_final
_form.pdf

Self-Help Resources, Judicial Council of Georgia, https://georgiacourts.gov/a2j/self-help
-resources-highlighted-by-a2j/

Law Libraries

Alexander Campbell King Law Library, School of Law, University of Georgia, http://
www.law.uga.edu/law-library

Athens-Clarke County Law Library, https://www.athensclarkecounty.com/1227/Law
-Library

Bibb County Superior Court Law Library, https://maconjudicialcircuitjudges.us/law-library

Chatham County Law Library, http://www.savannahga.gov/754/Libraries-Archival
-Repositories

Cobb County Law Library, https://www.cobbcounty.org/courts/law-library

DeKalb County Law Library, https://www.dekalbsuperiorcourt.com/law-library/about-the
-law-library/

Dougherty County Law Library, http://www.dougherty.ga.us/lawlibrary

Early County Law Library, https://earlycounty2055.com/index.php?page=about&family
=05—Living_Here&category=04—Libraries

Fulton County Law Library, https://www.fultoncourt.org/library/

Georgia State University Law Library, https://lawlibrary.gsu.edu/

Hall County Law Library, https://www.hallcounty.org/1037/Law-Library

Homer M. Stark Law Library, https://www.gcll.org/

Hugh F. Macmillan Law Library, Emory University Law School, http://library.law.emory
.edu/index.html

The Michael J. Lynch Law Library, Atlanta's John Marshall School of Law, http://john
marshall.libguides.com/library/library

Paulding County Law Library, https://www.paulding.gov/420/Law-Library

Richmond County Law Library, https://www.augustaga.gov/1992/Law-Library

United States Court of Appeals for the Eleventh Circuit Libraries, https://www.ca11
.uscourts.gov/eleventh-circuit-library

Legislative Resources

Constitution of the State of Georgia, https://advance.lexis.com/container?config=00JAAy
NDIyN2JjNC04NzBkLTRiNGQtYjcyNC04MjIxYTA1ZmI1OGYKAFBvZEN
hdGFsb2fj2wGx7D8FlWJs9VMmJTXe&crid=7ad6804b-10e5-45e5-ae98
-b3f9f6226484

Georgia General Assembly, http://www.legis.ga.gov/en-US/default.aspx

Legislation, Georgia General Assembly, http://www.legis.ga.gov/Legislation/en-US/Search
.aspx

Official Code of Georgia Annotated, https://advance.lexis.com/container?config=00JAA
zZDgzNzU2ZC05MDA0LTRmMDItYjkzMS0xOGY3MjE3OWNlODIKAFB
vZENhdGFsb2fcIFfJnJ2IC8XZi1AYM4Ne&crid=226db8f9-598a-485d-a3d9
-e6d7f2f7bc30

Judicial Resources

Court of Appeals Georgia, https://www.gaappeals.us/

Judicial Council of Georgia, https://georgiacourts.gov/

Rules, Court of Appeals Georgia, https://www.gaappeals.us/rules2/index.php

Rules, Supreme Court of Georgia, https://www.gasupreme.us/rules/

State Court Forms, Council of State Court Judges of Georgia, https://georgiacourts.gov
/statecourt/state-court-behind-the-bench/state-court-forms/

Supreme Court of Georgia, https://www.gasupreme.us/

Executive Resources

Executive Orders, Office of the Governor, https://gov.georgia.gov/executive-action/executive
-orders

Georgia Office of State Administrative Hearings, https://osah.ga.gov/

Office of the Governor, https://gov.georgia.gov/

Rules and Regulations of the State of Georgia, http://rules.sos.state.ga.us/cgi-bin/page.cgi

State Organizations, https://georgia.gov/state-organizations

Research Resources

American Association of Law Libraries, Public Library Toolkit: Georgia, https://www.aallnet
.org/lispsis/wp-content/uploads/sites/11/2018/01/LISPSIS-PLToolkit-Georgia.pdf

Library of Congress Guide to Law Online, Georgia, http://www.loc.gov/law/help/guide
/states/us-ga.php

Hawaii

Legal Aid and Self-Help Resources

Hawaii State Bar Association, Legal Assistance in the State of Hawaii, https://hsba.org
/HSBA/FOR_THE_PUBLIC/Legal_Assistance/HSBA/For_the_Public_
/Legal%20Assistance.aspx
Hawaii State Judiciary, Self-Help Resources, https://www.courts.state.hi.us/self-help/help
LawHelp.org/HI, https://www.lawhelp.org/hi/
Legal Aid Society of Hawaii, https://www.legalaidhawaii.org/
Volunteer Legal Services Hawaii, https://www.vlsh.org/

Law Libraries

Hawaii State Law Library System, https://histatelawlibrary.com/
State of Hawaii Legislative Reference Bureau, https://lrb.hawaii.gov/
University of Hawaii at Manoa Law Library, https://library.law.hawaii.edu/

Legislative Resources

Bills, https://www.capitol.hawaii.gov/
The Constitution of the State of Hawaii, https://lrb.hawaii.gov/constitution
Hawaii Revised Statutes, https://www.capitol.hawaii.gov/home.aspx
Hawaii State Legislature, https://www.capitol.hawaii.gov/

Judicial Resources

Circuit Court Standard Jury Instructions, Hawaii State Judiciary, https://www.courts.state
.hi.us/legal_references/circuit_court_standard_jury_instructions
Court Forms, Hawaii State Judiciary, https://www.courts.state.hi.us/self-help/courts/forms
/court_forms
Hawaii Appellate Court Opinions and Orders, Hawaii State Judiciary, https://www.courts
.state.hi.us/opinions_and_orders
Hawaii Rules of Court, Hawaii State Judiciary, https://www.courts.state.hi.us/legal
_references/rules/rulesOfCourt
Hawaii State Judiciary, https://www.courts.state.hi.us/

Executive Resources

Hawaii Administrative Rules, http://ltgov.hawaii.gov/the-office/administrative-rules/
Hawaii Administrative Rules Table and Directory, https://lrb.hawaii.gov/admin-rules
-directory
Hawaii State Agency Directory, https://stayconnected.hawaii.gov/
Office of the Governor, https://governor.hawaii.gov/

Research Resources

American Association of Law Libraries, Public Library Toolkit: Hawaii, https://www.aallnet
.org/lispsis/wp-content/uploads/sites/11/2018/01/LISPSIS-PLToolkit-Hawaii.pdf
Library of Congress Guide to Law Online, Hawaii, http://www.loc.gov/law/help/guide/states
/us-hi.php

Idaho

Legal Aid and Self-Help Resources

Idaho Legal Aid Services, https://www.idaholegalaid.org/
Idaho Pro Se Appellate Handbook, https://www.isc.idaho.gov/appeals-court/handbook
Idaho Volunteer Lawyers Program, https://isb.idaho.gov/ilf/ivlp/
State of Idaho Judicial Branch, Idaho Court Assistance Office and Self-Help Center, https://
courtselfhelp.idaho.gov/

Law Libraries

Arthur P. Oliver Law Library, Idaho State University, https://www.isu.edu/library/libandcoll
/oliver-law-library/
Idaho State Law Library, https://isll.idaho.gov/
United States Courts for the Ninth Circuit Library, https://www.ca9.uscourts.gov/library
/directory/
University of Idaho, College of Law Library, https://www.uidaho.edu/law/Library

Legislative Resources

Idaho Constitution, https://legislature.idaho.gov/statutesrules/idconst/
Idaho Legislature, https://legislature.idaho.gov/
Idaho Session Laws, https://legislature.idaho.gov/statutesrules/sessionlaws/
Idaho Statutes, https://legislature.idaho.gov/statutesrules/idstat/
Search All Current and Prior Legislation, Idaho Legislature, https://legislature.idaho.gov
/adv-legislation-search/

Judicial Resources

Civil Jury Instructions, https://isc.idaho.gov/main/civil-jury-instructions
Criminal Jury Instructions, https://www.isc.idaho.gov/main/criminal-jury-instructions
Forms, Court Assistance Office, https://courtselfhelp.idaho.gov/Forms
Idaho Court Rules, https://www.isc.idaho.gov/main/idaho-court-rules
Idaho Supreme Court and Court of Appeals Opinions, https://www.isc.idaho.gov/appeals
-court/opinions
State of Idaho Judicial Branch, https://www.idaho.gov/government/judicial-branch/

Executive Resources

A–Z Agency Directory, https://www.idaho.gov/agencies/
Executive Orders, https://gov.idaho.gov/executive-orders/

Idaho Administrative Bulletin, https://adminrules.idaho.gov/bulletin/index.html
Idaho Administrative Code, https://adminrules.idaho.gov/rules/current/index.html
Office of the Governor, https://gov.idaho.gov/

Research Resources

American Association of Law Libraries, Public Library Toolkit: Idaho, https://www.aallnet
.org/lispsis/wp-content/uploads/sites/11/2018/01/LISPSIS-PLToolkit-Idaho.pdf
Library of Congress Guide to Law Online, Idaho, http://www.loc.gov/law/help/guide/states
/us-id.php

Illinois

Legal Aid and Self-Help Resources

Ascend Justice, https://www.ascendjustice.org/
Chicago Volunteer Lawyer Services, https://www.cvls.org/
Citizen Self-Help, Illinois Courts, http://illinoiscourts.gov/citizen.asp
Illinois Legal Aid Online, https://www.illinoislegalaid.org/
Illinois Supreme Court, Access to Justice, http://www.illinoiscourts.gov/CivilJustice/Access
ToJustice.asp
Kane County Law Library and Self-Help Center, https://www.kclawlibrary.org/
Land of Lincoln Legal Aid, https://lincolnlegal.org/
Legal Aid Chicago, https://www.legalaidchicago.org/
Life Span, https://life-span.org/
Metropolitan Family Services, Legal Aid Society, https://www.metrofamily.org/legal-aid
-society/about-las/
Mil Mujeres, https://www.milmujeres.org/
Nineteenth Judicial Circuit Court, Lake County Illinois, Pro Se Litigants, http://www
.19thcircuitcourt.state.il.us/1409/Pro-Se-Litigants
Prairie State Legal Services, https://www.pslegal.org/default.asp
YWCA Evanston/North Shore, Support for Survivors of Domestic Violence, https://www
.ywca-ens.org/domestic-violence-program/support-services/

Law Libraries

Chicago-Kent College of Law Library, Illinois Institute of Technology, https://www.kent
law.iit.edu/library
Cook County Law Library, https://www.cookcountyil.gov/agency/law-library
David C. Shapiro Memorial Law Library, Northern Illinois University College of Law,
https://law.niu.edu/law/library/
DuPage County Law Library, https://www.dupageco.org/lawlibrary/
Illinois Supreme Court Library, http://www.illinoiscourts.gov/SupremeCourt/library.asp
Kane County Law Library and Self-Help Legal Center, https://www.kclawlibrary.org/
Lake County Law Library, https://www.19thcircuitcourt.state.il.us/1259/Law-Library
Library of the U.S. Courts of the Seventh Circuit, William J. Campbell Headquarters in
Chicago, http://www.lb7.uscourts.gov/ChicagoHome.html
Madison County Law Library, https://www.co.madison.il.us/departments/circuit_court/law
_library/index.php

McHenry County Law Library, https://www.mchenrycountyil.gov/county-government
/courts/22nd-judicial-circuit/law-library

Peoria County Law Library, https://www.peoriacounty.org/304/Law-Library-FAQ

Rinn Law Library, DePaul College of Law, https://law.depaul.edu/library/Pages/default.aspx

Rock Island County Law Library, https://www.rockislandcounty.org/LawLibrary/

Sangamon County Law Library, https://co.sangamon.il.us/departments/s-z/seventh-judicial
-circuit-court/law-library

School of Law Library, Southern Illinois University, https://law.siu.edu/lawlib/

University of Illinois College of Law Library, https://law.illinois.edu/academics/library/

Will County Law Library, https://www.willcountycourts.com/Law-Library-Main

Winnebago County Law Library, http://www.illinois17th.com/index.php?option=com
_content&task=view&id=292&Itemid=195

Legislative Resources

Bills and Resolutions, Illinois General Assembly, http://www.ilga.gov/legislation/default.asp

Constitution of the State of Illinois, http://www.ilga.gov/commission/lrb/conmain.htm

Illinois Compiled Statutes, http://www.ilga.gov/legislation/ilcs/ilcs.asp

Illinois General Assembly, http://www.ilga.gov/

Public Acts, Illinois General Assembly, http://www.ilga.gov/legislation/publicacts
/default.asp

Judicial Resources

Illinois Courts, http://www.illinoiscourts.gov/

Illinois Pattern Jury Instructions, Civil, http://www.illinoiscourts.gov/CircuitCourt/Civil
JuryInstructions/default.asp

Illinois Pattern Jury Instructions, Criminal, http://www.illinoiscourts.gov/CircuitCourt
/CriminalJuryInstructions/default.asp

Illinois Rules of Evidence, http://illinoiscourts.gov/SupremeCourt/Evidence/Evidence.asp

Illinois Supreme Court Rules, http://www.illinoiscourts.gov/SupremeCourt/Rules
/default.asp

Recent Appellate Court Opinions, Illinois Courts, http://www.illinoiscourts.gov/Opinions
/recent_appellate.asp

Recent Supreme Court Opinions, Illinois Courts, http://www.illinoiscourts.gov/Opinions
/recent_supreme.asp

Standardized State Forms, Illinois Supreme Court, http://illinoiscourts.gov/Forms/approved
/default.asp

Executive Resources

Administrative Hearings, https://www.cyberdriveillinois.com/departments/administrative
_hearings/home.html

Executive and Administrative Orders, https://www2.illinois.gov/government/executive
-orders

Illinois Administrative Code, http://www.ilga.gov/commission/jcar/admincode/titles.html

Illinois Register, https://www.cyberdriveillinois.com/departments/index/register/home
.html
Office of Governor, https://www2.illinois.gov/sites/GOV/Pages/default.aspx
Search Agencies, https://www2.illinois.gov/agencies/

Research Resources

American Association of Law Libraries, Public Library Toolkit: Illinois, https://www
.aallnet.org/lispsis/wp-content/uploads/sites/11/2018/01/LISPSIS-PLToolkit
-Illinois.pdf
Library of Congress Guide to Law Online, Illinois, http://www.loc.gov/law/help/guide
/states/us-il.php

Indiana

Legal Aid and Self-Help Resources

Indiana Judicial Branch, Information for the Public, https://www.in.gov/judiciary/2806
.htm
Indiana Judicial Branch, Self-Service Legal Center, https://www.in.gov/judiciary/self
service/
Indiana Legal Help, https://indianalegalhelp.org/find-legal-help/
Indiana Legal Services, https://www.indianalegalservices.org/
Legal Aid Corporation of Tippecanoe County, https://www.tclegalaid.org/

Law Libraries

Indiana Supreme Court Law Library, https://www.in.gov/judiciary/supreme/2329.htm
Jerome Hall Law Library, Maurer School of Law, Indiana University Bloomington,
https://www.law.indiana.edu/lawlibrary/index.shtml
Kresge Law Library, The Law School, University of Notre Dame, https://law.nd.edu/faculty
-scholarship/kresge-law-library/
Library of the U.S. Courts of the Seventh Circuit, Indianapolis Satellite, http://www.lb7
.uscourts.gov/IndianapolisHome.html
Ruth Lilly Law Library, Robert H. McKinney School of Law, Indiana University, https://
mckinneylaw.iu.edu/library/
William H. Miller Law Library, County of Vanderburgh, http://www.vanderburghgov.org
/county/topic/index.php?topicid=249&structureid=31

Legislative Resources

Bills, Indiana General Assembly, http://iga.in.gov/legislative/2020/bills/
Indiana Code, http://iga.in.gov/legislative/laws/2019/ic/titles/001
Indiana Constitution, http://iga.in.gov/legislative/laws/const/
Indiana General Assembly, http://iga.in.gov/
Session Laws, Indiana General Assembly, http://iga.in.gov/legislative/laws/acts/

Judicial Resources

Appellate Decisions, Indiana Judicial Branch, https://www.in.gov/judiciary/2730.htm
Indiana Judicial Branch, https://www.in.gov/judiciary/
Local Rules, Indiana Judicial Branch, https://www.in.gov/judiciary/2694.htm
Rules of Court, Indiana Judicial Branch, https://www.in.gov/judiciary/2695.htm

Executive Resources

Executive Orders, https://www.in.gov/gov/2384.htm
Find an Agency, IN.gov, https://www.in.gov/core/find_agency.html
Indiana Administrative Code, http://iac.iga.in.gov/iac/
Indiana Register, http://iac.iga.in.gov/iac//irtoc.htm
Office of the Governor, https://www.in.gov/gov/

Research Resources

American Association of Law Libraries, Public Library Toolkit: Indiana, https://www.aallnet
.org/lispsis/wp-content/uploads/sites/11/2019/10/LISPSIS-PLToolkit-Indiana.pdf
Library of Congress Guide to Law Online, Indiana, http://www.loc.gov/law/help/guide/states
/us-in.php

Iowa

Legal Aid and Self-Help Resources

Clinical Law Program at the University of Iowa, https://law.uiowa.edu/clinic
Drake Legal Clinic, https://www.drake.edu/law/clinics-centers/clinic/
Iowa Judicial Branch, Representing Yourself, https://www.iowacourts.gov/for-the-public
/representing-yourself/
Iowa Legal Aid, https://www.iowalegalaid.org/
Legal Aid of Story County, http://www.legalaidstory.com/
Muscatine Legal Services, http://www.muscatinelegal.com/
Polk County Bar Association, Volunteer Lawyer's Project, https://www.pcbaonline.org
/volunteer-lawyers-project/

Law Libraries

Drake University Law Library, https://www.drake.edu/law/library/
State Law Library of Iowa, https://www.statelibraryofiowa.org/services/collections/law
-library/index
University of Iowa Law Library, https://library.law.uiowa.edu/
U.S. Courts Library for the 8th Circuit, https://www.lb8.uscourts.gov:444/index1.htm

Legislative Resources

Find Legislation, Iowa Legislature, https://www.legis.iowa.gov/legislation/findLegislation
Iowa Acts and Passed Legislation, https://www.legis.iowa.gov/law/statutory/acts

Iowa Code, https://www.legis.iowa.gov/law/statutory
Iowa Constitution, https://www.legis.iowa.gov/law/statutory/constitution
Iowa Legislature, https://www.legis.iowa.gov/

Judicial Resources

Appellate Court Opinions, Iowa Judicial Branch, https://www.iowacourts.gov/iowa-courts
/court-of-appeals/court-of-appeals-court-opinions/
Court Forms, Iowa Judicial Branch, https://www.iowacourts.gov/for-the-public/court-forms/
Iowa Court Rules, https://www.legis.iowa.gov/law/courtRules
Iowa Judicial Branch, https://www.iowacourts.gov/
Supreme Court Opinions, Iowa Judicial Branch, https://www.iowacourts.gov/iowa-courts
/supreme-court/supreme-court-opinions/

Executive Resources

Executive Orders, Iowa Legislature, https://www.legis.iowa.gov/publications/otherResources
/executiveOrders
Executive Orders, Office of the Governor, https://governor.iowa.gov/executive-orders
Iowa Administrative Bulletin, https://www.legis.iowa.gov/law/administrativeRules/bullet
inSupplementListings
Iowa Administrative Code, https://www.legis.iowa.gov/law/administrativeRules/agencies
Office of the Governor, https://governor.iowa.gov/
Organizations List, Iowa Administrative Rules, https://rules.iowa.gov/Organization
Rules Open for Comment, Iowa Administrative Rules, https://rules.iowa.gov/

Research Resources

American Association of Law Libraries, Public Library Toolkit: Iowa (Basic), http://lib
guides.law.drake.edu/IowaBasic
American Association of Law Libraries, Public Library Toolkit: Iowa (Self-Represented
Litigant), http://libguides.law.drake.edu/selfrepresentedLitigant
Iowa Legal History, University of Iowa Law Library, http://libguides.law.uiowa.edu/iowa
legalhistory
Library of Congress Guide to Law Online, Iowa, http://www.loc.gov/law/help/guide/states
/us-ia.php

Kansas

Legal Aid and Self-Help Resources

Johnson County District Court Help Center, http://courts.jocogov.org/hc_selfhelp.aspx
Kansas Judicial Branch, Get Legal Help, https://www.kscourts.org/Public/Legal-Help
Kansas Judicial Branch, Public Resources, https://www.kscourts.org/Public
Kansas Legal Services, https://www.kansaslegalservices.org/
Legal Aid Clinic at the University of Kansas School of Law, https://law.ku.edu/legal-aid
-public
Washburn Law Clinic, http://washburnlaw.edu/aboutus/community/clinic/clients.html

Law Libraries

Johnson County Law Library, https://jocogov.org/dept/law-library/home
Kansas Legislative Research Department, http://www.kslegresearch.org/KLRD-web
    /Policy.html
Kansas Supreme Court Law Library, https://www.kscourts.org/About-the-Courts/Law
    -Library
Sedgwick County Law Library, https://www.wichitabar.org/page/SedgCoLawLibrary
Washburn University School of Law Library, http://washburnlaw.edu/library/index.html
Wheat Law Library, The University of Kansas School of Law, http://law.ku.edu/wheat
    -law-library

Legislative Resources

Bills, Kansas State Legislature, http://www.kslegislature.org/li/b2019_20/measures/bills/
Kansas Constitution, https://kslib.info/constitution
Kansas State Legislature, http://www.kslegislature.org/li/
Kansas Statutes, http://www.kslegislature.org/li/b2019_20/statute/
Session Laws of Kansas, https://sos.kansas.gov/lobbyist-legislative/session-laws/

Judicial Resources

Cases and Opinions, Kansas Judicial Branch, https://www.kscourts.org/Cases-Opinions
Find Court Forms, Kansas Judicial Branch, https://www.kscourts.org/Public/Find-a-Form
Forms, Kansas Judicial Council, https://www.kansasjudicialcouncil.org/legal-forms
Johnson County Court Forms, http://jocogov.org/dept/law-library/kansas-court-forms
Kansas Judicial Branch, https://www.kscourts.org/home
Rules and Orders, Kansas Judicial Branch, https://www.kscourts.org/Rules-Orders
Shawnee County Court Forms, http://www.shawneecourt.org/index.aspx?NID=27

Executive Resources

Executive Orders, Office of the Governor, https://governor.kansas.gov/newsroom/executive
    -orders/
Kansas Administrative Regulations, http://www.kssos.org/pubs/pubs_kar.aspx
Kansas Register, http://www.kssos.org/pubs/pubs_kansas_register.asp
Office of the Governor, https://governor.kansas.gov/
State Agency Listing, http://kanview.ks.gov/AgencyListing.aspx

Research Resources

American Association of Law Libraries, Public Library Toolkit: Kansas, https://www.aallnet
    .org/lispsis/wp-content/uploads/sites/11/2019/07/LISPToolkit-Kansas2019.pdf
Kansas Legal Forms, Wheat Law Library, http://guides.law.ku.edu/c.php?g=705127&p
    =5006965
Kansas Legislative History Guide, Washburn Law Library, http://www.washburnlaw.edu
    /library/research/guides/kansasleghistory.html

Library of Congress Guide to Law Online, Kansas, http://www.loc.gov/law/help/guide
/states/us-ks.php

Kentucky

Legal Aid and Self-Help Resources

Kentucky Court of Justice, Information for the Public, https://kycourts.gov/public/Pages
/default.aspx
Kentucky Legal Aid, https://www.klaid.org/
Legal Aid Network of Kentucky, http://kyjustice.org/
Legal Aid Society, https://www.yourlegalaid.org/

Law Libraries

Chase Law Library, Northern Kentucky University, https://chaselaw.nku.edu/current-students
/library.html
Eastern Kentucky University Law Library, https://library.eku.edu/law
Fayette County Law Library, https://kycourts.gov/courts/Fayette/Pages/lawlibrary.aspx
Jefferson County Public Law Library, https://www.jcpll.net/
Kentucky State Law Library, https://kycourts.gov/aoc/statelawlibrary/Pages/default.aspx
Louis D. Brandeis School of Law Library, University of Louisville, https://louisville.edu
/law/library
Murray State University James O. Overby Law Library, https://libguides.murraystate
.edu/law
Peggy King Legislative Reference Library, https://legislature.ky.gov/Public%20Services
/Pages/Legislative-Reference-Library.aspx
University of Kentucky Law Library, https://library.law.uky.edu/home
Western Kentucky University Law Collection, https://wku.edu/library/information
/departments/dlps/gov_law/law_collection.php

Legislative Resources

Acts of the Kentucky General Assembly, https://legislature.ky.gov/Law/Pages/KyActs.aspx
Bills, Kentucky General Assembly, https://legislature.ky.gov/Legislation/Pages/default.aspx
Constitution of Kentucky, https://apps.legislature.ky.gov/law/constitution
Enacted Legislation, Kentucky Secretary of State, https://www.sos.ky.gov/admin/Executive
/legislation/Pages/default.aspx
Kentucky General Assembly, https://legislature.ky.gov/Pages/index.aspx
Kentucky Revised Statutes, https://legislature.ky.gov/Law/Statutes/Pages/default.aspx

Judicial Resources

Kentucky Court of Justice, https://kycourts.gov/Pages/default.aspx
Legal Forms, Kentucky Court of Justice, https://kycourts.gov/resources/legalforms/Pages
/default.aspx

Local Rules of Practice, Kentucky Court of Justice, https://kycourts.gov/Pages/localrules
.aspx
Opinions, Kentucky Court of Justice, http://apps.courts.ky.gov/supreme/sc_opinions.shtm
Rules and Procedures, Kentucky Court of Justice, https://kycourts.gov/courts/supreme
/Pages/rulesprocedures.aspx

Executive Resources

Administrative Register of Kentucky, https://legislature.ky.gov/Law/kar/Pages/Registers
.aspx
Kentucky Administrative Regulations, https://legislature.ky.gov/Law/kar/Pages/default
.aspx
Office of the Governor, https://governor.ky.gov/
State Agencies, https://kentucky.gov/government/Pages/agency.aspx

Research Resources

American Association of Law Libraries, Public Library Toolkit: Kentucky, https://www
.aallnet.org/lispsis/wp-content/uploads/sites/11/2020/01/LISPSIS-PLToolkit
-Kentucky.pdf
Library of Congress Guide to Law Online, Kentucky, http://www.loc.gov/law/help/guide
/states/us-ky.php

Louisiana

Legal Aid and Self-Help Resources

Acandiana Legal Services Corporation, https://www.la-law.org/
The Family Court in and for the Parish of Baton Rouge, Self-Help Resources, http://www
.familycourt.org/main/inside.php?page=self-help_resources
LouisianaLawHelp, https://louisianalawhelp.org/
Louisiana State Bar Association, Self-Help Services and Legal Forms, https://www.lsba
.org/Public/FindLegalHelp/SelfRepresentation.aspx
Louisiana State University Law School, Louisiana Legal Aid Services, https://libguides
.law.lsu.edu/legalaid
Louisiana Supreme Court, Self-Represented Litigants, https://www.lasc.org/Judicial
_Administrator's_Office?p=SRL
Resources for Self-Represented Litigants, The Law Library of Louisiana, https://lasc
.libguides.com/resources-for-self-represented-litigants
Southeast Louisiana Legal Services, https://slls.org/

Law Libraries

The Law Library of Louisiana, https://lasc.libguides.com/home
Louisiana State University Law Library, https://www.law.lsu.edu/library
Tulane University Law School Library, https://library.law.tulane.edu/screens/index.html

United States Court of Appeals Library for the Fifth Circuit, Lafayette Satellite Library, https://www.lb5.uscourts.gov/Directory/?Lafayette

United States Court of Appeals Library for the Fifth Circuit, New Orleans Headquarters Library, https://www.lb5.uscourts.gov/Directory/?NewOrleans

United States Court of Appeals Library for the Fifth Circuit, Shreveport Satellite Library, https://www.lb5.uscourts.gov/Directory/?Shreveport

Legislative Resources

Bills, Louisiana State Legislature, http://www.legis.la.gov/legis/BillSearch.aspx?sid=last

Constitution of Louisiana, http://senate.legis.state.la.us/documents/constitution/

Laws, Louisiana State Legislature, http://www.legis.la.gov/legis/LawsContents.aspx

Louisiana Revised Statutes, https://legis.la.gov/Legis/Laws_Toc.aspx?folder=75&level =Parent

Louisiana State Legislature, https://legis.la.gov/legis/home.aspx

Judicial Resources

Code of Civil Procedure, http://www.legis.la.gov/legis/Laws_Toc.aspx?folder=68&level =Parent

Code of Criminal Procedure, http://www.legis.la.gov/legis/Laws_Toc.aspx?folder=69&level =Parent

Court Actions, Louisiana Supreme Court, https://www.lasc.org/CourtActions/2020

Court Rules, Louisiana Supreme Court, https://www.lasc.org/CourtRules

Guide to Free Online Cases, The Law Library of Louisiana, https://lasc.libguides.com/c .php?g=214725&p=1416848

Louisiana Judicial Branch, https://www.louisiana.gov/government/judicial-branch/

Louisiana Supreme Court, https://www.lasc.org/

Online Forms, The Law Library of Louisiana, https://lasc.libguides.com/c.php?g=129873 &p=2583986

Executive Resources

Agency Directory, https://www.louisiana.gov/government/agency-directory/

Executive Orders, https://www.doa.la.gov/Pages/osr/other/exord.aspx

Louisiana Administrative Code, https://www.doa.la.gov/Pages/osr/lac/books.aspx

Louisiana Register, https://www.doa.la.gov/Pages/osr/reg/register.aspx

Office of the Governor, https://gov.louisiana.gov/

Research Resources

American Association of Law Libraries, Public Library Toolkit: Louisiana, https://www .aallnet.org/lispsis/wp-content/uploads/sites/11/2020/01/LISPSIS-PLToolkit -Louisiana.pdf

Library of Congress Guide to Law Online, Louisiana, http://www.loc.gov/law/help/guide /states/us-la.php

Maine

Legal Aid and Self-Help Resources

Citizen Help, State of Maine Judicial Branch, https://www.courts.maine.gov/citizen_help
/index.shtml
HelpMELaw, https://helpmelaw.org/
Legal Services for the Elderly, https://www.mainelse.org/
Maine Equal Justice, https://maineequaljustice.org/
Pine Tree Legal Assistance, https://ptla.org/

Law Libraries

Garbrecht Law Library, University of Maine School of Law, https://mainelaw.maine.edu
/library/
Law Libraries, State of Maine Judicial Branch, https://www.courts.maine.gov/news
_reference/libraries/index.shtml
Maine State Law and Legislative Reference Library, http://legislature.maine.gov/lawlibrary/

Legislative Resources

Bills, Maine State Legislature, http://www.mainelegislature.org/legis/bills/
Legislative History Collections, Maine State Legislature, https://www.maine.gov/legis
/lawlib/lldl/legishistory.htm
Maine Revised Statutes, http://legislature.maine.gov/legis/statutes/
Maine Session Laws, http://legislature.maine.gov/ros/LawsOfMaine/#Law/129/R1/ACT
PUB/61
Maine State Constitution, http://legislature.maine.gov/ros/LawsOfMaine/#Const
Maine State Legislature, http://legislature.maine.gov/

Judicial Resources

Court Forms, State of Maine Judicial Branch, https://www.courts.maine.gov/fees_forms
/forms/index.shtml
Court Rules, State of Maine Judicial Branch, https://www.courts.maine.gov/rules_admin
orders/rules/index.shtml
Opinions and Orders, Maine Judicial Branch, https://www.courts.maine.gov/opinions
_orders/index.shtml
Probate Court Forms, Maine Probate Court, https://www.maineprobate.net/welcome
/probateforms-2019/
State of Maine Judicial Branch, https://www.courts.maine.gov/

Executive Resources

Executive Orders, Office of Governor, https://www.maine.gov/governor/mills/official
_documents
Office of Governor, https://www.maine.gov/governor/mills/
Rules by Department, https://www.maine.gov/sos/cec/rules/rules.html

State Agencies, https://www.maine.gov/portal/government/state-agencies/
Weekly Rule Making Notices, https://www.maine.gov/sos/cec/rules/notices.html

Research Resources

American Association of Law Libraries, Public Library Toolkit: Maine, https://www.aallnet
.org/lispsis/wp-content/uploads/sites/11/2019/01/LISPSIS-PLToolkit-Maine.pdf
Library of Congress Guide to Law Online, Maine, http://www.loc.gov/law/help/guide/states
/us-me.php

Maryland

Legal Aid and Self-Help Resources

Lawyer in the Library, Anne Arundel County Public Law Library, http://circuitcourt.org
/legal-help/lawyer-in-the-library
Legal Information Brochures, Maryland Bar Association, https://www.msba.org/for-the
-public/legal-information-brochures/
Legal Services Directory, The People's Law Library of Maryland, https://www.peoples
-law.org/directory
Maryland Courts, Family Law Self-Help Centers, https://mdcourts.gov/family/familyselfhelp
Maryland Courts, Legal Self-Help, https://www.courts.state.md.us/legalhelp
Maryland Courts, Self-Help Centers, https://www.courts.state.md.us/selfhelp
Maryland Court of Special Appeals, A Guide for Self-Representation, https://www.mdcourts
.gov/sites/default/files/import/cosappeals/pdfs/cosaguideselfrepresentation.pdf
Maryland Legal Aid, https://www.mdlab.org/
Maryland Legal Services Corporation, https://www.mlsc.org/
Maryland Volunteer Lawyers Service, https://mvlslaw.org/
The People's Law Library of Maryland, https://www.peoples-law.org/homepage
Thurgood Marshall State Law Library, https://www.mdcourts.gov/lawlib

Law Libraries

Maryland Law Libraries, https://mdcourts.gov/lawlib/using-library/for-librarians/maryland
-law-libraries
The People's Law Library of Maryland, https://www.peoples-law.org/homepage
Thurgood Marshall Law Library, University of Maryland Francis King Carey School of
Law, https://www.law.umaryland.edu/Thurgood-Marshall-Law-Library/
Thurgood Marshall State Law Library, Maryland Courts, https://mdcourts.gov/lawlib
United States Court of Appeals for the Fourth Circuit Library, https://www.ca4.uscourts
.gov/about-the-court/offices/about-the-fourth-circuit-library
University of Baltimore School of Law Library, http://law.ubalt.edu/library/

Legislative Resources

Maryland Code, http://mgaleg.maryland.gov/mgawebsite/laws/statutes
Maryland Code, Constitution, and Court Rules, https://advance.lexis.com/container?config
=00JAA1NTM5MzBmZC02MTg2LTQzNmEtYmI5Yy0yZWEwYzA1OGEwN

TYKAFBvZENhdGFsb2fdgr2eooaZj7MpSZGOIwWq&crid=a5d73095-003f
-4120-84ca-be8ff63a720d&prid=c25ed8a3-eeda-4739-aad3-15c758791cd0

Maryland Constitution, https://msa.maryland.gov/msa/mdmanual/43const/html/const.html

Maryland General Assembly, https://msa.maryland.gov/msa/mdmanual/07leg/html/ga
.html

Maryland House Bills, http://mgaleg.maryland.gov/mgawebsite/Legislation/Index/house

Maryland Senate Bills, http://mgaleg.maryland.gov/mgawebsite/Legislation/Index/senate

Session Laws, Maryland General Assembly, http://mgaleg.maryland.gov/mgawebsite

Judicial Resources

Court Forms, https://mdcourts.gov/courtforms?forms%5B0%5D=languages%3A59

Maryland Appellate Court Opinions, https://mdcourts.gov/opinions/opinions

Maryland Court Rules, https://advance.lexis.com/container?config=025156JABlOGU3N
WQ5Yi01NjljLTRjZmUtOWIxMC1jNWQwZjJlYjg3OWQKAFBvZENhdGFsb-
2d4ClCX0iZK6dHR8cd6gJaq&crid=7744f3bb-d7c5-4942-8a4b-7a5a67cb7e7e

Maryland Courts, https://www.courts.state.md.us/

Executive Resources

Code of Maryland Administrative Regulations, http://www.dsd.state.md.us/COMAR
/ComarHome.html

Executive Orders, Office of the Governor, https://governor.maryland.gov/category/executive
-orders/

Maryland Register, http://www.dsd.state.md.us/MDR/mdregister.html

Maryland State Agency Directory, https://www.maryland.gov/pages/agency_directory.aspx

Office of the Governor, https://governor.maryland.gov/

Research Resources

American Association of Law Libraries, Public Library Toolkit: Maryland, https://mdcourts
.gov/lawlib/using-library/for-librarians/public-library-toolkit

Library of Congress Guide to Law Online, Maryland, http://www.loc.gov/law/help/guide
/states/us-md.php

Massachusetts

Legal Aid and Self-Help Resources

De Novo: Center for Justice and Healing, https://www.denovo.org/

Greater Boston Legal Services, https://www.gbls.org/

Mass.gov, Finding Legal Help, https://www.mass.gov/service-details/finding-legal-help

Massachusetts Court System, Courts Self-Help, https://www.mass.gov/topics/courts-self
-help

MassLegalHelp, https://www.masslegalhelp.org/

MassLegalServices, Find Legal Aid, https://www.masslegalservices.org/findlegalaid

MetroWest Legal Services, https://mwlegal.org/

Prisoners' Legal Services of Massachusetts, https://www.plsma.org/
Volunteer Lawyer's Project, Boston Bar Association, https://vlpnet.org/

Law Libraries

Massachusetts Trial Court Law Libraries, https://www.mass.gov/orgs/trial-court-law-libraries
Northeastern School of Law Library, https://www.northeastern.edu/law/library/index.html
United States Court of Appeals for the First Circuit Library, https://www.ca1.uscourts.gov
/circuit-library
University of Massachusetts School of Law Library, https://www.umassd.edu/law/library/
Western New England University School of Law Library, https://www1.wne.edu/law
/library/?ql=true

Legislative Resources

Massachusetts Bills and Laws, https://malegislature.gov/Bills
Massachusetts Constitution, https://malegislature.gov/Laws/Constitution
Massachusetts General Laws, https://malegislature.gov/Laws/GeneralLaws
Massachusetts Legislature, https://malegislature.gov/
Massachusetts Session Laws, https://malegislature.gov/Laws/SessionLaws

Judicial Resources

Court Forms, Massachusetts Court System, https://www.mass.gov/topics/court-forms
Court Rules, Guidelines, and Standards, Massachusetts Court System, https://www.mass
.gov/court-rules-guidelines-and-standards
Massachusetts Court System, https://www.mass.gov/orgs/massachusetts-court-system
Model Jury Instructions, Massachusetts Court System, https://www.mass.gov/model-jury
-instructions
New Opinions, Massachusetts Court System, https://www.mass.gov/service-details/new
-opinions

Executive Resources

Code of Massachusetts Regulations, http://www.sec.state.ma.us/spr/sprcode/infocode.htm
Executive Orders, https://www.mass.gov/lists/executive-orders-issued-by-governor-baker
Massachusetts Register, http://www.sec.state.ma.us/spr/sprmareg/infosubscrition.htm
Massachusetts State Organizations, https://www.mass.gov/info-details/massachusetts
-state-organizations-a-to-z
Office of the Governor, https://www.mass.gov/orgs/office-of-the-governor

Research Resources

American Association of Law Libraries, Public Library Toolkit: Massachusetts, https://
www.aallnet.org/lispsis/wp-content/uploads/sites/11/2018/01/LISPSIS-PLToolkit
-Massachusetts.pdf

Library of Congress Guide to Law Online, Massachusetts, http://www.loc.gov/law/help
/guide/states/us-ma.php

Michigan

Legal Aid and Self-Help Resources

Lakeshore Legal Aid, https://lakeshorelegalaid.org/
Legal Aid and Defender Association Incorporated, http://ladadetroit.org/
Legal Aid of Western Michigan, https://lawestmi.org/
Legal Services of Eastern Michigan, http://www.lsem-mi.org/
Legal Services of Northern Michigan, http://www.lsnm.org/
Legal Services of South Central Michigan, https://lsscm.org/
Michigan Courts, Self-Help, https://courts.michigan.gov/self-help/pages/default.aspx
Michigan Indian Legal Services, https://www.mils3.org/
Michigan Legal Help, https://michiganlegalhelp.org/
State Bar of Michigan, Legal Programs by County, https://www.michbar.org/public
_resources/legalaid

Law Libraries

Directory of Michigan Libraries with Legal Collections, Library of Michigan, https://www
.michigan.gov/libraryofmichigan/0,9327,7-381-88854_89989_89990-52451—,00
.html

Legislative Resources

Bills, Michigan Legislature, http://www.legislature.mi.gov/(S(i2r5glras1do3agl1jqy5v4t))
/mileg.aspx?page=Bills
Constitution of Michigan, http://www.legislature.mi.gov/(S(i2r5glras1do3agl1jqy5v4t))
/mileg.aspx?page=GetObject&objectname=mcl-Constitution
Michigan Compiled Laws, http://www.legislature.mi.gov/(S(i2r5glras1do3agl1jqy5v4t))
/mileg.aspx?page=MCLBasicSearch
Michigan Legislature, https://www.legislature.mi.gov/(S(hrvf5jjsuac03bj1gyhqvyz0))
/mileg.aspx?page=home
Public Acts, Michigan State Legislature, http://www.legislature.mi.gov/(S(i2r5glras1do3a
gl1jqy5v4t))/mileg.aspx?page=PublicActs

Judicial Resources

Cases, Opinions, and Orders, Michigan Courts, https://courts.michigan.gov/opinions_orders
/Pages/default.aspx
Court Forms, Michigan Courts, https://courts.michigan.gov/administration/scao/forms/pages
/default.aspx
Court Rules, Michigan Courts, https://courts.michigan.gov/Courts/MichiganSupremeCourt
/rules/Pages/current-court-rules.aspx

Michigan Courts, https://courts.michigan.gov/Pages/default.aspx

Model Civil Jury Instructions, https://courts.michigan.gov/Courts/MichiganSupreme
Court/mcji/Pages/home.aspx

Model Criminal Jury Instructions, https://courts.michigan.gov/Courts/MichiganSupreme
Court/criminal-jury-instructions/Pages/default.aspx

Executive Resources

Departments, State of Michigan, https://www.michigan.gov/som/0,4669,7-192-29701_29702
_30045—,00.html

Executive Orders, Michigan Legislature, http://www.legislature.mi.gov/(S(i2r5glras1do3a
gl1jqy5v4t))/mileg.aspx?page=ExecutiveOrders

Executive Orders, Office of Governor, https://www.michigan.gov/whitmer/0,9309,7-387
-90499_90705—,00.html

Michigan Administrative Code, https://dtmb.state.mi.us/ARS_Public/AdminCode/Admin
Code

Michigan Register, https://www.michigan.gov/lara/0,4601,7-154-89334_10576_92306
_92312_92359—,00.html

Office of Governor, https://www.michigan.gov/whitmer/

Research Resources

American Association of Law Libraries, Public Library Toolkit: Michigan, https://www
.aallnet.org/lispsis/wp-content/uploads/sites/11/2019/03/LISPSIS-PLToolkit
-Michigan.pdf

Library of Congress Guide to Law Online, Michigan, http://www.loc.gov/law/help/guide
/states/us-mi.php

Minnesota

Legal Aid and Self-Help Resources

Anishinabe Legal Services, https://www.alslegal.org/

Central Minnesota Legal Services, https://www.centralmnlegal.org/

Immigrant Law Center of Minnesota, https://www.ilcm.org/

Judicare of Anoka County, http://www.anokajudicare.org/

LawHelpMN, https://www.lawhelpmn.org/

Legal Aid Services of Northeastern Minnesota, http://lasnem.org/

Legal Referrals by County, Minnesota State Law Library, https://mn.gov/law-library
/research-links/legal-referrals/legal-referrals-by-county.jsp

Legal Services of Northwest Minnesota, https://lsnmlaw.org/

Mid-Minnesota Legal Aid, https://mylegalaid.org/

Migrant Legal Services, http://www.legalassist.org/?id=87

Self-Help Centers, Minnesota Judicial Branch, http://www.mncourts.gov/Help-Topics/Self
-Help-Centers.aspx

Southern Minnesota Regional Legal Aid, https://www.smrls.org/

Law Libraries

Bush Memorial Library, Hamline University School of Law, https://www.hamline.edu
/bushlibrary/
County Law Libraries, Minnesota State Law Library, https://mn.gov/law-library/research
-links/county-law-libraries.jsp
Minnesota Legislative Reference Library, https://www.leg.state.mn.us/lrl/
Minnesota State Law Library, https://mn.gov/law-library/
University of Minnesota Law Library, https://www.law.umn.edu/library
U.S. Courts Library for the 8th Circuit, https://www.lb8.uscourts.gov:444/index1.htm
Warren E. Burger Law Library, Michell Hamline School of Law, https://mitchellhamline
.edu/library/

Legislative Resources

Bills, Minnesota State Legislature, https://www.leg.state.mn.us/leg/legis
Constitution of the State of Minnesota, https://www.revisor.mn.gov/constitution/
Minnesota Legislature, https://www.leg.state.mn.us/
Minnesota Session Laws, https://www.revisor.mn.gov/laws/
Minnesota Statutes, https://www.revisor.mn.gov/statutes/

Judicial Resources

Court Forms, Minnesota Judicial Branch, http://www.mncourts.gov/GetForms.aspx
Court of Appeals Opinions, Minnesota Judicial Branch, http://www.mncourts.gov/Court
OfAppeals/RecentOpinions.aspx
Forms Finder, Minnesota State Law Library, https://mn.gov/law-library/research-links
/forms.jsp
Minnesota Court Rules, https://www.revisor.mn.gov/court_rules/
Minnesota Judicial Branch, http://www.mncourts.gov/
Supreme Court Opinions, Minnesota Judicial Branch, http://www.mncourts.gov/Supreme
Court/RecentOpinions.aspx

Executive Resources

Executive Orders, Office of the Governor, https://mn.gov/governor/news/executiveorders.jsp
Minnesota Administrative Rules, https://www.revisor.mn.gov/rules/
Minnesota State Register, https://www.revisor.mn.gov/state_register/
Office of the Governor, https://mn.gov/governor/
State Agencies, Boards, Commissions, https://mn.gov/portal/government/state/agencies
-boards-commissions/

Research Resources

American Association of Law Libraries, Public Library Toolkit: Minnesota, https://www
.aallnet.org/lispsis/wp-content/uploads/sites/11/2019/03/LISPSIS-PLToolkit
-Minnesota.pdf

Legal Topics, Minnesota State Law Library, https://mn.gov/law-library/legal-topics/
Library of Congress Guide to Law Online, Minnesota, http://www.loc.gov/law/help/guide
/states/us-mn.php

Mississippi

Legal Aid and Self-Help Resources

Mississippi Access to Justice Commission, Legal Resources Help, http://www.msatjc.org/
The Mississippi Bar, Pro Bono Resources, https://www.msbar.org/for-the-public/pro-bono
-resources.aspx
Mississippi Center for Legal Services, http://www.mscenterforlegalservices.org/
MSLegalServices, https://www.mslegalservices.org/
North Mississippi Rural Legal Services, http://nmrls.com/
State of Mississippi Judiciary, Civil Legal Assistance, https://courts.ms.gov/Legal/Civil
Legal.php

Law Libraries

Harrison County Law Library, http://co.harrison.ms.us/departments/law%20library/
State Law Library of Mississippi, https://courts.ms.gov/research/statelibrary/library.php
State Law Library of Mississippi, Digital Library, https://msdiglib.org/sllm
University of Mississippi Grisham Law Library, http://library.law.olemiss.edu/

Legislative Resources

Bills, Mississippi Legislature, http://www.legislature.ms.gov/legislation/
Mississippi Code, https://www.sos.ms.gov/Education-Publications/Pages/Mississippi-Code
.aspx
Mississippi Code, https://advance.lexis.com/container?config=00JAAzNzhjOTYxNC0w
ZjRkLTQzNzAtYjJlYS1jNjExZWYxZGFhMGYKAFBvZENhdGFsb2cMlW-
40w5iIH7toHnTBIEP0&crid=71beea29-94d8-45e0-8784-ae777bec2f31&prid
=ce71c4ca-7b5e-48b6-97ad-ce8facd9285b
Mississippi Legislature, http://www.legislature.ms.gov/
Mississippi State Constitution, https://www.sos.ms.gov/Education-Publications/Pages
/Mississippi-Code.aspx
Mississippi State Constitution, https://advance.lexis.com/container?config=0155JABkOG
NiODRlYS01MDJhLTQ4MzEtODY5ZS1mNTgyYzliNGU5YzcKAFBvZEN-
hdGFsb2f5VdNz8RqsBWQtCGGS8cJt&crid=ae840fc5-a40c-4d75-983f
-dfdf24a534b7

Judicial Resources

Court of Appeals Decisions, State of Mississippi Judiciary, https://courts.ms.gov/appellate
courts/coa/coadecisions.php
Mississippi Model Jury Instructions, State of Mississippi Judiciary, https://courts.ms.gov
/research/research.php

Mississippi Rules of Court, https://courts.ms.gov/research/rules/rules.php
State of Mississippi Judiciary, https://courts.ms.gov/index.php
Supreme Court Decisions, State of Mississippi Judiciary, https://courts.ms.gov/appellate courts/sc/scdecisions.php
Trial Court Information and Forms, State of Mississippi Judiciary, https://courts.ms.gov /aoc/forms/personnelinfo.php

Executive Resources

Agencies, MS.gov, https://www.ms.gov/Agencies
Executive Orders, Office of Governor, https://governorreeves.ms.gov/covid-19/#executive Orders
Mississippi Administrative Bulletin, https://www.sos.ms.gov/adminsearch/default.aspx ?current_page=Bulletin
Mississippi Administrative Code, https://www.sos.ms.gov/adminsearch/default.aspx
Office of Governor, https://governorreeves.ms.gov/

Research Resources

American Association of Law Libraries, Public Library Toolkit: Mississippi, https://www .aallnet.org/lispsis/wp-content/uploads/sites/11/2018/01/LISPSIS-PLToolkit -Mississippi.pdf
Library of Congress Guide to Law Online, Mississippi, http://www.loc.gov/law/help/guide /states/us-ms.php

Missouri

Legal Aid and Self-Help Resources

Legal Aid of Western Missouri, https://lawmo.org/
Legal Services of Eastern Missouri, https://lsem.org/
Missouri Courts, Initiating an Appeal, https://www.courts.mo.gov/page.jsp?id=842
Missouri Courts, Representing Yourself in a Family Law Case, https://www.courts.mo .gov/page.jsp?id=5240
Missouri Legal Services, https://www.lsmo.org/
Sixteenth Circuit Court of Jackson, Missouri, Self-Representation, https://www.16thcircuit .org/#self-tab

Law Libraries

Law Library Association of Saint Louis, https://llastl.org/
Leon E. Bloch Law Library, University of Missouri, Kansas City, https://law.umkc.edu/law -library/index.html
Library of the U.S. Courts of the Seventh Circuit, East St. Louis Satellite Library, http:// www.lb7.uscourts.gov/ESLHome.html
Missouri University School of Law Library, https://mulaw.missouri.edu/library/
Saint Louis County Law Library, https://wp.stlcountycourts.com/law-library/

Supreme Court Library, https://www.courts.mo.gov/page.jsp?id=218
United States Courts Library, 8th Circuit, https://www.lb8.uscourts.gov:444/index1.htm
Vincent C. Immel Law Library, Saint Louis University, https://www.slu.edu/law/library/

Legislative Resources

Bills, Missouri General Assembly, https://house.mo.gov/billcentral.aspx
Missouri Constitution, https://revisor.mo.gov/main/Home.aspx?constit=y
Missouri General Assembly, https://www.mo.gov/government/legislative-branch/
Missouri Revised Statutes, https://revisor.mo.gov/main/Home.aspx

Judicial Resources

Court Forms, Missouri Courts, https://www.courts.mo.gov/page.jsp?id=103116
Jury Instructions and Charges, https://www.courts.mo.gov/page.jsp?id=589
Missouri Courts, https://www.courts.mo.gov/
Pending Cases and Decisions, Missouri Courts, https://www.courts.mo.gov/page.jsp?id
=103122
Rules, Court Operating Rules, and Orders Affecting Rules, https://www.courts.mo.gov
/page.jsp?id=46

Executive Resources

Executive Orders, https://www.sos.mo.gov/library/reference/orders/default
Missouri Code of State Regulations, https://www.sos.mo.gov/adrules/csr/csr.asp
Missouri Register, https://www.sos.mo.gov/adrules/moreg/moreg.asp
Office of Governor, https://governor.mo.gov/

Research Resources

Library of Congress Guide to Law Online, Missouri, http://www.loc.gov/law/help/guide
/states/us-mo.php

Montana

Legal Aid and Self-Help Resources

Montana Judicial Branch, Court Help Program, https://courts.mt.gov/selfhelp
Montana Law Help, https://www.montanalawhelp.org/
Montana Legal Services Association, https://www.mtlsa.org/

Law Libraries

Montana Judicial Branch, State Law Library of Montana, https://courts.mt.gov/library
Montana State Legislature Legislative Reference Center, https://leg.mt.gov/reference/

William J. Jameson Law Library, University of Montana Law School, http://www.umt.edu
/law/library/default.php

Legislative Resources

Bill and Session Information, Montana State Legislature, http://laws.leg.mt.gov/legprd
/LAW0200W$.Startup?P_SESS=20191
The Constitution of the State of Montana, https://leg.mt.gov/bills/mca/title_0000/chapters
_index.html
Montana Code Annotated, https://leg.mt.gov/statute/
Montana State Legislature, https://leg.mt.gov/

Judicial Resources

Court Rules, Montana Judicial Branch, https://courts.mt.gov/Courts/rules
District Court Rules, Montana Judicial Branch, https://courts.mt.gov/courts/dcourt/about
Forms, Montana Judicial Branch, https://courts.mt.gov/Forms
Montana Judicial Branch, https://courts.mt.gov/
Standards of Review Handbook, Montana Judicial Branch, https://courts.mt.gov/sorh
Supreme Court Daily Orders/Opinions, Montana Judicial Branch, https://courts.mt.gov
/Portals/189/orders/dailyorders.html

Executive Resources

Administrative Rules of Montana, https://sosmt.gov/arm/#arm
Agency Websites, https://mt.gov/govt/agencylisting.aspx
Executive Orders, Office of the Governor, http://governor.mt.gov/Home/Governor/eo
Montana Administrative Register, https://sosmt.gov/arm/#arm
Office of the Governor, http://governor.mt.gov/

Research Resources

American Association of Law Libraries, Public Library Toolkit: Montana, https://www
.aallnet.org/lispsis/wp-content/uploads/sites/11/2018/01/LISPSIS-PLToolkit
-Montana.pdf
Library of Congress Guide to Law Online, Montana, http://www.loc.gov/law/help/guide
/states/us-mt.php

Nebraska

Legal Aid and Self-Help Resources

Legal Aid of Nebraska, https://www.legalaidofnebraska.org/
Legal Aid Services in Nebraska, AccessNebraska, http://nebraskaccess.ne.gov/legal
aid.asp

Nebraska Judicial Branch Assistance and Other Information for Self-Represented Litigants, Schmid Law Library, http://schmidguides.unl.edu/c.php?g=796452&p=5859846

State of Nebraska Judicial Branch, Nebraska Online Legal Self-Help Center, https://supreme court.nebraska.gov/self-help

Law Libraries

Klutznick Law Library, Creighton University, https://law.creighton.edu/academics/law -library

Nebraska State Law Library, https://supremecourt.nebraska.gov/administration/state -library

Schmid Law Library, University of Nebraska, https://law.unl.edu/library/

Legislative Resources

Nebraska Constitution, https://nebraskalegislature.gov/laws/browse-constitution.php

Nebraska Legislature, https://nebraskalegislature.gov/

Nebraska Revised Statutes, https://nebraskalegislature.gov/laws/browse-statutes.php

Search Bills, Nebraska Legislature, https://nebraskalegislature.gov/bills/

Search Laws, Nebraska Legislature, https://nebraskalegislature.gov/laws/laws.php

Judicial Resources

Forms, State of Nebraska Judicial Branch, https://supremecourt.nebraska.gov/forms?field _language_tid=288

Nebraska Supreme Court Rules, https://supremecourt.nebraska.gov/supreme-court-rules

Opinions, State of Nebraska Judicial Branch, https://www.nebraska.gov/apps-courts-epub /public/

State of Nebraska Judicial Branch, https://supremecourt.nebraska.gov/

Executive Resources

Agencies, https://www.nebraska.gov/agencies/

Executive Orders, http://govdocs.nebraska.gov/docs/pilot/pubs/EOIndex.html

Nebraska Administrative Code, https://www.nebraska.gov/rules-and-regs/regsearch/Rules /index.cgi

Office of the Governor, https://governor.nebraska.gov/

Proposed Rules and Regulations Docket, https://www.nebraska.gov/nesos/rules-and-regs /regtrack/index.cgi

Research Resources

American Association of Law Libraries, Public Library Toolkit: Nebraska, http:// schmidguides.unl.edu/NebraskaPublicLibraryToolkit

Library of Congress Guide to Law Online, Nebraska, http://www.loc.gov/law/help/guide /states/us-ne.php

Nevada

Legal Aid and Self-Help Resources

Legal Aid Center of Southern Nevada, https://www.lacsn.org/

Nevada Judiciary, Clark County Civil Law Self-Help Center, https://www.civillawselfhelp
center.org/

Nevada Judiciary, Clark County Family Law Self-Help Center, https://www.familylawself
helpcenter.org/

Nevada Judiciary, Washoe County Family Law Self-Help Center, https://www.washoe
courts.com/LawLibrary/SelfHelp

Nevada Law Help, https://nevadalawhelp.org/

Nevada Legal Services, https://nlslaw.net/

United States Courts for the Ninth Circuit Library, https://www.ca9.uscourts.gov/library
/directory/

Washoe Legal Services, https://washoelegalservices.org/

Law Libraries

Churchill County Law Library, http://www.churchillcounty.org/212/Law-Library

Clark County Law Library, https://www.clarkcountynv.gov/LawLibrary/Pages/default.aspx

Douglas County Law Library, https://douglasdistrictcourt.com/law-library/

Elko County Law Library, http://www.elkocountylibrary.org/use/law-library

Nevada Legislature Research Library, https://www.leg.state.nv.us/Division/Research/Library
/index.html

Supreme Court of Nevada Law Library, https://nvcourts.gov/LawLibrary/

Washoe County Law Library, https://www.washoecourts.com/LawLibrary

Wiener-Rogers Law Library, University of Nevada Las Vegas William S. Boyd School of
Law, https://law.unlv.edu/law-library

Legislative Resources

The Constitution of the State of Nevada, https://www.leg.state.nv.us/Const/NVConst.html

Nevada Legislature, https://www.leg.state.nv.us/

Nevada Revised Statutes and Statutes of Nevada, https://www.leg.state.nv.us/law1.cfm

Session Information, Nevada Legislature, https://www.leg.state.nv.us/Session/

Judicial Resources

Advance Opinions, Supreme Court of Nevada, https://nvcourts.gov/Supreme/Decisions
/Advance_Opinions/

Appellate Practice Forms, https://nvcourts.gov/Supreme/Appellate_Practice_Forms/

Court Rules of Nevada, https://www.leg.state.nv.us/CourtRules/

Nevada Judiciary, https://nvcourts.gov/

Executive Resources

Executive Orders, Office of the Governor, http://gov.nv.gov/News/Executive_Orders
/Executive_Orders/

Nevada Administrative Code and Register, https://www.leg.state.nv.us/lawl.cfm
Office of the Governor, http://gov.nv.gov/
State Agencies and Departments, http://nv.gov/agencies

Research Resources

American Association of Law Libraries, Public Library Toolkit: Nevada, https://nvcourts
.gov/Law_Library/Documents/How_to_Locate_the_Law_-_A_Guide_to_Locating
_Nevada_Law_and_Legal_Resources/
Library of Congress Guide to Law Online, Nevada, http://www.loc.gov/law/help/guide
/states/us-nv.php
Supreme Court of Nevada, Law Library, Nevada Legal Resources, https://nvcourts.gov
/Law_Library/Resources/Self_Represented/Nevada_Legal_Resources/

New Hampshire

Legal Aid and Self-Help Resources

New Hampshire Judicial Branch, Self-Help Center, https://www.courts.state.nh.us/selfhelp
/index.htm
New Hampshire Legal Aid, https://nhlegalaid.org/
New Hampshire Legal Assistance, https://www.nhla.org/

Law Libraries

The John W. King New Hampshire Law Library, New Hampshire Judicial Branch, https://
www.courts.state.nh.us/lawlibrary/index.htm

Legislative Resources

Bills, The General Court of New Hampshire, http://gencourt.state.nh.us/bill_Status/
The General Court of New Hampshire, http://www.gencourt.state.nh.us/
New Hampshire Revised Statutes, http://www.gencourt.state.nh.us/rsa/html/indexes
/default.html
New Hampshire State Constitution, https://www.nh.gov/glance/constitution.htm

Judicial Resources

Circuit Court District Division, Forms, https://www.courts.state.nh.us/district/forms
/index.htm
Circuit Court Family Division, Forms, https://www.courts.state.nh.us/fdpp/forms/index
.htm
Circuit Court Probate Divisions, Forms, https://www.courts.state.nh.us/probate/pcforms
/index.htm
New Hampshire Court Rules, https://www.courts.state.nh.us/rules/index.htm
New Hampshire Judicial Branch, https://www.courts.state.nh.us/
Superior Court Forms, New Hampshire Judicial Branch, https://www.courts.state.nh.us
/superior/forms/index.htm

Supreme Court Opinions, New Hampshire Judicial Branch, https://www.courts.state.nh
.us/supreme/opinions/index.htm

Supreme Court, Appeal and Other Forms, New Hampshire Judicial Branch, https://www
.courts.state.nh.us/supreme/forms/index.htm

Executive Resources

Executive Orders, Office of the Governor, https://www.governor.nh.gov/news-and-media
?category=Executive%20Order

New Hampshire Code of Administrative Rules, http://www.gencourt.state.nh.us/rules
/about_rules/listagencies.htm

New Hampshire Rulemaking Register, http://www.gencourt.state.nh.us/rules/register
/default.htm

Office of the Governor, https://www.governor.nh.gov/

State Government Agencies, https://www.nh.gov/government/agencies.htm

Research Resources

American Association of Law Libraries, Public Library Toolkit: New Hampshire, https://
www.aallnet.org/lispsis/wp-content/uploads/sites/11/2019/12/LISPSIS-PLToolkit
-Newhampshire.pdf

Library of Congress Guide to Law Online, New Hampshire, http://www.loc.gov/law/help
/guide/states/us-nh.php

New Jersey

Legal Aid and Self-Help Resources

American Friends Service Committee, https://www.afsc.org/office/newark-nj

Community Health Law Project, http://www.chlp.org/Home%20Page

Essex County Legal Aid Association, https://eclaanj.org/

Legal Services of New Jersey, https://www.lsnj.org/

LSNJLAW, Legal Services of New Jersey, https://www.lsnjlaw.org/Pages/Default.aspx

New Jersey Courts, Self-Help Center, https://njcourts.gov/selfhelp/index.html

Northeast New Jersey Legal Services, https://www.northeastnjlegalservices.org/

Partners for Women and Justice, https://pfwj.org/

Seton Hall, Center for Social Justice Legal Clinics, https://law.shu.edu/clinics/about.cfm

Law Libraries

Law Library, New Jersey State Library, https://www.njstatelib.org/research_library/legal
_resources/

The New Jersey Digital Legal Library, http://njlegallib.rutgers.edu/njar/njarhome.htm

New Jersey State Library, https://www.njstatelib.org/

Rutgers Law Library, http://library.law.rutgers.edu/rutgers-law-library

United States Court of Appeals for the Third Circuit Library, https://www.ca3.uscourts
.gov/circuit-libraries

Legislative Resources

Bills, New Jersey Legislature, https://www.njleg.state.nj.us/bills/bills0001.asp

Chapter Laws, New Jersey Legislature, https://www.njleg.state.nj.us/lawsconstitution/chapter.asp

New Jersey General and Permanent Statutes, https://lis.njleg.state.nj.us/nxt/gateway.dll?f=templates&fn=default.htm&vid=Publish:10.1048/Enu

New Jersey Legislature, https://www.njleg.state.nj.us/

New Jersey State Constitution, https://www.njleg.state.nj.us/lawsconstitution/consearch.asp

Judicial Resources

Forms, New Jersey Courts, https://www.njcourts.gov/selfhelp/catalog.html

New Jersey Courts, https://njcourts.gov/

Opinions, New Jersey Courts, https://njcourts.gov/attorneys/opinions.html

Rules of Court, New Jersey Courts, https://njcourts.gov/attorneys/rules.html

Executive Resources

Departments and Agencies, https://nj.gov/nj/gov/deptserv/

Executive Orders, Office of Governor, https://nj.gov/infobank/eo/056murphy/approved/eo_archive.html

New Jersey Administrative Code, https://advance.lexis.com/container?config=00JAA5O TY5MTdjZi11MzYxLTQxNTEtOWFkNi0xMmU5ZTViODQ2M2MKAFBv ZENhdGFsb2coFSYEAfv22IKqMT9DIHrf&crid=8eb5d7bf-8669-456e-ad4e -958b3b1ed463&prid=3a76c748-86bd-463f-8b9b-d8a255c2f586

New Jersey Register, https://advance.lexis.com/container?config=00JABkMGM5YTky OS1IZWRkLTRmMTktOTAxMS03YzU0MTU1ZWY0OWYKAFBvZENhd GFsb2deD7LQBBLcCbuY7q4FNupa&crid=f5e7dc44-7184-4614-9646-5a5164 0d50c8

Office of Governor, https://nj.gov/governor/

Research Resources

American Association of Law Libraries, Public Library Toolkit: New Jersey, http://libguides.law.rutgers.edu/c.php?g=812549

Legal Services of New Jersey Publications, https://www.lsnj.org/publicationsvideos.aspx

Library of Congress Guide to Law Online, New Jersey, http://www.loc.gov/law/help/guide/states/us-nj.php

New Jersey State and Local Governments, Rutgers University Libraries, https://libguides.rutgers.edu/nj_government

New Mexico

Legal Aid and Self-Help Resources

DNA, People's Legal Services, https://dnalegalservices.org/

Enlace Communitario, https://www.enlacenm.org/

Law Help New Mexico, https://www.lawhelpnewmexico.org/
New Mexico Courts, Self-Help, https://self-help.nmcourts.gov/
New Mexico Courts, Self-Help Guide, https://www.nmcourts.gov/Self-Help/self-help-guide
    .aspx
New Mexico Immigrant Law Center, https://nmilc.org/
New Mexico Legal Aid, https://www.newmexicolegalaid.org/
Pegasus Legal Services for Children, http://pegasuslaw.org/
Senior Citizen's Law Office, http://sclonm.org/
Southwest Women's Law Center, https://swwomenslaw.org/
United South Broadway Corporation, https://www.unitedsouthbroadway.org/

Law Libraries

New Mexico Courts, Supreme Court Law Library, https://lawlibrary.nmcourts.gov/default
    .aspx
University of New Mexico Law Library, http://lawlibrary.unm.edu/

Legislative Resources

Bills, New Mexico Legislature, https://www.nmlegis.gov/Legislation/Bill_Finder
Constitution of the State of New Mexico, https://laws.nmonesource.com/w/nmos/const-n
    m#!fragment//BQCwhgziBcwMYgK4DsDWszIQewE4BUBTADwBdoByCgSg
    BpltTCIBFRQ3AT0otokLC4EbDtyp8BQkAGU8pAELcASgFEAMioBqAQQ
    ByAYRW1SYAEbRS2ONWpA
New Mexico Legislature, https://www.nmlegis.gov/
New Mexico Session Laws, https://nmonesource.com/nmos/nmsl/en/nav_date.do
New Mexico Statutes Annotated, https://nmonesource.com/nmos/nmsa/en/nav_date.do

Judicial Resources

Court of Appeals of New Mexico Opinions, https://nmonesource.com/nmos/nmca/en/nav
    _date.do
Court Forms, https://nmonesource.com/nmos/forms/en/nav_date.do
Court Forms, New Mexico Courts, https://www.nmcourts.gov/forms.aspx
Court Rules, https://nmonesource.com/nmos/nmra/en/nav_date.do
New Mexico Courts, https://www.nmcourts.gov/
Supreme Court of New Mexico Opinions, https://nmonesource.com/nmos/nmsc/en/nav
    _date.do

Executive Resources

Executive Orders, Office of Governor, https://www.governor.state.nm.us/about-the-governor
    /executive-orders/
New Mexico Administrative Code, http://164.64.110.134/nmac/
New Mexico Register, http://www.srca.nm.gov/new-mexico-register/
Office of Governor, https://www.governor.state.nm.us/
State Agencies, http://newmexico.gov/A_to_Z.aspx

Research Resources

American Association of Law Libraries, Public Library Toolkit: New Mexico, https://
www.aallnet.org/lispsis/wp-content/uploads/sites/11/2019/08/LISPSIS
-PLToolkit-Newmexico.pdf

Library of Congress Guide to Law Online, New Mexico, http://www.loc.gov/law/help/guide
/states/us-nm.php

New Mexico Legal Research Guide, University of New Mexico Law Library, http://lib
guides.law.unm.edu/NM

New Mexico Legislative History Quick Guide, University of New Mexico Law Library,
http://libguides.law.unm.edu/legislativehistoryquickguide

New York

Legal Aid and Self-Help Resources

City Bar Justice Center, https://www.citybarjusticecenter.org/get-help/

Empire Justice Center, https://empirejustice.org/

Law Help NY, https://www.lawhelpny.org/

Legal Aid Society of New York, https://www.legalaidnyc.org/

Legal Assistance of Western New York, https://www.lawny.org/

Legal Services NYC, https://www.learningcenter.legalservicesnyc.org/

Legal Services of the Hudson Valley, https://lshv.org/

Nassau Suffolk Law Services, https://www.nslawservices.org/

Neighborhood Legal Services, https://nls.org/

New York State Unified Court System, Representing Yourself, https://www.nycourts.gov
/courthelp/

New York State Unified Court System, Court Help Centers and Community Organizations,
https://www.nycourts.gov/CourtHelp/GoingToCourt/helpcenters.shtml

Rural Law Center of New York, http://www.rurallawcenter.org/

Law Libraries

Charles B. Sears Law Library, University at Buffalo, https://law.lib.buffalo.edu/

Cornell University Law Library, https://law.library.cornell.edu/

Public Access Law Library, New York State Unified Court System, http://ww2.nycourts
.gov/lawlibraries/publicaccess.shtml

Schaffer Law Library, Albany Law School, https://www.albanylaw.edu/academic-life
/academic-resources/schaffer-law-library

Syracuse University College of Law Library, http://www.law.syr.edu/law-library/

United States Court of Appeals for the Second Circuit Research and Library Services,
https://www.ca2.uscourts.gov/library/research_services.html

Legislative Resources

Bills, New York State Assembly, https://nyassembly.gov/leg/

Bills, New York State Senate, https://www.nysenate.gov/legislation

Constitution of the State of New York, https://www.dos.ny.gov/info/constitution.htm

New York Consolidated Laws, https://www.nysenate.gov/legislation/laws/CONSOLIDATED

New York State Assembly, https://nyassembly.gov/
New York State Senate, https://www.nysenate.gov/

Judicial Resources

Administrative Rules of the Unified Court System and Uniform Rules of the Trial Courts,
    New York State Unified Court System, http://ww2.nycourts.gov/rules/index.shtml
Decisions, New York State Unified Court System, http://ww2.nycourts.gov/decisions/index
    .shtml
DIY Forms, New York State Unified Court System, https://www.nycourts.gov/CourtHelp
    /DIY/index.shtml
Forms, New York State Unified Court System, http://www.nycourts.gov/forms/index.shtml
New York State Unified Court System, https://www.nycourts.gov/

Executive Resources

Executive Orders, Office of Governor, https://www.governor.ny.gov/executiveorders
New York Codes, Rules, and Regulations, https://govt.westlaw.com/nycrr/index?__lrTS=2
    0200601164130925&transitionType=Default&contextData=%28sc.Default%29
New York State Agencies, https://www.ny.gov/agencies
New York State Register, https://www.dos.ny.gov/info/register.htm
Office of Governor, https://www.governor.ny.gov/

Research Resources

American Association of Law Libraries, Public Library Toolkit: New York, https://www
    .aallnet.org/lispsis/wp-content/uploads/sites/11/2018/01/LISPSIS-PLToolkit
    -Newyork.pdf
Library of Congress Guide to Law Online, New York, http://www.loc.gov/law/help/guide
    /states/us-ny.php
New York Lawz, http://www.nylawz.com/

North Carolina

Legal Aid and Self-Help Resources

Charlotte Center for Legal Advocacy, https://charlottelegaladvocacy.org/
Law Help NC, https://www.lawhelpnc.org/
Legal Aid of North Carolina, https://www.legalaidnc.org/
North Carolina Judicial Branch, Going to Court, https://www.nccourts.gov/going-to-court
North Carolina Judicial Branch, Help Topics, https://www.nccourts.gov/help-topics
North Carolina Justice Center, https://www.ncjustice.org/
North Carolina Victim Assistance Network, http://www.nc-van.org/

Law Libraries

Buncombe County Law Library, https://www.buncombecounty.org/governing/depts/library
    /branch-locations/buncombe-county-law.aspx

Elon Law Library, https://www.elon.edu/u/law/academics/library/

Goodson Law Library, Duke University Law School, https://law.duke.edu/lib/

Katherine R. Everett Law Library, University of North Carolina Law School, https://library.law.unc.edu/

North Carolina Central University, School of Law Library, http://ncculaw.libguides.nccu.edu/lawlibrary

North Carolina Legislative Library, https://sites.ncleg.gov/library/

United States Court of Appeals for the Fourth Circuit Library, https://www.ca4.uscourts.gov/about-the-court/offices/about-the-fourth-circuit-library

Legislative Resources

Bills and Laws, North Carolina General Assembly, https://www.ncleg.gov/Legislation

North Carolina General Assembly, https://www.ncleg.gov/

North Carolina General Statutes, https://www.ncleg.gov/Laws/GeneralStatutes

North Carolina State Constitution, https://www.ncleg.gov/Laws/Constitution

Session Laws, North Carolina General Assembly, https://www.ncleg.gov/Laws/SessionLaws

Judicial Resources

Appellate Court Opinions, North Carolina Judicial Branch, https://www.nccourts.gov/documents/appellate-court-opinions

Court Rules, North Carolina Judicial Branch, https://www.nccourts.gov/courts/supreme-court/court-rules

Forms, North Carolina Judicial Branch, https://www.nccourts.gov/documents/forms

North Carolina Judicial Branch, https://www.nccourts.gov/

Executive Resources

Agencies, https://www.nc.gov/agencies

Executive Orders, Office of Governor, https://governor.nc.gov/news/executive-orders

North Carolina Administrative Code, http://reports.oah.state.nc.us/ncac.asp

North Carolina Register, https://www.oah.nc.gov/rules-division/north-carolina-register

Office of Governor, https://governor.nc.gov/

Research Resources

American Association of Law Libraries, Public Library Toolkit: North Carolina, https://www.aallnet.org/lispsis/wp-content/uploads/sites/11/2018/01/LISPSIS-PLToolkit-Ncarolina.pdf

Library of Congress Guide to Law Online, North Carolina, http://www.loc.gov/law/help/guide/states/us-nc.php

North Dakota

Legal Aid and Self-Help Resources

Legal Services of North Dakota, http://www.legalassist.org/

Migrant Legal Services, http://www.legalassist.org/?id=87

State of North Dakota Courts, Legal Self-Help Center and Forms, https://www.ndcourts
.gov/legal-self-help

Law Libraries

North Dakota Supreme Court Law Library, https://www.ndcourts.gov/legal-resources/law
-library
Thormodsgard Law Library, University of North Dakota Law School, https://law.und.edu
/library/

Legislative Resources

The Constitution of North Dakota, https://www.legis.nd.gov/constitution
Legislative Bill Tracking System, North Dakota Legislative Branch, https://www.legis.nd
.gov/legislative-bill-tracking-system
North Dakota Century Code, https://www.legis.nd.gov/general-information/north-dakota
-century-code
North Dakota Legislative Branch, https://www.legis.nd.gov/
Session Laws, North Dakota Legislative Branch, https://www.legis.nd.gov/session-laws

Judicial Resources

Legal Self-Help Center and Forms, State of North Dakota Courts, https://www.ndcourts
.gov/legal-self-help
North Dakota Rules of Court, State of North Dakota Courts, https://www.ndcourts.gov
/legal-resources/rules
Opinions, State of North Dakota Courts, https://www.ndcourts.gov/supreme-court/opinions
Pattern Jury Instructions, State of North Dakota Courts, https://www.ndcourts.gov/legal
-self-help/pattern-jury
State of North Dakota Courts, https://www.ndcourts.gov/

Executive Resources

Agency by Alphabet, https://www.nd.gov/government/state-government/agency-alphabet
Executive Orders, Office of Governor, https://www.governor.nd.gov/executive-orders
North Dakota Administrative Code, https://www.legis.nd.gov/agency-rules/north-dakota
-administrative-code
Office of Governor, https://www.governor.nd.gov/

Research Resources

American Association of Law Libraries, Public Library Toolkit: North Dakota, https://
www.aallnet.org/lispsis/wp-content/uploads/sites/11/2018/01/LISPSIS-PLToolkit
-Ndakota.pdf
Library of Congress Guide to Law Online, North Dakota, http://www.loc.gov/law/help
/guide/states/us-nd.php

Ohio

Legal Aid and Self-Help Resources

Advocates for Basic Legal Equality, Legal Aid of Western Ohio, http://www.ablelaw.org/
Community Legal Aid, https://www.communitylegalaid.org/
Legal Aid Society of Cleveland, https://lasclev.org/
Legal Aid Society of Columbus, https://www.columbuslegalaid.org/
Legal Aid Society of Greater Cincinnati, https://www.lascinti.org/
Ohio Legal Help, https://www.ohiolegalhelp.org/
The Supreme Court of Ohio and Ohio Judicial System, Domestic Relations and Juvenile
    Standardized Forms, http://www.supremecourt.ohio.gov/JCS/CFC/DRForms
    /default.asp

Law Libraries

Adams County Law Library, https://www.ohiolegalhelp.org/resource/adams-county-law
    -library
Ashland County Law Library, http://www.ashlandlawlibrary.org/
Ashtabula County Law Library, http://www.co.ashtabula.oh.us/534/Law-Library
Athens County Law Library, https://www.ohiolegalhelp.org/resource/athens-county-law
    -library
Auglaize County Law Library, https://www2.auglaizecounty.org/departments/law-library
Brown County Law Library, https://www.bclawlibrary.org/
Butler County Law Library, http://www.bclawlib.org/index.shtml
Case Western Reserve University School of Law Library, https://case.edu/law/our-school
    /library
Champaign County Law Library, http://hubbiz.com/w/champaign-county-law-library-oh-17
Clark County Law Library, https://www.ohiolegalhelp.org/resource/clark-county-law-library
Clermont County Law Library, https://www.clermontlawlibrary.com/
Cleveland-Marshall College of Law Library, Cleveland State University, https://www.law
    .csuohio.edu/lawlibrary/
Columbiana County Law Library, https://www.columbianacountylawlibrary.org/
Cuyahoga County Law Library, https://www.ohiolegalhelp.org/resource/cuyahoga-county
    -law-library
Darke County Law Library, https://www.ohiolegalhelp.org/resource/darke-county-law-library
Fairfield County Law Library, https://www.govserv.org/US/Lancaster/495291607338598
    /Fairfield-County-Law-Library
Franklin County Law Library, https://lawlibrary.franklincountyohio.gov/
Fulton County Law Library, https://www.ohiolegalhelp.org/resource/fulton-county-law
    -library
Gallia County Law Library, https://www.ohiolegalhelp.org/resource/gallia-county-law
    -library
Greene County Law Library, https://www.ohiolegalhelp.org/resource/greene-county-law
    -library   .
Hamilton County Law Library, https://lawlibrary.hamiltoncountyohio.gov/
Hancock County Law Library, https://co.hancock.oh.us/government-services/law-library
Hardin County Law Library, https://www.ohiolegalhelp.org/resource/hardin-county-law
    -library

Highland County Law Library, https://www.ohiolegalhelp.org/resource/highland-county-law-library

Huron County Law Library, http://www.huroncountybar.org/content/law-library

Jefferson County Law Library, https://jeffersoncountyoh.com/law-library

Knox County Law Library, https://www.ohiolegalhelp.org/resource/knox-county-law-library

Lake County Law Library, https://lakecountyohio.libguides.com/c.php?g=684991&p=4839893

Lavalley Law Library, University of Toledo, https://www.utoledo.edu/law/library/

Lawrence County Law Library, https://www.ohiolegalhelp.org/resource/lawrence-county-law-library

Lorain County Law Library, https://www.lorainlawlib.org/

Lucas County Law Library, http://co.lucas.oh.us/1885/Lucas-County-Law-Library

Mahoning County Law Library, https://mahoninglawlibrary.org/

Marion County Law Library, http://www.marionlawlibrary.org/

Medina County Law Library, https://www.ohiolegalhelp.org/resource/medina-county-law-library

Meigs County Law Library, https://www.ohiolegalhelp.org/resource/meigs-county-law-library

Montgomery County Law Library, https://www.mcohio.org/government/county_agencies/law_library/index.php

Moritz Law Library, Ohio State University Moritz College of Law, https://law.onu.edu/library

Morrow County Law Library, https://www.ohiolegalhelp.org/resource/morrow-county-law-library

Muskingum County Law Library, https://www.ohiolegalhelp.org/resource/muskingum-county-law-library

Perry County Law Library, https://www.ohiolegalhelp.org/resource/perry-county-law-library

Pickaway County Law Library, https://www.ohiolegalhelp.org/resource/pickaway-county-law-library

Portage County Law Library, http://www.portagecountylawlibrary.com/

Preble County Law Library, https://www.ohiolegalhelp.org/resource/preble-county-law-library

Richland County Law Library, http://richlandcourtsoh.us/lawlibrary.php

Robert S. Marx Law Library, University of Cincinnati, https://law.uc.edu/education/library.html

Ross County Law Library, https://www.ohiolegalhelp.org/resource/ross-county-law-library

Sandusky County Law Library, https://sanduskycountyoh.gov/index.php?page=law-library

Scioto County Law Library, https://sciotolawlibrary.org/

Stark County Law Library, https://www.starkcountyohio.gov/law-library

Summit County / Akron Law Library, https://akronlawlib.summitoh.net/

The Supreme Court of Ohio and Ohio Judicial System, Supreme Court Law Library, http://www.supremecourt.ohio.gov/LegalResources/LawLibrary/default.asp

Taggart Law Library, Ohio Northern University Pettit College of Law, https://law.onu.edu/library

Trumbull County Law Library, http://lawlibrary.co.trumbull.oh.us/

Tuscarawas County Law Library, http://co.tuscarawas.oh.us/LawLibrary.htm

Union County Law Library, https://www.co.union.oh.us/Law-Library/

United States Court of Appeals for the Sixth Circuit Library, https://www.ca6.uscourts
.gov/sixth-circuit-library
The University of Akron School of Law Library, https://www.uakron.edu/law/about-us
/law-library.dot
Warren County Law Library, https://www.ohiolegalhelp.org/resource/warren-county-law
-library
Washington County Law Library, https://www.washingtongov.org/148/Law-Library
Wayne County Law Library, https://sites.google.com/site/waynecountylawlibrary/
Wood County Law Library, https://www.co.wood.oh.us/lawlibrary/
Zimmerman Law Library, University of Dayton, https://udayton.edu/law/library/index.php

Legislative Resources

Acts, Ohio Legislature, https://www.legislature.ohio.gov/legislation/acts
Legislation, Ohio Legislature, https://www.legislature.ohio.gov/legislation/search
Ohio Constitution, https://www.legislature.ohio.gov/laws/ohio-constitution
Ohio Legislature, https://www.legislature.ohio.gov/
Ohio Revised Code, http://codes.ohio.gov/orc/

Judicial Resources

Ohio Rules of Court, The Supreme Court of Ohio and the Ohio Judicial System, http://
www.supremecourt.ohio.gov/LegalResources/Rules/default.asp
Ohio Trial Courts and Local Rules, The Supreme Court of Ohio and the Ohio Judicial
System, http://www.supremecourt.ohio.gov/JudSystem/trialCourts/default.asp
Opinions, The Supreme Court of Ohio and the Ohio Judicial System, http://www.supreme
court.ohio.gov/Rod/docs/
The Supreme Court of Ohio and the Ohio Judicial System, http://www.supremecourt.ohio
.gov/
The Supreme Court of Ohio Rules of Practice, http://www.supremecourt.ohio.gov/Legal
Resources/Rules/practice/rulesofpractice.pdf

Executive Resources

Executive Orders, Office of the Governor, https://governor.ohio.gov/wps/portal/gov/governor
/media/executive-orders/
Office of the Governor, https://governor.ohio.gov/wps/portal/gov/governor/
Ohio Administrative Code, http://codes.ohio.gov/oac/
The Register of Ohio, http://www.registerofohio.state.oh.us/
State Agencies, https://ohio.gov/wps/portal/gov/site/government/state-agencies

Research Resources

American Association of Law Libraries, Public Library Toolkit: Ohio, https://www.aallnet
.org/lispsis/wp-content/uploads/sites/11/2018/01/LISPSIS-PLToolkit-Ohio.pdf
Library of Congress Guide to Law Online, Ohio, http://www.loc.gov/law/help/guide/states
/us-oh.php

Oklahoma

Legal Aid and Self-Help Resources

Legal Aid OK, https://oklaw.org/
Legal Aid Services of Oklahoma, https://www.legalaidok.org/
Oklahoma Bar Association, Legal Resources, https://www.okbar.org/legalresources/
Oklahoma Indian Legal Services, http://www.oilsonline.org/
Oklahoma State Court Network, Forms, https://www.oscn.net/static/forms/start.asp

Law Libraries

Chickasaw Nation Law Library, Oklahoma City University School of Law, https://law
    .okcu.edu/law-library/
Donald E. Pray Law Library, University of Oklahoma Law Center, http://jay.law.ou.edu
    /library/
Oklahoma County Law Library, https://oklaw.org/organization/oklahoma-county-law-library
Oklahoma Department of Libraries, Law and Legislative Reference, https://libraries.ok
    .gov/law-legislative-reference/
Oklahoma State Court Network, The Electronic Law Library for Oklahoma, https://www
    .oscn.net/applications/oscn/start.asp?viewType=LIBRARY
Tulsa County Law Library, https://www.tulsacounty.org/TulsaCounty/dynamic.aspx?id=738

Legislative Resources

Bills, Oklahoma State Legislature, http://www.oklegislature.gov/BasicSearchForm.aspx
Oklahoma Constitution, https://www.oscn.net/applications/oscn/Index.asp?ftdb=STOKCN
    &level=1
Oklahoma Session Laws, https://www.oscn.net/applications/oscn/Index.asp?ftdb=STOKLG
    &level=1
Oklahoma State Legislature, http://www.oklegislature.gov/
Oklahoma Statutes, https://www.oscn.net/applications/oscn/index.asp?ftdb=STOKST
    &level=1

Judicial Resources

Legal Forms, https://www.oscn.net/static/forms/start.asp
Oklahoma Cases, https://www.oscn.net/applications/oscn/Index.asp?ftdb=STOKCS
    &level=1
Oklahoma Court Rules, https://www.oscn.net/applications/oscn/Index.asp?ftdb=STOKRU
    &level=1
Oklahoma State Court Network, https://www.oscn.net/v4/
Oklahoma Uniform Jury Instructions, https://www.oscn.net/applications/oscn/Index.asp
    ?ftdb=STOKJU&level=1

Executive Resources

Executive Orders, https://www.sos.ok.gov/gov/execorders.aspx
Office of the Governor, https://www.governor.ok.gov/

Oklahoma Administrative Code and Register, http://www.oar.state.ok.us/oar/codedoc02
.nsf/frmMain?OpenFrameSet&Frame=Main&Src=_75tnm2shfcdnm8pb4dthj0c
hedppmcbq8dtmmak3lctijujrgcln50ob7ckj42tbkdt374obdcli00_

State Agencies, https://www.ok.gov/portal/agency.php

Research Resources

American Association of Law Libraries, Public Library Toolkit: Oklahoma, https://lib
guides.okcu.edu/c.php?g=225271.pdf

Library of Congress Guide to Law Online, Oklahoma, http://www.loc.gov/law/help/guide
/states/us-ok.php

Oregon

Legal Aid and Self-Help Resources

Lane County Legal Aid/Oregon Law Center, http://lclac.org/

Legal Aid Services of Oregon, https://lasoregon.org/

Oregon Judicial Department, Self-Help Center, https://www.courts.oregon.gov/help/Pages
/default.aspx

Oregon Law Center, https://oregonlawcenter.org/

Oregon Law Help, https://oregonlawhelp.org/

Law Libraries

John E. Jaqua Law Library, University of Oregon, https://library.uoregon.edu/law

J. W. Long Law Library, Willamette University School of Law, https://willamette.edu/law
/longlib/index.html

Oregon Council of County Law Libraries, http://www.oregoncountylawlibraries.org/

Paul L. Boley Library, Lewis and Clark Law School, https://library.lclark.edu/law?b=g&d
=a&group_id=11380

State of Oregon Law Library, https://soll.libguides.com/index

United States Courts for the Ninth Circuit Library, https://www.ca9.uscourts.gov/library
/directory/

Legislative Resources

Bills, Oregon State Legislature, https://www.oregonlegislature.gov/citizen_engagement
/Pages/Find-a-Bill.aspx

Oregon Constitution, https://www.oregonlegislature.gov/bills_laws/Pages/OrConst.aspx

Oregon Revised Statutes, https://www.oregonlegislature.gov/bills_laws/Pages/ORS.aspx

Oregon State Legislature, https://www.oregonlegislature.gov/

Session Laws, Oregon State Legislature, https://www.oregonlegislature.gov/bills_laws
/Pages/Oregon-Laws.aspx

Judicial Resources

Court of Appeals Opinions, Oregon Judicial Department, https://www.courts.oregon.gov
/publications/coa/Pages/default.aspx

Forms Center, Oregon Judicial Department, https://www.courts.oregon.gov/forms/Pages
    /default.aspx
Interactive Online Forms, Oregon Judicial Department, https://www.courts.oregon.gov
    /services/online/Pages/iforms.aspx
Oregon Judicial Department, https://www.courts.oregon.gov/Pages/default.aspx
Rules Center, Oregon Judicial Department, https://www.courts.oregon.gov/rules/Pages
    /default.aspx
Supreme Court Opinions, Oregon Judicial Department, https://www.courts.oregon.gov
    /publications/sc/Pages/default.aspx

Executive Resources

Agencies: A to Z, https://www.oregon.gov/pages/a_to_z_listing.aspx
Executive Orders, Office of Governor, https://www.oregon.gov/gov/admin/Pages/executive
    -orders.aspx
Office of Governor, https://www.oregon.gov/gov/Pages/index.aspx
Oregon Administrative Rules, https://sos.oregon.gov/archives/Pages/oregon_administrative
    _rules.aspx
The Oregon Bulletin, https://sos.oregon.gov/archives/Pages/oregon-bulletin.aspx

Research Resources

American Association of Law Libraries, Public Library Toolkit: Oregon, https://www.aallnet
    .org/lispsis/wp-content/uploads/sites/11/2018/01/LISPSIS-PLToolkit-Oregon.pdf
Library of Congress Guide to Law Online, Oregon, http://www.loc.gov/law/help/guide/states
    /us-or.php

Pennsylvania

Legal Aid and Self-Help Resources

Community Legal Services, https://clsphila.org/
Court of Common Pleas, Lancaster County, Self-Help Center, https://www.court.co
    .lancaster.pa.us/35/Self-Help-Center
Jenkins Law Library, Self-Help, https://www.jenkinslaw.org/research/guides/self-help/you
    -begin
Legal Aid of Southeastern PA, https://www.lasp.org/
Mid Penn Legal Services, https://www.midpenn.org/
Neighborhood Legal Services, https://www.nlsa.us/
North Penn Legal Services, https://www.northpennlegal.org/
Northwestern Legal Services, https://www.nwls.org/
PA Law Help, https://www.palawhelp.org/
Pennsylvania Health Law Project, https://www.phlp.org/en/
Pennsylvania Legal Aid Network, https://palegalaid.net/
Philadelphia Legal Assistance, https://www.philalegal.org/
Southwestern Pennsylvania Legal Aid, https://spla.org/

Law Libraries

Barco Law Library, University of Pittsburgh, https://www.library.law.pitt.edu/

Center for Legal Information, Duquesne University Law School, https://www.duq.edu
/academics/schools/law/center-for-legal-information-(law-library)

Charles Widger School of Law Library, Villanova University, https://www1.villanova.edu
/villanova/law/library.html

Jenkins Law Library, https://www.jenkinslaw.org/

Law Libraries in Pennsylvania, PA Law Help, https://www.palawhelp.org/issues/children-
and-families/self-help-pro-se-forms-and-information?channel=law%2Dlibraries
&location=all&format=link

State of Pennsylvania Law Library, https://www.statelibrary.pa.gov/GeneralPublic
/Collections/More-About-the-Collections/Pages/Law-Library.aspx

United States Court of Appeals for the Third Circuit Library, https://www.ca3.uscourts
.gov/circuit-libraries

Legislative Resources

Bills and Amendments, Pennsylvania General Assembly, https://www.legis.state.pa.us
/cfdocs/legis/home/bills/

Constitution of Pennsylvania, https://www.legis.state.pa.us/cfdocs/legis/LI/consCheck
.cfm?txtType=HTM&ttl=0

Consolidated Statutes of Pennsylvania, https://www.legis.state.pa.us/cfdocs/legis/LI/Public
/cons_index.cfm

Pennsylvania General Assembly, https://www.legis.state.pa.us/

Session Information, Pennsylvania General Assembly, https://www.legis.state.pa.us/cfdocs
/legis/home/session.cfm

Judicial Resources

Court Opinions and Postings, Unified Judicial System of Pennsylvania, http://www
.pacourts.us/courts/supreme-court/court-opinions/

Forms, Unified Judicial System of Pennsylvania, http://www.pacourts.us/forms

Minor Court Civil Rules, http://www.pacodeandbulletin.gov/Display/pacode?file=/secure
/pacode/data/246/partItoc.html&d=

Philadelphia County Local Court Rules, https://www.philacourts.us/localrules/

Rules of Appellate Procedure, http://www.pacodeandbulletin.gov/Display/pacode?file=
/secure/pacode/data/210/partItoc.html&d=

Rules of Civil Procedure, http://www.pacodeandbulletin.gov/Display/pacode?titleNumber
=231&file=/secure/pacode/data/231/231toc.html

Rules of Criminal Procedure, http://www.pacodeandbulletin.gov/Display/pacode?title
Number=234&file=/secure/pacode/data/234/234toc.html

Rules of Evidence, http://www.pacodeandbulletin.gov/Display/pacode?titleNumber=225
&file=/secure/pacode/data/225/225toc.html

Unified Judicial System of Pennsylvania, http://www.pacourts.us/

Executive Resources

Directory of Agencies, https://www.pa.gov/directory/
Executive Orders, Office of Governor, https://www.governor.pa.gov/topic/executive
-order/
Office of Governor, https://www.governor.pa.gov/
Pennsylvania Administrative Code and Bulletin, http://www.pacodeandbulletin.gov/

Research Resources

American Association of Law Libraries, Public Library Toolkit: Pennsylvania, https://
www.jenkinslaw.org/research/guides?field_research_categories_tid=479.pdf
Library of Congress Guide to Law Online, Pennsylvania, http://www.loc.gov/law/help
/guide/states/us-pa.php

Rhode Island

Legal Aid and Self-Help Resources

Help RI Law, Rhode Island Legal Services, https://www.helprilaw.org/
Rhode Island Judiciary, Public Resource Links, https://www.courts.ri.gov/PublicResources
/Pages/publicResources.aspx
Rhode Island Legal Services, http://www.rils.org/

Law Libraries

Rhode Island Judiciary, State Law Library, https://www.courts.ri.gov/Courts/Supreme
Court/StateLawLibrary/Pages/default.aspx

Legislative Resources

Constitution of the State of Rhode Island, http://www.rilin.state.ri.us/riconstitution/Pages
/constintro.aspx
Legislative Information, State of Rhode Island General Assembly, http://www.rilin.state
.ri.us/pages/legislation.aspx
State of Rhode Island General Assembly, http://www.rilin.state.ri.us/Pages/Default.aspx
State of Rhode Island General Laws, http://webserver.rilin.state.ri.us/Statutes/

Judicial Resources

Forms, Rhode Island Judiciary, https://www.courts.ri.gov/PublicResources/forms/Pages
/default.aspx
Rhode Island Judiciary, https://www.courts.ri.gov/Pages/default.aspx
Superior Court Decisions, https://www.courts.ri.gov/Courts/SuperiorCourt/Pages/Decisions
%20and%20Orders.aspx
Supreme Court Opinions and Orders, https://www.courts.ri.gov/Courts/SupremeCourt
/Pages/Opinions%20and%20Orders.aspx

Supreme Court Rules, https://www.courts.ri.gov/Courts/SupremeCourt/Pages/Supreme %20Court%20Rules. aspx

Executive Resources

Executive Orders, Office of Governor, https://governor.ri.gov/newsroom/orders/
Office of Governor, https://governor.ri.gov/
Rhode Island Agencies, https://www.ri.gov/guide/
Rhode Island Code of Regulations, https://rules.sos.ri.gov/organizations

Research Resources

American Association of Law Libraries, Public Library Toolkit: Rhode Island, https:// www.aallnet.org/lispsis/wp-content/uploads/sites/11/2019/11/LISPSIS-PLToolkit -Rhodeisland.pdf
Library of Congress Guide to Law Online, Rhode Island, http://www.loc.gov/law/help /guide/states/us-ri.php

South Carolina

Legal Aid and Self-Help Resources

Law Help SC, https://www.lawhelp.org/sc
South Carolina Judicial Branch, Self-Help Resources, https://www.sccourts.org/selfHelp /index.cfm
South Carolina Legal Services, https://sclegal.org/

Law Libraries

South Carolina Judicial Branch, Supreme Court Law Library, https://www.sccourts.org /supreme/library.cfm
University of South Carolina School of Law Library, https://www.sc.edu/study/colleges _schools/law/law_library/index.php

Legislative Resources

Legislation, South Carolina Legislature, https://www.scstatehouse.gov/legislation.php
South Carolina Code of Law, https://www.scstatehouse.gov/code/statmast.php
South Carolina Constitution, https://www.scstatehouse.gov/scconstitution/scconst.php
South Carolina Legislature, https://www.scstatehouse.gov/

Judicial Resources

Court of Appeals Published Opinions, South Carolina Judicial Branch, https://www .sccourts.org/opinions/indexCOAPub.cfm
Court Forms, South Carolina Judicial Branch, https://www.sccourts.org/forms/

Court Rules, South Carolina Judicial Branch, https://www.sccourts.org/courtReg/
South Carolina Judicial Branch, https://www.sccourts.org/
Supreme Court Published Opinions, South Carolina Judicial Branch, https://www.sccourts
.org/opinions/indexSCPub.cfm

Executive Resources

Agency Listing, https://sc.gov/agency-listing
Executive Orders, https://governor.sc.gov/executive-branch/executive-orders
Office of Governor, https://governor.sc.gov/
South Carolina Code of Regulations, https://www.scstatehouse.gov/coderegs/statmast.php
State Register, https://www.scstatehouse.gov/state_register.php

Research Resources

American Association of Law Libraries, Public Library Toolkit: South Carolina, http://
guides.law.sc.edu/CircuitRiders
Library of Congress Guide to Law Online, South Carolina, http://www.loc.gov/law/help
/guide/states/us-sc.php

South Dakota

Legal Aid and Self-Help Resources

Dakota Plains Legal Services, https://www.dpls.org/
East River Legal Services, https://erlservices.org/
South Dakota Law Help, https://www.sdlawhelp.org/
South Dakota Legal Self-Help, https://ujslawhelp.sd.gov/
University of South Dakota School of Law, Legal Form Helpline, https://ujs.sd.gov/uploads
/general/LegalFormHelpLine.pdf

Law Libraries

South Dakota Supreme Court Law Library, https://ujs.sd.gov/uploads/sc/SCLawLibrary.pdf
University of South Dakota School of Law Library, https://www.usd.edu/law/law-library

Legislative Resources

Bills, South Dakota Legislature, https://sdlegislature.gov/Legislative_Session/Bills/Default
.aspx?Session=2020
Codified Laws, South Dakota Legislature, https://sdlegislature.gov/Statutes/Codified_Laws
/default.aspx
Constitution, https://sdlegislature.gov/Statutes/Constitution/default.aspx
Session Laws, South Dakota Legislature, https://sdlegislature.gov/statutes/Session_Laws
/Foreword.aspx?Session=2020
South Dakota Legislature, https://sdlegislature.gov/

Judicial Resources

Law Help and Forms, https://ujslawhelp.sd.gov/
Rules of Civil Procedure, https://sdlegislature.gov/Statutes/Codified_Laws/DisplayStatute.aspx?Type=Statute&Statute=15
Rules of Criminal Procedure, https://sdlegislature.gov/Statutes/Codified_Laws/DisplayStatute.aspx?Type=Statute&Statute=23A
South Dakota Supreme Court Opinions, https://ujs.sd.gov/Supreme_Court/Opinions.aspx
South Dakota Supreme Court Rules, https://ujs.sd.gov/Supreme_Court/Rules.aspx
South Dakota Unified Justice System, https://ujs.sd.gov/

Executive Resources

Administrative Rules, https://sdlegislature.gov/Rules/RulesList.aspx
Executive Orders, https://sdsos.gov/general-information/executive-actions/executive-orders/search/Default.aspx
Office of the Governor, https://governor.sd.gov/
Register, https://sdlegislature.gov/Rules/RegisterArchive.aspx

Research Resources

American Association of Law Libraries, Public Library Toolkit: South Dakota, https://www.aallnet.org/lispsis/wp-content/uploads/sites/11/2018/01/LISPSIS-PLToolkit-Sdakota.pdf
Library of Congress Guide to Law Online, South Dakota, http://www.loc.gov/law/help/guide/states/us-sd.php

Tennessee

Legal Aid and Self-Help Resources

Legal Aid of East Tennessee, https://www.laet.org/
Tennessee Alliance for Legal Services, https://www.tals.org/
Tennessee State Courts, Self-Help Center, https://tncourts.gov/programs/self-help-center
West Tennessee Legal Services, https://www.wtls.org/

Law Libraries

Alyne Queener Massey Law Library, Vanderbilt University, https://www.library.vanderbilt.edu/law/
Belmont University College of Law Library, http://www.belmont.edu/law/library/index.html
Joel A. Katz Law Library, University of Tennessee Knoxville College of Law, https://law.utk.edu/library/
Knox County Governmental Law Library, https://www.knoxbar.org/index.cfm?pg=legalresourceguidelegalresearch
Shelby County Law Library, https://www.shelbycountylawlibrary.com/

Legislative Resources

Acts and Resolutions, Tennessee Secretary of State, https://sos.tn.gov/division-publications
/acts-and-resolutions
The Constitution of Tennessee, https://advance.lexis.com/container?config=00JAA0ZTgy
OTUyMC0zMmVkLTQ0OGQtODZmMi01ZjVkMWYwMmRjNzIKAFBv
ZENhdGFsb2fzAVhmp1UzFFtyIYU8iKWI&crid=df40545a-392e-408e-9d61
-ce9ba3f2aa20
Legislation, Tennessee General Assembly, http://www.capitol.tn.gov/legislation/
Tennessee Code, https://advance.lexis.com/container?config=014CJAA5ZGVhZjA3NS0
2MmMzLTRlZWQtOGJjNC00YzQ1MmZlNzc2YWYKAFBvZENhdGFsb2e9
zYpNUjTRaIWVfyrur9ud&crid=47136162-c0c3-4674-9cfb-6442a534d1ca
&prid=73add634-88cb-40fc-9edd-012f8ebbdeb7
Tennessee General Assembly, http://www.legislature.state.tn.us/

Judicial Resources

Appellate Court Opinions, Tennessee State Courts, http://www.tncourts.gov/opinionsview/all
Court Rules, Tennessee State Courts, http://www.tncourts.gov/courts/rules
Forms and Publications, Tennessee State Courts, https://tncourts.gov/forms-publications
Tennessee State Courts, https://tncourts.gov/

Executive Resources

Administrative Register, Tennessee Secretary of State, https://sos.tn.gov/products/division
-publications/administrative-register
Effective Rules and Regulations of the State of Tennessee, Tennessee Secretary of State,
https://sos.tn.gov/effective-rules
Executive Orders, Tennessee Secretary of State, https://sos.tn.gov/products/division-publi
cations/executive-orders
Office of Governor, https://www.tn.gov/governor.html
State Agency Websites, https://www.tn.gov/careers/about-state-agencies—redirect/about
-state-agencies.html

Research Resources

American Association of Law Libraries, Public Library Toolkit: Tennessee, https://www
.aallnet.org/lispsis/wp-content/uploads/sites/11/2018/01/LISPSIS-PLToolkit
-Tennessee.pdf
Library of Congress Guide to Law Online, Tennessee, http://www.loc.gov/law/help/guide
/states/us-tn.php

Texas

Legal Aid and Self-Help Resources

Legal Aid of Northwest Texas, https://internet.lanwt.org/en-us
Lone Star Legal Aid, http://www.lonestarlegal.org/

Texas Advocacy Project, https://www.texasadvocacyproject.org/
Texas Judicial Branch, Self-Help, http://www.txcourts.gov/programs-services/self-help
/self-represented-litigants/
Texas Law Help, https://texaslawhelp.org/
Texas Legal Services Center, https://www.tlsc.org/
Texas Rio Grande Legal Aid, https://www.trla.org/
Travis County Law Library and Self-Help Center, https://lawlibrary.traviscountytx.gov/
United States Court of Appeals Library for the Fifth Circuit, Houston Satellite Library,
https://www.lb5.uscourts.gov/Directory/?Houston
United States Court of Appeals Library for the Fifth Circuit, San Antonio Satellite Library,
https://www.lb5.uscourts.gov/Directory/?SanAntonio
Volunteer Legal Services of Central Texas, http://www.vlsoct.org/

Law Libraries

Baylor University Law Library, https://www.baylor.edu/law/library/index.php?id=931623
County Law Libraries of Texas, http://www.sll.texas.gov/self-help/where-to-go-for-help
/law-libraries-of-texas/
Dee J. Kelly Law Library, Texas A&M University School of Law, https://law.tamu.edu
/current-students/library/
O'Quinn Law Library, University of Houston Law Center, http://www.law.uh.edu/libraries/
Sarita Kenedy East Law Library, St. Mary's University, http://lawlib.stmarytx.edu/
Tarlton Law Library, University of Texas Jamail Center for Legal Research, http://tarlton
.law.utexas.edu/home?b=g&d=a&group_id=7861
Texas State Law Library, https://www.sll.texas.gov/
Texas State Library and Archive Commission, https://www.tsl.texas.gov/ref/fedinfo/index
.html
Texas Tech School of Law Library, http://www.depts.ttu.edu/law/lawlibrary/index.php
Thurgood Marshall Law Library, Texas Southern University, http://www.tsulaw.edu
/library/index.html
Underwood Law Library, Southern Methodist Dedman School of Law, https://www.smu
.edu/Law/Library

Legislative Resources

Bills, Texas Legislature, https://www.legis.state.tx.us/Search/BillSearch.aspx
Texas Constitution, https://statutes.capitol.texas.gov/
Texas Legislature, https://capitol.texas.gov/
Texas Statutes, https://statutes.capitol.texas.gov/
Texas Statutes by Date, https://statutes.capitol.texas.gov/StatutesByDate.aspx

Judicial Resources

Forms, Texas Judicial Branch, http://www.txcourts.gov/rules-forms/forms/
Orders and Opinions, Supreme Court, Texas Judicial Branch, http://www.txcourts.gov
/supreme/orders-opinions/
Rules and Standards, Texas Judicial Branch, http://www.txcourts.gov/rules-forms/rules
-standards/
Texas Judicial Branch, http://www.txcourts.gov/

Executive Resources

Office of Governor, https://gov.texas.gov/
State Agencies, https://www.tsl.texas.gov/apps/lrs/agencies/index.html
Texas Administrative Code, https://www.sos.state.tx.us/tac/index.shtml
Texas Register, https://www.sos.state.tx.us/texreg/index.shtml

Research Resources

American Association of Law Libraries, Public Library Toolkit: Texas, https://www.aallnet
    .org/lispsis/wp-content/uploads/sites/11/2018/01/LISPSIS-PLToolkit-Texas.pdf
Library of Congress Guide to Law Online, Texas, http://www.loc.gov/law/help/guide/states
    /us-tx.php

Utah

Legal Aid and Self-Help Resources

Disability Law Center, http://disabilitylawcenter.org/
Legal Aid Society of Salt Lake, https://www.legalaidsocietyofsaltlake.org/
Utah Courts, Legal Clinics, https://www.utcourts.gov/howto/legalclinics/
Utah Courts, Online Court Assistance Program, https://www.utcourts.gov/ocap/index.html
Utah Courts, Self-Help Center, https://www.utcourts.gov/selfhelp/contact/index.html
Utah Courts, Self-Help Resources/Self-Represented Parties, https://www.utcourts.gov
    /selfhelp/
Utah Legal Services, https://www.utahlegalservices.org/

Law Libraries

Brigham Young University Hunter Law Library, https://lawlibrary.byu.edu/
James E. Faust Library, The University of Utah S. J. Quinney College of Law, https://law
    .utah.edu/library/
Utah State Law Library, https://www.utcourts.gov/lawlibrary/

Legislative Resources

Bills, Utah State Legislature, https://le.utah.gov/bills/bills_By_Session.jsp
Online Court Assistance Program, https://www.utcourts.gov/ocap/
Session Laws, Utah State Legislature, https://le.utah.gov/asp/passedbills/passedbills.asp
Utah Code and Constitution, https://le.utah.gov/Documents/code_const.htm
Utah State Legislature, https://le.utah.gov/

Judicial Resources

Appellate Court Opinions, Utah Courts, https://www.utcourts.gov/opinions/
Utah Court Rules, https://www.utcourts.gov/resources/rules/
Utah Courts, https://www.utcourts.gov/

Executive Resources

Executive Documents, https://rules.utah.gov/executive-documents/
Office of Governor, https://governor.utah.gov/
State Agencies, https://www.utah.gov/government/agencylist.html
Utah Administrative Code, https://rules.utah.gov/publications/utah-adm-code/
Utah State Bulletin, https://rules.utah.gov/publications/utah-state-bull/

Research Resources

American Association of Law Libraries, Public Library Toolkit: Utah, https://www.aallnet
      .org/lispsis/wp-content/uploads/sites/11/2020/02/LISPSIS-PLToolkit-Utah.pdf
Library of Congress Guide to Law Online, Utah, http://www.loc.gov/law/help/guide/states
      /us-ut.php

Vermont

Legal Aid and Self-Help Resources

Legal Services Vermont, https://legalservicesvt.org/
Vermont Judiciary, Self-Help Center, https://www.vermontjudiciary.org/self-help
Vermont Legal Aid, https://www.vtlegalaid.org/
Vermont's Legal Help Website, https://vtlawhelp.org/

Law Libraries

Vermont Department of Libraries, Law and Government Publications, https://libraries
      .vermont.gov/law
Vermont Law School Community Legal Information Center, https://www.vermontlaw
      .edu/academics/library/CLIC

Legislative Resources

Acts and Resolves, Vermont General Assembly, https://legislature.vermont.gov/bill/acts
      /2020
Bills, Vermont General Assembly, https://legislature.vermont.gov/bill/released/2020
Constitution of the State of Vermont, https://legislature.vermont.gov/statutes/constitution
      -of-the-state-of-vermont/
Vermont General Assembly, https://legislature.vermont.gov/
Vermont Statutes, https://legislature.vermont.gov/statutes/

Judicial Resources

Court Forms, Vermont Judiciary, https://www.vermontjudiciary.org/court-forms
Court Rules, https://advance.lexis.com/container?config=00JABhZTg3NTMzOS1Nzdl L
      TQ4NDYtYjQ3ZC0zMjlmYjMzYWZkNGYKAFBvZENhdGFsb2fEw1feWzA-
      GCzOJpfhDH4YW&crid=35d6af2a-b674-427a-b896-db21b8eadb0f

Opinions, Decisions, and Order Library, https://www.vermontjudiciary.org/opinions
-decisions
Vermont Judiciary, https://www.vermontjudiciary.org/

Executive Resources

Agency A–Z, https://www.vermont.gov/government/agency-a-z
Executive Orders, Office of Governor, https://governor.vermont.gov/document-types
/executive-orders
Office of Governor, https://governor.vermont.gov/
Proposed Rules, https://secure.vermont.gov/SOS/rules/
Vermont Administrative Code, https://advance.lexis.com/container?config=0147JAAzNT
M4MTQxMS04MjI5LTQxN2QtODFjMy1hNWQ1OGExMjc3ZTUKAFBvZEN
hdGFsb2e0UpKanB5ifXeRwqlwuxNP&crid=17991c1c-2d86-44bb-ae06-acaa4e
9183eb&prid=a6e6e942-5dae-432a-a318-fc3e8fbfc7f6

Research Resources

American Association of Law Libraries, Public Library Toolkit: Vermont, https://www
.aallnet.org/lispsis/wp-content/uploads/sites/11/2020/01/LISPSIS-PLToolkit
-Vermont.pdf
Library of Congress Guide to Law Online, Vermont, http://www.loc.gov/law/help/guide
/states/us-vt.php

Virginia

Legal Aid and Self-Help Resources

Blue Ridge Legal Services, http://brls.org/
Central Virginia Legal Aid Society, http://cvlas.org/
Legal Aid and Justice Center, https://www.justice4all.org/
Legal Services of Northern Virginia, http://www.lsnv.org/
VA Legal Aid, https://www.valegalaid.org/
Virginia Legal Aid Society, http://vlas.org/
Virginia Poverty Law Center, https://vplc.org/
Virginia's Judicial System Court Self-Help, https://selfhelp.vacourts.gov/

Law Libraries

Appalachian School of Law Library, http://www.asl.edu/library/
Arthur J. Morris Law Library, University of Virginia School of Law, https://law.richmond
.edu/library/index.html
Regent University School of Law Library, https://www.regent.edu/school-of-law/about
/regent-law-library/
United States Court of Appeals for the Fourth Circuit Libraries, https://www.ca4.uscourts
.gov/about-the-court/offices/about-the-fourth-circuit-library
Virginia's Judicial System, State Law Library, http://www.courts.state.va.us/courtadmin
/library/home.html

Virginia's Judicial System, Virginia Public Law Libraries, http://www.courts.state.va.us
/courtadmin/library/virginia_public_lib.html
Washington and Lee School of Law Library, https://law.wlu.edu/library
William Taylor Muse Law Library, University of Richmond School of Law, https://law
.richmond.edu/library/index.html
Wolf Law Library, William & Mary Law School, https://law.wm.edu/library/index.php

Legislative Resources

Bills and Resolutions, Virginia's Legislative Information System, https://lis.virginia.gov
/cgi-bin/legp604.exe?201+men+BIL&201+men+BIL
Code of Virginia, https://law.lis.virginia.gov/vacode/
Constitution of Virginia, https://law.lis.virginia.gov/constitution/
Virginia General Assembly, https://virginiageneralassembly.gov/

Judicial Resources

Forms, Virginia's Judicial System, http://www.courts.state.va.us/forms/home.html
Opinions, Virginia's Judicial System, http://www.courts.state.va.us/opinions/home.html
Rules of the Supreme Court of Virginia, http://www.courts.state.va.us/courts/scv/rules.html
Virginia Model Jury Instructions, Civil, http://www.courts.state.va.us/courts/circuit
/resources/model_jury_instructions_civil.pdf
Virginia Model Jury Instructions, Criminal, http://www.courts.state.va.us/courts/circuit
/resources/model_jury_instructions_criminal.pdf
Virginia's Judicial System, http://www.courts.state.va.us/

Executive Resources

Administrative Code, https://law.lis.virginia.gov/admincode/
Agencies, https://www.virginia.gov/agencies/
Executive Actions, Office of Governor, https://www.governor.virginia.gov/executive-actions/
Office of Governor, https://www.governor.virginia.gov/
Virginia Register of Regulations, http://register.dls.virginia.gov/

Research Resources

American Association of Law Libraries, Public Library Toolkit: Virginia, https://www.aallnet
.org/lispsis/wp-content/uploads/sites/11/2018/01/LISPSIS-PLToolkit-Virginia.pdf
Library of Congress Guide to Law Online, Virginia, http://www.loc.gov/law/help/guide
/states/us-va.php

Washington

Legal Aid and Self-Help Resources

Columbia Legal Services, https://columbialegal.org/
Equal Justice Coalition, http://www.ejc.org/

Legal Foundation of Washington, https://legalfoundation.org/
Northwest Justice, https://nwjustice.org/home
TeamChild, https://teamchild.org/
Washington Courts, Courthouse Facilitators, http://www.courts.wa.gov/committee/?fa
=committee.home&committee_id=108
Washington Courts, Self-Help Resources, http://www.courts.wa.gov/newsinfo/index.cfm
?fa=newsinfo.displayContent&theFile=content/selfhelp
Washington Courts, Self-Help Resources from the State Law Library, http://www.courts
.wa.gov/library/?fa=library.display&fileID=dspSelfHelpResources
Washington Law Help, https://www.washingtonlawhelp.org/

Law Libraries

Chastek Law Library, Gonzaga University School of Law, https://www.gonzaga.edu/school
-of-law/academics/chastek-library
Gallagher Law Library, University of Washington Law School, https://lib.law.uw.edu/
Seattle University School of Law Library, https://law.seattleu.edu/library
United States Courts for the Ninth Circuit Library, https://www.ca9.uscourts.gov/library
/directory/
Washington Courts, State Law Library, http://www.courts.wa.gov/library/?fa=library.home
Washington State County Law Libraries Directory, http://wacll.weebly.com/directory.html

Legislative Resources

Bill Information, Washington State Legislature, https://app.leg.wa.gov/billinfo/
Revised Code of Washington, https://app.leg.wa.gov/rcw/
Session Laws, http://leg.wa.gov/CodeReviser/Pages/session_laws.aspx
Washington State Constitution, http://leg.wa.gov/CodeReviser/Pages/WAConstitution.aspx
Washington State Legislature, http://leg.wa.gov/

Judicial Resources

Court Forms, Washington Courts, http://www.courts.wa.gov/forms/?fa=forms.home&dis=y
Opinions, Washington Courts, http://www.courts.wa.gov/opinions/
Pattern Jury Instructions, Washington Courts, https://www.courts.wa.gov/index.cfm?fa
=home.contentDisplay&location=PatternJuryInstructions
Washington Courts, http://www.courts.wa.gov/
Washington State Court Rules, Washington Courts, http://www.courts.wa.gov/court_rules/

Executive Resources

Executive Orders, Office of Governor, https://www.governor.wa.gov/office-governor/official
-actions/executive-orders
Office of Governor, https://www.governor.wa.gov/
State Agencies, Board, and Commissions, https://access.wa.gov/agency.html
Washington Administrative Code, https://app.leg.wa.gov/wac/

Washington State Register, http://leg.wa.gov/CodeReviser/Pages/Washington_State
_Register.aspx

Research Resources

American Association of Law Libraries, Public Library Toolkit: Washington, https://
www.aallnet.org/lispsis/wp-content/uploads/sites/11/2018/01/LISPSIS-PLToolkit
-Washington.pdf
Library of Congress Guide to Law Online, Washington, http://www.loc.gov/law/help/guide
/states/us-wa.php

West Virginia

Legal Aid and Self-Help Resources

Legal Aid of West Virginia, https://www.lawv.net/
West Virginia Senior Legal Aid, http://www.wvseniorservices.gov/StayingSafe/WestVir
giniaSeniorLegalAid/tabid/82/Default.aspx

Law Libraries

West Virginia Judiciary, State Law Library, http://www.courtswv.gov/public-resources/law
-library/law-library-home.html
West Virginia University College of Law Library, https://www.law.wvu.edu/library

Legislative Resources

Bills, West Virginia Legislature, http://www.wvlegislature.gov/Bill_Status/bill_status.cfm
Constitution of West Virginia, http://www.wvlegislature.gov/WVCODE/WV_CON.cfm
West Virginia Code, http://code.wvlegislature.gov/
West Virginia Legislature, https://www.wvlegislature.gov/

Judicial Resources

Court Forms, West Virginia Judiciary, http://www.courtswv.gov/legal-community/court
-forms.html
Court Rules, West Virginia Judiciary, http://www.courtswv.gov/legal-community/court
-rules.html
Opinions, West Virginia Judiciary, http://www.courtswv.gov/supreme-court/opinions.html
West Virginia Judiciary, http://www.courtswv.gov/

Executive Resources

Agencies, https://www.wv.gov/agencies/Pages/default.aspx
Code of State Rules, http://apps.sos.wv.gov/adlaw/csr/
Executive Records, West Virginia Secretary of State, https://sos.wv.gov/admin-law/Pages
/ExeRec.aspx

Office of Governor, https://governor.wv.gov/Pages/default.aspx
State Register, http://apps.sos.wv.gov/adlaw/registers/

Research Resources

American Association of Law Libraries, Public Library Toolkit: West Virginia, https://www.aallnet.org/lispsis/wp-content/uploads/sites/11/2018/01/LISPSIS-PLToolkit-Wvirginia.pdf
Library of Congress Guide to Law Online, West Virginia, http://www.loc.gov/law/help/guide/states/us-wv.php

Wisconsin

Legal Aid and Self-Help Resources

Badger Law, http://www.badgerlaw.net/
Legal Action of Wisconsin, https://www.legalaction.org/
Wisconsin Court System, Self-Help Law Center, https://www.wicourts.gov/services/public/selfhelp/index.htm
Wisconsin Equal Justice Fund, http://www.e-justice.org/
Wisconsin Judicare, http://www.judicare.org/

Law Libraries

Ray and Kay Eckstein Law Library, Marquette University Law School, https://law.marquette.edu/law-library/eckstein-law-library
University of Wisconsin Law School Library, https://library.law.wisc.edu/
Wisconsin Law Libraries Open to the Public, Law Libraries Association of Wisconsin, http://chapters.aallnet.org/llaw/publications/wilawlib.html
Wisconsin State Law Library, https://wilawlibrary.gov/

Legislative Resources

Acts, Wisconsin State Legislature, https://docs.legis.wisconsin.gov/2019/related/acts
Annotated Wisconsin Constitution, https://docs.legis.wisconsin.gov/constitution/wi
Wisconsin State Legislature, https://legis.wisconsin.gov/
Wisconsin Statutes, https://docs.legis.wisconsin.gov/statutes/prefaces/toc

Judicial Resources

Forms, Wisconsin Court System, https://www.wicourts.gov/forms1/index.htm
Opinions, Wisconsin Court System, https://www.wicourts.gov/opinions/index.htm
Rules, Wisconsin Court System, https://www.wicourts.gov/scrules/index.htm
Wisconsin Court System, https://www.wicourts.gov/

Executive Resources

Agencies, https://www.wisconsin.gov/Pages/AllAgencies.aspx
Executive Orders, Office of Governor, https://evers.wi.gov/Pages/Newsroom/Executive
     -Orders.aspx
Office of Governor, https://evers.wi.gov/Pages/Home.aspx
Wisconsin Administrative Code, https://docs.legis.wisconsin.gov/code/admin_code
Wisconsin Administrative Register, https://docs.legis.wisconsin.gov/code/register

Research Resources

American Association of Law Libraries, Public Library Toolkit: Wisconsin, https://www
     .aallnet.org/lispsis/wp-content/uploads/sites/11/2019/04/LISPSIS-PLToolkit
     -Wisconsin.pdf
Library of Congress Guide to Law Online, Wisconsin, http://www.loc.gov/law/help/guide
     /states/us-wi.php

Wyoming

Legal Aid and Self-Help Resources

Equal Justice Wyoming, https://equaljustice.wy.gov/index.php
Legal Aid of Wyoming, https://www.lawyoming.org/
University of Wyoming, Civil Legal Services Clinic, http://www.uwyo.edu/law/experiential
     /clinics/civil-legal-serv-clinic.html
Wyoming Judicial Branch, Legal Assistance and Self-Help Forms, https://www.courts
     .state.wy.us/legal-assistances-and-forms/

Law Libraries

George W. Hopper Law Library, University of Wyoming College of Law, http://www.uwyo
     .edu/lawlib/
Wyoming Judicial Branch, State Law Library, https://www.courts.state.wy.us/state-law
     -library/

Legislative Resources

Constitution of the State of Wyoming, https://advance.lexis.com/container?config=00JAA
     4NTk4NDdiZC1jMjc2LTQ3N2MtOGEyZi01NTZkNzlkYWExMWEKAFBv
     ZENhdGFsb2eAj5drJzoaO6wDnG9XTLWC&crid=20e39bef-423e-4690-ae23
     -88a12a39450d
Legislation, State of Wyoming Legislature, https://www.wyoleg.gov/Legislation
State of Wyoming Legislature, https://www.wyoleg.gov/
Wyoming Statutes Annotated, https://advance.lexis.com/container?config=00JAAzZmQ5Yj
     BjOC1hNDdjLTQxNGMtYmExZi0wYzZlYWIxMmM5YzcKAFBvZENhdGFsb-
     2cJAHazmy52H3XVa9c97KcS&crid=3977a0ee-289e-4c63-8c1f-e6cea55299ff

Judicial Resources

Court Rules, Wyoming Judicial Branch, https://www.courts.state.wy.us/supreme-court/court -rules/

Court Self-Help Forms, Wyoming Judicial Branch, https://www.courts.state.wy.us/legal -assistances-and-forms/court-self-help-forms/

Opinions, Wyoming Judicial Branch, https://www.courts.state.wy.us/opinions/

Wyoming Judicial Branch, https://www.courts.state.wy.us/

Executive Resources

Administrative Rules, https://rules.wyo.gov/

Agencies, http://www.wyo.gov/agencies

Executive Orders, Office of Governor, https://governor.wyo.gov/state-government/executive -orders

Office of Governor, https://governor.wyo.gov/

Research Resources

American Association of Law Libraries, Public Library Toolkit: Wyoming, https://www .aallnet.org/lispsis/wp-content/uploads/sites/11/2018/01/LISPSIS-PLToolkit -Wyoming.pdf

Library of Congress Guide to Law Online, Wyoming, http://www.loc.gov/law/help/guide /states/us-wy.php

Glossary

Access to Justice—A movement of various legal service providers who are working to make courts and legal processes more accessible to self-represented litigants.

Administrative courts—Decision-making bodies located in government agencies that can hear disputes.

Administrative law—Laws that cover how government agencies operate.

Amendment—A change to the text of a piece of legislation.

Annotated—Notes added to a document to provide clarification or background.

Annotations (American Law Reports)—A summary and analysis of an area of law that includes citations, relevant cases, statutes, regulations, and law-review articles.

Authorities—Sources cited within a judicial opinion.

Authority—In legal research four types of authority will guide legal reasoning: primary, secondary, binding, and persuasive. Primary authority are the laws themselves; secondary authority are sources that explain the law; binding authority comes from the jurisdiction in question; persuasive authority may be from a different jurisdiction or a lower court.

Bill—A draft of proposed legislation.

Binding authority—Laws from the relevant jurisdiction.

Case law—Court decisions that make up the law generated by the judicial branch. Cases published as law are cases that change legal precedent and come from appeals-level courts and higher. Also known as decisions or opinions.

Citator service—A service like Shepard's Citations or KeyCite that will tell you if a case is good law or if it has been overturned by a later case.

Citing references—Within case-law research, citing references will cite a particular case positively, neutrally, or negatively.

Civil law—Generally concerns matters of private laws. Disputes will be between individuals or individual entities (like a business).

Code—Laws from the legislative branch that have been organized by topic.

Committee prints—Publications issued by congressional committees that include topics related to their legislative or research activities as well as other matters such as memorial tributes.

Committee reports—Reports generated by various congressional committees during the process of crafting and considering legislation.

Common law—The body of law created by judicial decisions and precedent rather than laws created by statute.

Concurrent resolution—A resolution that does not have the force of law but is adopted by both houses of Congress.

Constitution—The overriding document that outlines the powers of government and provides the scope of what laws can be created. It also outlines the rights of the individual.

Court rules—Laws that outline how the courts operate.

Criminal law—Generally concerns matters of public laws. In criminal cases, the plaintiff will always be the government.

Defendant—The person who is being sued in a lawsuit.

Digest—In case-law research, a set of books that will help you find cases by topic.

Enabling statute—The law or laws created by the legislature that allow a government agency to create regulations in a specific area.

Executive order—A directive from the president or a governor that carries the force of law.

Headnotes—Notes at the beginning of a legal opinion that outline the various points of law addressed in the case.

Hornbook—A type of legal secondary source. It is usually a single-volume source that will delve into a particular type of law and is geared toward a law-student audience.

Independent regulatory agencies—Government agencies that are created by statute rather than falling under one of the executive departments.

Joint resolution—A legislative measure, similar to a bill, that requires passage by both houses of Congress and that needs presidential approval in order to become a law.

Jurisdiction—The power of the government to make laws and have authority over its designated geographical area.

Justice gap—The difference between civil legal needs and the resources to meet them.

Key Number System—Developed by West Publishing, an indexing system to classify case law by legal topic area.

KeyCite—The citator service built into the legal research database WestlawNext that will tell you if a case has been overturned, who else has cited the case, and what authorities the case uses.

Official publication—The publication of laws sanctioned by the government. In some cases the government is the publisher; in others, it may be a commercial publisher.

Opinions—*See* Case law.

Ordinance—Laws passed by a municipal government.

Parallel citation—In legal publishing, when a case has been published in multiple reporters it will have more than one citation.

Persuasive authority—Laws from another jurisdiction that may provide insight, but are not binding.

Plaintiff—The party bringing forward a lawsuit.

Pocket veto—An indirect veto that occurs when the president or governor does not sign a bill by the time the legislative session ends.

Practice aids—A type of legal secondary source geared toward attorneys. These are usually multivolume sets that provide practice tips, forms, information on key laws, and more.

Precedent—Earlier case decisions that guide the courts in how to rule on a matter.

Primary authority—The law itself.

Private law—Laws that generally tend to be about the relationship between individuals.

Pro bono—Free legal representation. To obtain pro bono representation, clients usually need to meet income requirements and have a certain type of case.

Pro se—One acting in his own legal interest.

Public law—Laws that generally tend to be about the relationship between the state and the individual.

Regulations/rules—Laws created by the government agencies in the executive branch. Regulations must have an enabling statute before they can be created.

Regulatory law—Involves matters concerning regulations and their enabling statutes. The government will be the plaintiff in these cases.

Reporter—A series of books that contain judicial opinions.

Resolution (simple resolution)—A legislative measure that is passed by only one house of Congress, that is not signed by the president, and therefore does not carry the force of law.

Revised statutes—A codification of statutes of a general and permanent nature where they are organized by topic.

Secondary authority—Resources that explain what the laws mean.

Self-represented litigant—One representing herself in court.

Session law—A law created by the legislature and approved by the president or governor from a particular legislative session.

Shepard's Citations—A citator service from LexisNexis that will tell you if a case has been overturned, who else has cited the case, and what authorities the case uses.

Statutes—Laws from the legislative branch that are signed into law by the president or governor.

Statutes at large—A permanent collection of the laws passed each session by Congress.

Titles—Topical categories used to organize laws.

Treatises—A type of legal secondary source that will deal with one type of law in depth.

Unauthorized practice of law—Practicing law without a license. This is prohibited in all fifty states.

Uniform laws—Unofficial laws drafted by the Uniform Law Commissions that states can use for legislation.

Unofficial publication—Publication of laws produced by an outside commercial publisher. These publications will retain the same text of the law but may have different annotations or editor's notes.

Veto—The power or right of one branch of government to unilaterally stop an official action, usually occurring in the case of the president stopping the passage of legislation.

Index

About the Author

DEBORAH A. HAMILTON is the strategic services librarian who oversees the law collection at Pikes Peak Library District. She has served as president, vice president, and secretary for the Colorado Association of Law Libraries. She sits on the board of directors for the Pikes Peak Justice and Pro Bono Center, a nonprofit that provides free and low-cost legal services, and is a member of the Access to Justice Committee for Colorado's Fourth Judicial District. She has published in *The Relevant Library: Essays on Adapting to Changing Needs* and *The Complete Guide to Using Google in Libraries: Instruction, Administration, and Staff Productivity (Volume 1)*.